# DETROIT on STAGE

# GREAT LAKES BOOKS

*A complete listing of the books in this series can be found online at wsupress.wayne.edu*

*Editors*

PHILIP P. MASON
*Wayne State University*

CHARLES K. HYDE
*Wayne State University*

*Advisory Editors*

JEFFREY ABT
*Wayne State University*

SUSAN HIGMAN LARSEN
*Detroit Institute of Arts*

SIDNEY BOLKOSKY
*University of Michigan—Dearborn*

NORMAN MCRAE
*Detroit, Michigan*

SANDRA SAGESER CLARK
*Michigan Historical Center*

WILLIAM H. MULLIGAN JR.
*Murray State University*

JOHN C. DANN
*University of Michigan*

ERIK C. NORDBERG
*Michigan Technological University*

DE WITT DYKES
*Oakland University*

GORDON L. OLSON
*Grand Rapids, Michigan*

JOE GRIMM
*Detroit Free Press*

MICHAEL O. SMITH
*Wayne State University*

RICHARD H. HARMS
*Calvin College*

MICHAEL D. STAFFORD
*Cranbrook Institute of Science*

LAURIE HARRIS
*Pleasant Ridge, Michigan*

JOHN VAN HECKE
*Grosse Pointe Farms, Michigan*

ARTHUR M. WOODFORD
*Harsen's Island, Michigan*

# DETROIT on STAGE
## The Players Club, 1910–2005

MARIJEAN LEVERING

WAYNE STATE UNIVERSITY PRESS   DETROIT

© 2007 by Wayne State University Press, Detroit, Michigan 48201.

Library of Congress Cataloging-in-Publication Data
Levering, Marijean.
Detroit on stage : the Players Club, 1910–2005 / Marijean Levering.
p. cm. — (Great lakes books)
Includes bibliographical references and index.
ISBN 978-0-8143-4322-7 (paperback)
ISBN 978-0-8143-4323-4 (ebook)
1. Players Club (Detroit, Mich.)—History—20th century.
2. Theater—Michigan—Detroit—History—20th century. I. Title.
PN2297.P53L48 2007
792.09774'340904—dc22
2007006704

The publication of this volume in a freely accessible digital format has been made possible by a major grant from the National Endowment for the Humanities and the Mellon Foundation through their Humanities Open Book Program.

All photos in this book appear by permission of The Players.

Contact The Players
3321 E. Jefferson Avenue
Detroit, MI 48207
Ph (313) 259-3385; Fax (313) 259-0932
e-mail: players-office@sbcglobal.net

*Designed by Elizabeth Pilon*
*Typeset by Maya Rhodes*

http://wsupress.wayne.edu/

This is dedicated to all of the Players, past, present, and future.

*Nunquam Renig*

# Contents

List of Illustrations   ix
Preface   xi
Acknowledgments   xiii

Introduction   1

## 1
### Ancestry: Club and Theatre Movements That Produced The Players   5

## 2
### The Strolling Players: The Early Years, 1910–1929   17

## 3
### The Players during the Depression and World War II   59

## 4
### The Long Run: Postwar Prosperity   83

## 5
### The Long Run Ends: Changing America and Changing Players   117

## 6
### The Players Today   161

Conclusion   181

Appendix A: Players Timeline   189
Appendix B: Membership List   199
Appendix C: Famous Players   231
Notes   257
Index   287

# Illustrations

Player seal and motto    xiv
Cover page of the first edition of *The Player*    31
"Farewell to Bacchus"    37
Exterior of the Playhouse    50
Interior of the Playhouse (Stage)    51
Interior of the Playhouse (Auditorium)    52
Paul Honoré mural    54
Detail of the auditorium    55
Lobby of the Playhouse    56
A New Deal    64
*Roller Skates Must Be Mended* (1937)    69
*Men Working* (1937)    71
*What the Heil* (1940)    74
First Minge caricature (1946)    87
*The Trial of Anne Boleyn* (1954)    96
Vice-President Nixon's visit to The Players (1954)    97
First Schafer caricature (1959)    106
Backstage crew in tuxedos and lab coats    111
Pre-frolic prep    112
*The Tridget of Greva*    125
First Greene caricature (1975)    131
First Monley caricature (1983)    140
Unidentified society "ladies"    144
Lee Carroll caricature    147
Michigan historical marker for the Players Playhouse    153
Jim Turnbull's "A Selkirk Christmas"    159
Chorus "girls"    165
Bill Rohloff caricature    176
Membership gathered for a frolic    179

# Preface

The Players is an all-male social club whose main activity is the production and enjoyment of theatre by members, for members. During my research on this club, I was asked regularly a few specific questions when describing my work. One of them was "How did you find out about The Players?" (And before you assume that this is a typo, the official name of the club includes the capitalized article "the.") Even members of the club were surprised that I knew about their small organization.

I grew up in Detroit, the home of The Players. I must have passed by the club many times without even realizing it was there. I was seventeen when I started college, so I spent one semester at a university near home before going away to school in Chicago. While still in Detroit, I wanted to be as involved in theatre as possible, so I became the stage manager/assistant director for a new children's theatre, which I was able to join because I was not yet eighteen. We rehearsed at one of the member's homes, but our performances were held at The Players Playhouse. It was a beautiful space. I spent two and a half months running up and down the stairs, in and out of the dressing rooms, and perched in the tech booth running the lights. I even spent a little time onstage when I ran the Sunday audience warm-ups before the show to help the kids in the audience get out the wiggles.

After some time in the space, I started to notice details on the caricatures that cover the hallway past the dressing rooms—such as the hairy legs on the chorus girls. Then I noticed the size 13 women's heels in the dressing room, and finally I asked, "Exactly what kind of theatre club is this?"

I was fascinated by The Players, but I soon left the area to pursue my education. I came back to Detroit to pursue my Ph.D. in theatre at Wayne State University. My department had an excellent policy with its doctoral students. The very first week, they start talking to you about the dissertation process. Everyone is immediately encouraged to pick a physically accessible topic, so that we would be in a better position to actively engage in research and thus be more likely to complete the dissertation. I was in Detroit, I was interested in theatre history, and I knew about a club that had been around since the early twentieth century. I thought it was a perfect fit, and luckily, so did my department.

The other frequent question I am asked is some variation on, "It's an all-male club—why did they let you do the research?" This misconception was widespread and frequently voiced. The general assumption about an all-male club is that its only function is to exclude women while men plot to control the world. Although this may sound somewhat facetious, this was an almost constant belief of nearly anyone with whom I spoke about my research. Not only is this idea patently false, but also it has very little to do with the values of this organization. My advisor contacted a member of the club who, in turn, notified the board of governors of my interest, and I was invited to attend a board meeting to discuss the project. The board was excited that anyone would take an interest in the club and opened the archives to me.

In addition, I had frequent access to the membership that was eager to share their stories and in turn to ask questions of me. I have attended two of the performances that are open to a general audience, but not one of the monthly performances (frolics) that are all-male, although I have seen tapes of these shows. I never wanted to attend the closed performances because I believe my presence would have altered the experience for everyone, defeating the purpose of such a visit. Whenever I needed help or information, the members, presidents, board members, and office managers (mostly women) have been extraordinarily accommodating and very forthright about their club and its activities.

Quite honestly, I feel lucky. Not just because of the experience of writing a history from original sources that have been overlooked (a scholar's dream), but because of the people I met in the process, for they are the true soul and purpose of the club.

# Acknowledgments

Thanks to everyone at Wayne State University Press for their help, particularly Kathryn Wildfong, who patiently answered my *many* questions, and thanks to the anonymous readers for their helpful suggestions. Special mention goes to Mary Tederstrom, Dora Maillaro-Tomalonis, and Craig Nelson for reading the manuscript when I could no longer see the weak spots, making this a much clearer work. Thanks to Wayne for being an occasional research Sherpa while I toiled in various archives. Much appreciation to my mom, my family, and friends who encouraged me while I was writing this.

I am indebted to my dissertation committee at Wayne State University, who originally saw this in a much rougher form and offered invaluable advice: Dr. David Magidson (my advisor), Dr. Blair Anderson, Dr. Phil Mason, and Dr. James Thomas. Also, I am deeply grateful to Charles K. Hyde and Arthur Woodford, who were kind enough to help me with the membership numbers for the Detroit Athletic Club and the Detroit Club. Thanks also to Utica College for supporting this research with a summer fellowship.

Finally, thanks to all the Players who made this possible, particularly the boards of governors from 1998 to 2006, Players Thomas Brunk (without whom this may never have come to pass in either form), Bill Rohloff, Bob O'Leary, J. J. Jorgensen, Al Shelden Jr., Geno Pirrami, Larry Smith, Chuck Steltenkamp, Bill Turnbull, Bill Champion, and Peter Dawson. Thanks in particular to the many office managers who have helped me at the Playhouse, whose insight and advice helped shape the final work: Marleen Tulas, Ruth Scoles, Diane Blake, and Robin Francis.

Player seal and motto

# DETROIT on STAGE

# Introduction

On a cold Saturday night in February 1920 members arrive for their monthly club meeting. It is a formal affair, with the men attired in tuxedos, which they still call "dinner jackets." Founded ten years prior, in 1910, the club lacks a home of its own, and they meet at the Detroit Society of Arts and Crafts. Unlike the other arts and crafts societies in the United States, the one in Detroit has a room uniquely suited for these meetings—a theatre. Called simply "The Players," the club's sole purpose is for the production and enjoyment of theatre by members, for members. Players design, direct, and act in the shows, including the female roles. Stagehands are hired to help move scenery, but this function will also be assumed by members during the Depression. The club is private, so members also make up the audience, although there are a few invited guests. Like the rest of the membership, they will also be men, and if the friends who invited them do their jobs, they will also be in formal attire for the evening's "frolic," as these events are called. Tonight there are three one-act plays on the bill, which is fairly standard for a frolic. Two of the plays were written by members.

Player Lee Anderson is a prolific writer of one acts for The Players and other local groups in his time away from his advertising company that specializes in automotive advertising. Tonight's piece by Anderson is *In the Thousands of Years to Come*, a social and political satire on government interference in private life set one hundred years in the future. In this brave new world, constitutional amendments have so regulated everyday life that clothing and floor coverings are mandated by government edict. Prohibition is obviously the root of this issue, as the plot centers around the discovery of a bottle of mysterious liquid along with a recipe for its manufacture. A chemist discerns that the unknown substance is liquor, long ago prohibited by the Eighteenth Amendment. The central characters sample their find in the name of science, and as they begin to feel its effects, they cannot understand why it was ever banned.

This piece is greeted with laughter and is made all the more amusing by the fact that the members are enjoying their own illicit beer, despite the fact that several Players are judges and elected Detroit officials who will be enforcing Prohibition as part of their jobs come Monday morning. Like the tuxedos, beer is a tradition at the frolics.

Let us visit The Players another Saturday night, this time in 1946. Players are again gathering, but this time they are in their own home, The Playhouse, on Jefferson Avenue, a large Detroit thoroughfare that runs parallel to the Detroit River. The membership is again attired in tuxedos, although they still joke about the smell of mothballs. Conspicuous consumption was frowned upon during the war, and the tuxes have only been out of the closet a few times since it ended. This time, the Players' wives and families are gathering with them to share in the fun. This is the May Show, more formally know as the Spring Invitational. This is the only show that ladies could attend each year for several decades, and the members go all out to reproduce the best shows of the preceding season for invited guests.

Although Players tend to perform comedies, this program includes a Player-written drama. This patriotic play, set during the Revolutionary War, should not be mistaken for leftover war fervor. One Player admitted that the show left him "with the longing for a man of George Washington's stature in a high place right now."[1] Not wishing to be taken too seriously, the invitational closes with a rollicking, Player-authored comedy of manners. This show included some "society ladies," as Players are well aware that the invited audience loves a chance to see the members in dresses and wigs.

Let us move forward in time once again to the night of December 6, 1975. Although it is four days early, Players are celebrating the sixty-fifth year of their club and the fiftieth anniversary of the opening of the Playhouse. Members love traditions, so they will be performing *Doing Stratford*, a Player-written musical originally created to celebrate the opening of the Playhouse in 1925. Despite the problems Detroit has faced since the race riots eight years earlier, membership is almost to capacity. There are Players who have been members for decades, plus others who have been members like their fathers, grandfathers, and uncles before them, and they will continue their membership, even if it means driving in from the suburbs. People and businesses have left the city, but this is their "home," and the thought of moving the club never crosses their minds.

# INTRODUCTION

The year 2000 is another anniversary year for Players and a celebration of survival. Membership rolls at The Players, like most similar clubs, declined steadily through the late seventies and into the nineties. Many clubs did not survive the changing interests and demographics of American society. Clubs were originally founded in now aging downtowns. They no longer appeal to a new generation that regularly travels an hour or more to get to their workplace downtown, but commuters have no desire to do the same on nights or weekends. Increased crime rates and the general fear they engender further drive down membership rolls for those who would not come into the city at all if they could help it. Numbers are further eroded by an inclusive society that sees old private clubs as the last bastions of the "old boys'" network.

Most clubs either adapted or closed their doors. In 1986, the esteemed Detroit Athletic Club opened its membership rolls to women for the first time. Conversely, The Players today, for the most part, resembles the same club it was decades ago. A Player from the twenties could attend a frolic today and feel comfortable. Although membership rolls are smaller and more diverse than they were in some decades past, the essential nature of the club remains the same: it is a small group of men who love theatre and who get out their tuxedos one Saturday a month, October through May, to drink beer and enjoy the shows at the frolic.

This book explores the history of The Players—who they were, what they did, and what made them unique—as a means to discover who they are today, what traditions they still hold dear, and why they have survived relatively unscathed and unaltered through changes that have shuttered older and more venerable institutions. It is important to examine the period before The Players made its debut on the Detroit stage to understand how the development of social clubs, the growth of Detroit's automotive industry, and changing theatre practices intersected to produce The Players.

# 1

# Ancestry

## Club and Theatre Movements That Produced The Players

The Players came into being at a moment in time that was ripe for its development. The year 1910 marked the intersection of the closing of the golden age for private clubs and the beginning of the Community and Little Theatre movements. A proliferation of clubs and activities in Detroit was spurred on by the "new-money" elite created by the auto industry. The members of the new-money elite believed they needed to acquire the trappings of culture, and, as they had the money and leisure time to do so, multiple organizations that supported the arts came into existence. Several Detroit arts associations originated within four years: The Players, the Fine Arts Society, the Detroit Society of Arts and Crafts, the Scarab Club, and the Theatre Arts Club. Despite the assertions of the decline in membership in voluntary organizations since the 1980s in such books as Robert D. Putnam's *Bowling Alone*, of these groups only the Detroit Society of Arts and Crafts has ceased to exist, and even this society is survived by the school that it founded, the College for Creative Studies.

The *Concise Oxford Dictionary* (9th ed.) defines a club as "an association of persons united by a common interest, usually meeting periodically for a shared activity." This definition accurately covers everything from a country club to a sewing circle. Another way of examining clubs is not merely by their purpose (the particular activity around which they center) or by the external benefits that members receive for their association with a specific club (social or business connections), but more importantly by what members experience on a personal level from their involvement in a club (friendship, a creative outlet, education, etc.). Urban historian Peter Clark's *British Clubs and Societies, 1580–1800* lists the following reasons why men join clubs: "A desire for recognition, to enjoy male fellowship and heavy drinking, to make friends and have something to do, to escape from an uncongenial home or work environment, or to pick up business contacts, to insure against a rainy day, acquire new skills and manners, take part in politics, music and sporting activity, or support some kind of public improvement."[1] Clubs have been offering these services to their members for both longer and in greater variety than most people are aware. Many people immediately connect the idea of a "club" to the exclusive "old boys' clubs" of Victorian England and America that existed during the height of exclusive clubs and societies. This particular concept of a club is white, Protestant, male, elitist, highly proper, and located in a club building that, at the very least, includes a room with leather armchairs and a bar.[2] This is an accurate description of socially prominent clubs of the Victorian era, but it ignores the breadth of clubs that catered to just about every social bracket, gender, race, religion, and interest.

Clubs were not new to society even in the Victorian age, however. Most histories of club life, such as John Timbs's *Clubs and Club Life in London*, date the advent of clubs to ancient Greece.[3] Clark also connects medieval trade guilds and fraternities to the history of clubs, since they both began as voluntary organizations with a common purpose of promoting a profession, promoting a religion, or helping to support the local parish. A study of these early organizations helps to dispel some of the major misconceptions about clubs. Overall, these groups were neither overtly elitist nor wealthy. Although some of them were all male, this was not a requirement of membership. Women participated in the fraternities and confraternities that supported parish life. While it is true that members of the trade guilds were male and that most of the guilds promoted standards in their field, this was not in and of itself elitist, nor was it true of all organizations.[4]

Clubs as we know them originated from English drinking establishments at the end of the sixteenth century. Coffeehouses, chocolate houses, inns, and taverns provided a social hub for the local community through food, drink, and a variety of entertainments that ranged from card games to concerts to plays. These establishments often hosted a group of regulars who originally banded together to share the cost of food and drink, plus a back or private room in which they could socialize.[5] Once clubs moved into these spaces, social rules prevented women from attending by themselves, thus limiting their presence unless they were escorted or in large groups.[6] According to Frank Ernest Hill in his book on the educational activity of men's clubs, it was only "natural that with time certain of the groups should take on characteristics reflecting the particular interests of their members."[7] It is also important to note that these locations were public places, not exclusive bastions for a wealthy class. Clubs, wherever they met, existed to serve a broad range of social classes.

The exclusive clubs, whose main purpose was to bar all but the "right" people, arose in part as a response to the blurring of class lines that occurred in rapidly expanding urban areas after the Industrial Revolution. Sudden wealth granted businessmen the trappings of the upper class—mansions, art, and possessions—but not the heightened status they desired. Old money used clubs as a means to limit new money's access to status. Only those who had the manners or the connections that made them acceptable or desirable were granted membership to the elite clubs.[8] Those who were not admitted would often establish their own institutions, and this pattern was followed in Detroit. The Detroit Athletic Club was founded in part as a response to the refusal of the old-money members of the Detroit Club to allow any of the new-money members to be part of the club's leadership. In essence, old-money members of the Detroit Club would take their new money, but the old guard would not allow the new-money members a say in club matters. In addition, Packard's Henry B. Joy, a prime mover behind the founding of the current Detroit Athletic Club (there was an earlier Detroit Athletic Club that had folded), hoped that providing a club for the still somewhat rough members of the automotive industry would help to "civilize" them.[9] This was not an unusual desire. For those people who were not part of the elite, one of the major benefits of being a member of a prominent club was that it could help them acquire the polish necessary to navigate the upper echelon of society. Although he is speaking of the benefits of club life for a much earlier time period, Clark's description still holds true: "Meetings helped members to refine their manners, their dress sense, conversational and debating skills, as well as genteel speech and gestures. Acquiring the trappings of genteel respectability, members won access to a wider social universe."[10]

Clubs came to America with other elements of British culture. Originally, these may have taken the form of aid or religious societies. Various clubs vie for the title of "first" in the colonies: Clark mentions that in Boston in 1717 a fire club was founded whose main purpose was to put out fires at subscribers' homes and to help them rebuild after such an occurrence. Timbs gives the honor to the Junto, a club founded by Benjamin Franklin in 1727 to "hold weekly discussions on morals, politics, and natural philosophy; and that out of its discussions there should come action for the public good."[11] James M. Mayo's history of country clubs in the United States gives the honor to the South River Club, a dining club founded in 1700 near Annapolis, Maryland.[12]

Theatre was also not new to club life, either in England or in the United States. Medieval guilds supported the production of religious plays on feast days as part of their contribution to civic life. Plays were produced as part of the entertainments at taverns and inns, and private, socially exclusive theatrical clubs were also not unusual. Although theatre clubs do not have as high a profile as general social clubs, they have been widespread throughout the history of clubs in the United States and England. The earliest theatrical club in the United States was the Thalians, established in 1800. Their organization had some of the same characteristics as The Players. It was all male, produced theatre, and included influential members of the community:

> [The Thalian Association was] begotten in Wilmington, North Carolina, about 1800. It had a perpetual lease on the lower floor of some sort of school, and later on it built a theatre for itself. The second birth-record of the Thalian Association—there have been at least four rebirths—includes in the list of its actors a governor of the state, a lawyer, a banker, a railroad man, a colonel, and five doctors, one of whom was a "bold and brilliant operator" in the days before anesthetics. But the Thalians appear to have welcomed no women to their casts; they had a female impersonator who later turned out to be a bishop.[13]

Other such clubs included the Chicago Theatre Society (founded 1907), Plays and Players of Philadelphia (1911), the Players Club of Columbus, Ohio (1923), and in New Orleans, the Petit Théâtre du Vieux Carré (1919).[14]

Another club that still produces theatre today was not originally formed with stage production in mind. The Bohemian Club in

San Francisco was founded in 1872, primarily by journalists and by men who loved the arts for the purpose of association of like-minded people.[15] Soon thereafter, however, businessmen had to be admitted to pay the bills. As of 1994, with more than two thousand all-male members and a fifteen-year waiting list, the club epitomizes the stereotype of old boys' clubs.[16] Peter Martin Phillips's work on the sociology of the club focuses on the concentration of wealth and power in the membership rolls, which have included prominent men from across the country and the world, including most of the Republican presidents since Theodore Roosevelt.[17]

Today, the Bohemian Club still promotes an interest in art. On an almost weekly basis, there is a theatrical event at the club that can range from a comedy to a variety show, and it also hosts musical performances and art shows.[18] The club holds its Midsummer Encampment in July in the Bohemian Grove, a 2,800-acre, redwood forest retreat in Sonoma County owned and maintained by the club. The retreat gets its name from an actual grove on the property of old-growth redwoods, some of which are more than two thousand years old.[19] Art is omnipresent at the encampment, which boasts a 2,500-seat amphitheatre and has its own orchestra, chorus, and various smaller musical groups composed solely of members. The encampment opens with a highly theatrical "Cremation of Care" ceremony where "Dull Care" is literally burned in effigy.[20] Part of the summer activities is an annual "Grove Play." In the chapter on the Bohemian Grove in his book on American subcultures, W. Hampton Sides describes the Grove Play as "an extravagant epic drama written and performed exclusively by Bohemian talent and usually starring an odd cast of sprites and wood nymphs played by men in drag. Though a Grove Play typically carries a price tag upward of thirty thousand dollars, it is performed only once."[21] The encampment and its play are parodied in *Teddy Bears' Picnic*, a 2002 movie directed by Harry Shearer.

Artists are still an important part of the club membership invited to join at reduced rates, although Sides calls the arrangement a "latter-day version of Europe's court patronage system," because the artists are "expected to put out" by employing their talents in service of the club's entertainments. Lest this appear to be some kind of artistic slavery, he admits that all members, "even the rich and untalented ones," are expected to participate in the hands-on work involved in the artistic endeavors of the club.[22]

Theatrical clubs also existed on college campuses. The oldest one in the United States, founded in 1795 and also still in existence, is Harvard's Hasty Pudding Club. Hasty Pudding began their theatricals by performing mock trials that soon became elaborate affairs with costumes. In 1844, a senior wrote a parody of a popular musical burlesque and substituted it for the expected mock trial. It was so well-received that the club continued to mount plays. Hasty Pudding still puts on an elaborate yearly musical described by the club's web site as "a no-holds-barred drag burlesque, with men playing both the male and the female roles." Although only men are onstage, women undertake roles behind the scenes of the productions.[23]

Stage professionals did not form clubs for themselves until well into the 1800s, although they were often members of general social clubs. For instance, Shakespeare met with other literary figures at the Mermaid Tavern, while Ben Jonson founded a club at the Devil Tavern.[24] In England, one of the first and most famous theatrical clubs was the Garrick, founded in 1831. The Garrick was a successor to the Garrick Society, formed in 1779 after the death of renowned actor David Garrick. Its main purpose was to bring together actors and "men of education and refinement to meet on equal terms"[25] in a social space that provided areas for dining, reading, smoking, and card playing, its rooms boasting an extensive collection of theatre portraits and pictures.[26]

In the United States, the Lambs was the first club established for professional actors, founded in 1874 as "an all male dining club for actors" and named after a similar club then flourishing in London. Still active today, the now coed club's main purpose continues to be social, although members do perform for each other's enjoyment and as a means to hone their craft.[27] More than a decade later, the Players Club in New York was founded in 1888 by the actor Edwin Booth, who described its purpose in elevating terms: "It will be a beacon, I hope, to incite emulation in the 'poor player'—to lift up himself to a higher social grade than the Bohemian level that so many worthy members of my profession now grovel on from sheer lack of incentive to 'go up higher.'"[28] The Friars Club in New York, also a fraternity of performers, was founded not long after, in 1907. Both still in existence today, the New York Friars and the Players clubs' main purpose is to provide a place for professionals to socialize, so they do not focus on creative activities such as performing. Most likely, this noncreative objective resulted from the fact that the members who founded and supported the clubs worked in theatre for a living, and so probably did not want to rely on performing as their primary social activity. In fact, both New York clubs seem to restrict club-sponsored performances to fund-raising purposes. All of the New York Players' performances were held to raise money for the upkeep and perpetuation of their club and its buildings. Although the Friars Club continues to hold roasts to honor members—which can become performances in themselves—actual scripted performances by the club also appear to be predominately for fund-raising purposes.[29]

Although perceived as unique today, The Players club in Detroit shares many characteristics with other similar clubs beyond its primary function of producing theatre. It is all male (not unusual for being founded in 1910) and, as was standard with most clubs, its activities usually involve the consumption of food and drink. Beer is served at its performances, which are usually followed by supper (and more beer). Another club tradition that The Players upheld is having individualized mugs for drinking of said beer.[30] The Players' version of this is a white stein with the club's seal, the member's name, and the year in which he joined. In addition to an affinity for food and drink, many clubs have a dress code for their events, which serves to "create a social atmosphere that instill[s] proper decorum and distinctiveness."[31] Following this tradition, members of The Players attend performances in formal attire, lending a sense of elegance to their productions.

The Players came into existence about the same time as several other Detroit clubs. It appears to have been based on an earlier coed Detroit theatrical society called the Comedy Club, which folded in 1903.[32] The Fine Arts Society, founded in 1906, brought together "professional and amateur lovers of the Arts" for performances (both theatrical and musical) and for dinner dances.[33] The Theatre Arts Club, a women's theatrical society, was founded in 1910, the same year in which The Players was founded. The two women behind it were an actress, Nellie Peck Saunders, and Lillie Larned, whose family owned the Whitney Opera House in Detroit and whose husband, Charles, was one of the founding members of The Players.[34] The ladies got the jump on the gentlemen by holding their first performance in May of that year. The Players did not organize until December.

Two other arts organizations were founded around this time in response to the Arts and Crafts movement that had originated in England and had now spread to the United States. The movement began as a reaction against the mass-produced, machine-made goods and processes of the Industrial Revolution and valued handmade, functional objects that brought beautiful pieces into ordinary homes for everyday use. In W. Hawkins Ferry's *The Buildings of Detroit: A History*, he credits expanding industry in Detroit for making the area conducive to a new art movement by attracting "creative minds that were receptive to new ideas."[35]

The Arts and Crafts movement came to Detroit in two waves. The first wave broke in 1904 with a small exhibit of Arts and Crafts pieces at the Detroit Museum of Art. The second arrived with another exhibit the following year. The organizers of the two exhibits responded to the interest shown by the public by forming the Detroit Society of Arts and Crafts in 1906, with the mission of encouraging "good and beautiful work as applied to useful service."[36] The Detroit society was distinct from other American societies in that it expressed an interest in theatre. Starting in 1910, the society performed masques (described later) and plays. When members designed their first purpose-built home in 1915 (the first Arts and Crafts society to do so), they included a small theatre as part of the structure.[37] In fact, several members of The Players were also members of the Arts and Crafts society, including one of the two architects that designed the building. From the time the new building was opened in 1916 until the gallery closed its doors in 1941, the Detroit Society of Arts and Crafts was a leader both in the country and in Detroit. It was the first Arts and Crafts society to hold an exhibit on the "Art of the Automobile" and was also the first venue in which many Detroiters saw the work of such artists as Alex Calder, Matisse, Monet, Picasso, and Georgia O'Keefe.[38]

The other arts organization founded around the same time, the Hopkins Club, was started in 1907 as a means for artists to promote themselves and their art. The club took its name from a Detroit marine painter, Robert Hopkins. In 1913, the members formalized the club by creating bylaws and electing a board of directors. At the same time, they also changed their name to the Scarab Club after the Egyptian scarab, a symbol of "resurrection" demonstrating "the club's commitment to the renewal of arts in Detroit."[39] In addition, they also formalized their mission, declaring that their purpose was "to promote the mutual acquaintance of art lovers and art workers; to stimulate and guide toward practical expression the artistic sense of the people of Detroit; to advance the knowledge and love of the fine arts in every possible manner; and to maintain a clubhouse for entertainment and social purposes as well as to provide working and exhibit facilities for artist members."[40] With the construction of their headquarters in the Detroit Cultural Center, the club was now able to offer classrooms, individual studios for artists, gallery space for exhibits for members and other Michigan artists, and a lounge and garden for socializing and more formal events.

Membership rolls among these arts organizations share many names. The Detroit Society of Arts and Crafts is of particular interest to a study of The Players. The Arts and Crafts society produced its first major theatrical venture in June 1910. The "Masque of Arcadia," written by Arts and Crafts member Alexandrine McEwen and held at the estate of the department store entrepreneur, J. L. Hudson,[41] was performed pageant style: short pieces of dialogue interspersed with dances. Masques are usually comprised of large casts with elaborate costumes and allegorical subject matter, and this one included characters such as Mother Nature, Summer, and a Chorus of the Pleasures.[42] The event was successful enough to encourage further masques by the society.

As part of their mission to bring new art to Detroit, the Arts and Crafts society, along with such groups as The Players and the Fine Arts Society, arranged for an exhibit of stage models representing the "new stagecraft" to come to the Detroit Museum of Art.[43] Having studied stage design in Europe with one of its main proponents, Gordon Craig, Sam Hume was chosen to organize the exhibit. The new stagecraft moved the emphasis of stage design from realism to a simplified design that reflected the core message of the play. This new trend in design was a reflection of the Art Theatre movement that arrived in the United States at this time.

The Art Theatre movement, sometimes called the Little Theatre movement, began in the latter part of the nineteenth century in Europe. It reflected a turn away from melodramatic spectacles performed in enormous theatres and focused on an intimate theatre that embraced quality scripts and an imaginative, cohesive vision when staging them. Art theatres, often run by dedicated amateurs, encouraged new playwrights, experimentation, innovative staging of classic plays, and in particular, an emphasis on quality and coherence in all aspects of performance and design as a means of creating a harmonious work of art out of the many aspects of a play's production. The first little theatres in America were both founded in 1915: the Provincetown Players, where the playwright Eugene O'Neill got his start, and the Washington Square Players. This same year, George G. Booth, the first president of the Detroit Society of Arts and Crafts, invited Hume to Detroit to produce another masque to dedicate the scaled-down Greek theatre he had built on the grounds of his estate. The masque was a great success, garnering a profit of sixteen hundred dollars to outfit the theatre in the new Arts and Crafts society building, and Hume was asked to be the director of the new facility.

Hume had a hand in the design of the space and equipment, in addition to planning the seasons at the Arts and Crafts Little Theatre.[44] It quickly became one of the premiere little theatres in America, attracting Sheldon Cheney, another progressive theatre professional, who founded *Theatre Arts Magazine* at the Detroit Society of Arts and Crafts, with funding provided by its board of directors. He also wrote the seminal work on the art theatre in the United States, aptly titled *The Art Theatre*. The 1917 edition not only extensively describes the productions at the Arts and Crafts Little Theatre but also includes its 1916–17 season and cast lists as examples of how a little theatre should be run.[45] The 1925 edition still discusses the Detroit theatre, but the cast lists and photos have been replaced with those of other little theatres across the country.

Why is this relevant to The Players? The cast lists for that first season of the Arts and Crafts Little Theatre are littered with names of Players. Of the nineteen shows performed, only three do not include men who were either at the time or soon afterward members of The Players. Considering the overlap of membership between the two organizations, it seemed logical that The Players would be heavily influenced by the Little Theatre movement in how it chose and produced its shows. In its early decades, members of The Players believed that their activities helped to further the movement:

> Critics may carp about our plays and players but one grand thing about Players' Night is that these prominent Detroit businessmen who give of their time and talents so freely toward cultural development and the advancement of the Little Theatre movement, have just as good a time when the plays are not so good as when they are tops. It's our private party and we like it whether we are good or bad. It's a tough job to pick

plays, cast them, rehearse them and do them unusually well—only once.⁴⁶

Despite the possible mutual influence, however, most of the stage designs at The Players did not reflect the new stagecraft. The Players' designers could get creative with sets, but they also had no qualms about using a stock dining room set multiple times. As to play choice, The Players tends toward the lighter, popular fare mostly shunned by the Art Theatre, although it did produce quite a few O'Neill plays in its early years, as much because the casts were heavily male as for the quality of writing. Hume was known for leaning toward more mainstream plays and buffering an experimental piece with two more accessible pieces. Cheney described Hume's choices in balder terms:

> It was in choice of plays that Hume compromised. He sandwiched the plays of limited appeal between thrillers and farce-comedies. He frankly wanted to please his audiences (and his backers), and he added a certain number of somewhat shallow plays with a wide and obvious appeal to those that were clearly in the art theatre field.⁴⁷

> An analysis of that season's bill at the Arts and Crafts Theatre shows that only six of the nineteen plays produced were at all unusual or specialized in appeal. One of these appeared on each of the six programs of the season—which indicates that when Hume wished to try something a little "advanced" on his audiences, he sandwiched it between things of more obvious appeal.⁴⁸

It is unclear why The Players did not follow the art theatre path. It may have been too serious for a club whose members hoped to enjoy themselves and relax. It may also have been because the Arts and Crafts Little Theatre only lasted two seasons, and its ideals did not have enough time to take hold. In 1918, Hume left the society when he received an offer for an assistant professorship at the University of California, and the society abandoned the idea of running its own theatre after his departure; not only did they believe that it was not the "function" of their society to do so, but also they did not like the idea of the theatre's being "run as a more or less independent organization within the Society and only partially controlled by it."⁴⁹ Outside groups such as The Players continued to rent the space until it was destroyed by fire in 1928.

Despite the impact of the Little Theatre movement, The Players is more closely allied with the ideals of another trend that came to the United States about the same time as the Art and Little Theatre movements: the Community Theatre movement. The Community Theatre movement is very much rooted in a specific location and group of people (not a requirement for an art theatre), and unlike the experimentation integral to art theatre, community theatre's main purpose is to "expose a community to continuing living theatre, and to provide a participation outlet for such theatre talents as may exist in a particular community."[50] When discussing the community theatre in their book on the subject, Robert E. Gard and Gertrude S. Burley emphasize the participation of the group in the process: "The essential consideration is the necessary involvement of the community itself in the well-being and continuation of the group as a recognized community enterprise in which the citizens take pride, and to which they may look for theatrical entertainment."[51] This captures the essence of productions at The Players: activities in which everyone can participate, whether in the audience, on the stage, or behind the scenes.

Despite the multifaceted historical influences that helped shape the club's present character, The Players still shares one central feature with those early clubs begun in taverns and coffeehouses. It is a group of men who want to get together over a mug, relax, socialize, and be entertained; at the heart of The Players is the same camaraderie shared across centuries of clubs. But there were many clubs like The Players at one time, so the question of why it survived when so many others did not still bears asking. I present here a history of a living organization that could have become a cautionary tale at several points in its story. This is therefore not merely a record of the club but also an exploration of why the experience was and still is worthwhile to its members. As the arts come under constant attack in our culture, it is valuable to understand why members of the business elite once invested so much of their time and talents in an arts-related endeavor. As society and the makeup of the club has changed, why has this group of men from various backgrounds continued to come together to produce theatre? The answers to these questions not only allow us a more detailed portrait of the club but also may provide avenues in which to perpetuate its existence and models that may save similar organizations in the future.

# 2

# The Strolling Players
## The Early Years, 1910–1929

The idea of forming a theatrical club in Detroit developed over several years. Around the turn of the twentieth century, the coed Comedy Club had produced theatrical works, but it disbanded in 1903 due to lack of interest and participation. In 1906, the Fine Arts Society was formed "to bring together professional and amateur lovers of the Arts,"[1] picking up the theatrical torch by including plays in its arts-related club activities. In addition, other Detroit social clubs such as the University Club and the Detroit Boat Club presented skits or plays by and for their members.[2]

The Players was the brainchild of Guy Brewster Cady, who started out in the wholesale grocery business and then moved into designing advertising displays for windows and counters.[3] In a brief history on the founding of the club, he revealed that the "idea of a Dramatic Club for gentlemen only" had been on his mind for years.[4] Alexander K. Gage described the meeting, in the fall of 1909, at which Cady approached him with the idea for a new club:

> I was visiting Guy Brewster Cady in his "Emporium of Nick Nacks" on Library Avenue, just off John R Street, one afternoon and he broached the idea of an organization like the old Comedy Club in which we both had been active; but with a membership of men—and no women. The Fine Arts Society with its membership, composed of ladies and gentlemen, was doing a fine job dramatically as well as musically. It had taken over much of the interest of many of the more active members of the Comedy Club.
>
> But it seemed that there was room for a Club of men. There were a number of similar organizations in other cities. One or the other of us was more or less familiar with several: The Lambs, The Hermits, The Bohemian Club, and also the Sock and Buskin, the Hasty Pudding, the Jesters and the Mask and Wig among the Colleges and Universities.[5]

Alexander agreed, and it took a little more than a year for Cady to finalize the idea.

The club was born on the evening of 10 December 1910, in Richter's, a German restaurant on State Street just west of Woodward Avenue in Detroit. According to Player William B. Gregory, Richter's was "a sterling pre-prohibition emporium for the dispensing of liquid cheer." It was the "haunt of the actresses and actors from the old Garrick Theatre—favorite hangout for the staff of the *Detroit* News."[6] Cady invited several men that he thought would be interested in a new club, but of the twelve invited, only four were in attendance. Besides Cady and Gage, H. J. Maxwell Grylls, Leonard R. Carley, and William W. Talman were in attendance that night. A second meeting was held eleven days later where Charles P. Larned, Kirkland B. Alexander, and Frederick S. Stearns joined. They discussed writing the club's constitution, and Larned, Carley, and Cady were assigned to write the first draft. By 4 January 1911 two more men had joined in the proceedings, Walter C. Boynton and Ernest S. Witbeck, thus providing the necessary ten charter members to form the club. The attending members made some small changes to the drafted constitution, and on 11 January 1911, at the University Club of Detroit, the ten charter members read and accepted the revised constitution and signed the Articles of Association. Three days later, they set about the business of the club, electing officers (Larned was the first president), setting up committees, and looking for a place to meet. According to the Articles of Association, the purpose of The Players was "for the encouragement and development of amateur dramatic talent and for the presentation of stage entertainments."[7] Membership was originally divided into three categories: active, associate, and nonresident. The initiation fee was fifteen dollars and the yearly dues were ten dollars, although associate dues were raised to fifteen dollars in 1914.[8] In 1913, honorary members were added for the same fifteen-dollar initiation fee and yearly dues of fifteen dollars.[9] Although the minutes record "an evening of vaudeville [during which] each and every member had some little 'stunt' to do" in May 1911,[10] the first official "frolic," as their performances were soon named, was held at the Twentieth Century Club on 26 October 1911. It was a vaudeville piece (basically a collection of variety acts) probably because it was the easiest genre of theatre to produce with little rehearsal and no set. It is interesting to note that the Twentieth Century Club was a women's social club, whose "Drama Coterie" had become active enough that the club had decided to build its own theatre.[11]

The Players soon built upon this foundation, and the next month's entertainment consisted of "a playlet, some music by about eight of the Players, and a sketch by three members in a Dutch dialect" to be held at the University Club.[12] In the early years of the club, the board typically decided on the plays the club performed and who would be cast in them. By 1916, this had become a somewhat unwieldy task, and the board established a Plays Committee (later called the Script Committee) to read and recommend scripts to the board, who would then choose which scripts and in what order they would be performed, although casting still fell to the board.[13] This arrangement stood until 1953, when the committee became "Script and Casting," which has remained the major body through which plays and casts are chosen.[14]

Initially, frolics were limited to members only. Upon later discussion, the performers voiced their desire to perform to a moderately sized crowd. Because The Players had only twenty-seven members at the time, the board of governors allowed invited guests to the December frolic.[15] Not long after this performance, the club discussed the idea of public performances, or at least the possibility of one in April."[16] This was the first mention of the Spring Invitational, soon to become the traditional—and for many years the only—public performance of The Players' best work. As the members wanted to put on the best show possible, they decided that the April performance should consist of three one-act plays, each of which would be performed separately at the January, February, and March frolics as a kind of dress rehearsal that allowed for suggestions and criticism from the other Players.[17]

The precedent for the composition of the May Show (officially known as the Spring Invitational, but seldom called that by the members) was set later by the 1914–15 board. When that board debated the possible content, Player Walter C. Boynton hit upon a solution that was roundly accepted. The board had tossed around the idea of performing a musical of some kind, but Boynton told them to "give up the idea of a musical opera and give a performance made up of the best of the monthly shows of that season at the public performance."[18] This allowed the club to maintain its private nature, but held out the possibility that if the show was good, family and friends would still get to see it in May. A 1917 copy of *The Player* (the Club's newsletter) finally settled the objective of the May Show: "Beyond being an anniversary affair, [it] should be to give our friends an idea of the sort of entertainment we indulge in at our regular stag performances."[19] What was left unsaid, but can be inferred with a fair amount of certainty, is that it was also an opportunity for Players to prove to their wives and other loved ones that they really were telling the truth about what occurred at the monthly frolics.

The first time the possibility of a public performance was discussed, the question of getting women to take the female roles was raised, but no definitive action was taken. Because their club was founded as an exclusively male society, to admit women into their main social activity would have fundamentally altered the nature of the club. There were other less exclusive opportunities for theatre experiences and a variety of gender mixes. The Fine Arts Society provided an outlet for men and women to produce theatre, and an all-female social club, Theatre Arts, had also formed in 1910 to produce drama. Many of the early members of the Theatre Arts Club were wives or daughters of Players and were also members of the Fine Arts Society. One of the Theatre Arts Club's founding members, Lillie Whitney Larned, was married to Charles P. Larned, one of the founding Players. According to Alice Tarbell Crathern's book that chronicles the contributions of women to Detroit, Lillie's brothers "owned and ran the Whitney Opera House, so she came naturally by her interest in the theatre."[20] All-male societies were the norm in club life, but the Fine Arts Society and the Theatre Arts Club provided other types of companionship combined with theatre.

The Players functioned like most private clubs. As was standard, new members had to be proposed by current members, and for many years, a single blackball could keep a prospective member out of the club. Guests had to be invited by the board of governors and would be turned away at the door if the Players inviting them had not forewarned the board. Thus the exclusive nature of the club made it possible for a select group of men with a common purpose to socialize in comfort: the members of The Players could feel free to drink beer, watch a show, and relax among their friends.

Unfortunately, interest in the club appears to have dropped off shortly after the minutes entry discussing the possibility of a Spring Invitational in February 1912, and there are no more minutes until January 1913. Because the minutes were religiously kept from the beginning in 1910, and were again kept faithfully after this ten-month gap until 1981, it is relatively safe to assume that there were problems that interfered with Player activities. In addition, the first minutes that resume in 1913 note that it was necessary to "revivify" the club. These minutes record "[a barn-storming] party that the Players offered their friends ... at the Century Building. [Following the party] most of the members of the Club, having the welfare of the Club at heart, met at the University Club. After a discussion relative to the present condition of the Club it was suggested that a new Board of Governors be elected who should devote their energies to the revivifying of the society."[21] This appeared to work, as the club has not lapsed since.

That year, the board made several decisions about how The Players would be run and whether it would be a truly amateur organization. The first major Player invitational occurred on 11 April 1913 at the Garden Theatre in Detroit for one of its first big successes, *Hairlooms*.[22] *Hairlooms* was a musical comedy, with music written by Player Willard S. Hill and libretto by Players Horace B. Peabody and Kirkland B. Alexander. "The plot, what there was of it, dealt with the travels of an American millionaire who fell into the hands of a pair of scheming Spaniards who feel entitled to some of his money, but this, of course, was lost sight of completely upon any excuse whatever."[23] The unidentified author of the *Detroit News* article reviewing the production seemed almost surprised at how well the show was put together. "It was anything but amateurish as a production, however. There was a catchy swing to the music and abundant cleverness in the lines, the settings were thoroughly adequate, and above all, the entire company showed careful training and real talent."[24]

This show not only proved that the members of The Players could put on a successful show but also displayed some of their sense of humor. In the section of the program normally reserved for acknowledgments, The Players listed an aside:

> We desire to thank the management of the Garden Theatre for risking the play house in our hands. Consequently we request the audience to postpone any retaliatory measures until we're out of the theatre.
>
> We desire to thank the Police Commissioner for charitable forbearance.
>
> For certain essential but indefinable portions of the costumerie, we desire to thank certain ladies who, at this moment, being members of

> the audience, are viewing the maltreatment of their raiment with logical misgivings.
>
> Most of all, we desire to thank the audience for its optimism and self control. This perhaps is premature. But we'll take a chance.[25]

It is worth noting that The Players' crest is a comedy mask, and its ancestry is rooted in the Comedy Club. Members of The Players want to enjoy themselves, and although they work hard, they refuse to take themselves too seriously.

The successful *Hairlooms* production prompted discussion of a public performance for a paying audience, and a general meeting of all those of active membership status was called in April 1913 to discuss the matter: "It was the sense of the meeting that any performances in the future, given by THE PLAYERS should not be given for any money consideration. It was argued that such a policy would put the club on a unique basis and keep it free from the charge that there was any professionalism about the Organization. It would mean that the performances would be given solely for the enjoyment of the invited guests of the Club Members."[26]

The next board meeting settled this position by voting unanimously that "it be the future policy of THE PLAYERS that all performances be by invitations only—that no tickets to performances be sold."[27] The board decided at the same time that there would be one big performance every year in the spring, though the minutes do not specifically say that this performance would be open to invited guests. The minutes record that a "Frolic or Stunt Night" was held for a few invited guests in May 1913, but no record of what was performed remains.

This refusal to open Player performances to the public clearly illustrates the nature of the club. Admitting the public would have changed the feel of the occasion for the members in the audience and for those onstage. When the audience is composed solely of Players, it is a very intimate and convivial atmosphere. Even if something goes wrong onstage, it is often just part of the fun to see how the performers will get out of the bind. Jokes often take on a special significance due to the shared history that exists between the performers and the audience. In essence, everyone is an insider; no one is excluded from any of the meanings in any of the performances. The pressure of a paying public audience would have detracted from the social nature of the club. It did not wish to be a community theatre but rather a gentleman's club.

Although there have always been a handful of members who have worked professionally in the entertainment industry, few of the rest of the membership have any training or experience. Some members merely enjoyed watching theatre and preferred to be audience members. The categories of active and associate membership had been created to accommodate just such a division. Associates would pay higher dues and provide the audience while actives would pay lower dues and provide the labor for the shows. At first, all members were active; no associates show up in the minutes until 1913.[28] The actives' efforts in producing the club's entertainments made up the monetary difference between the two categories, and this division was not unusual among other private theatrical clubs.[29] Although every member enjoyed good theatre, not everyone was the most accomplished artist. By removing the possibility of a non-Player audience except for only the most polished performances, ardent amateurs whose enthusiasm may have outweighed ability had a chance to participate in something they enjoyed for an understanding audience.

Although The Players is devoted to remaining an amateur organization, it does not take participation in plays lightly. For many years, when the board of governors chose plays for the frolics and cast them, they did so frolic by frolic, even after the Script Committee was established. It would be decades before the Script and Casting Committee chose the entire season ahead of time. Even when membership numbers were low in the early years, failure to accept an assignment without a suitable explanation in writing would lead to an immediate transfer to associate status.[30] Because the active status members participated in the production of plays and committees, they held the only vote on club matters. Associates provided the audience but had no official vote. This system was, however, altered to allow associates to vote in 1941.

This insistence on participation is reflected in the club motto, *Nunquam Renig*, which has been translated *very* roughly by Al Weeks as "None Shall Refuse"[31] and by others as "Never Refuse," although "Never Renig" is a closer translation. The motto is normally invoked whenever there is a job that needs to be done or a crisis that needs to be solved. Its exact origins are unclear, but it became part of The Players very early and was incorporated into The Player crest by Edgar Bowen. The best explanation of the motto appears in the 26 January 1952 edition of *The Player*. W. E. Kapp wrote a brief synopsis of the early history of The Players and provides the following insight (the slightly inaccurate quote from Al Weeks is from the introduction to *The Players Book of One Act Plays* published in 1928):

> These Founder Players at the very beginning made The Players not just another dramatic society with serious slogans—"The Play's the Thing"—"The Show must go on," but a group with a motto "Numquam *sic*] Renig" on which we quote Player Al Weeks—"It has been pointed out that the motto of the club is not the best Latin. It is not intended to be even bad Latin. The Players does not pretend to teach or elevate anybody. Its sole object is to entertain. And so its motto is a combination of Latin and American slang, thereby removing any suspicion that it is a little group of serious thinkers."[32]

The Players was only one of many clubs and social activities that demanded a member's attention. It was typical at the time to belong to several clubs that catered to various needs, whether they were social or business, so it was not unusual that many of the members were both supporters of the arts and members of the other organizations devoted to the arts in Detroit. In addition, membership in the more exclusive clubs (such as the Yondotega, the Detroit Athletic Club, and the Detroit Club) raised one's social status and allowed one to meet the "right" people. The rapid development of the auto industry in Detroit had made several men millionaires and raised the profile of the city in general, but this created a situation in which new money wanted to be accepted by old money. Membership in the right clubs helped this transition, but so did supporting the pet cultural and charitable institutions of the old elite.

Supporting cultural and charitable institutions was particularly critical in Detroit in the early twentieth century. Except for the Detroit Museum of Art (established in 1888), all of the major cultural and civic institutions were formed between 1905, when the Detroit Orchestral Association was founded to bring orchestras to the city, and 1928, when the Detroit Historical Museum, the Henry Ford Museum, Greenfield Village, and the Detroit Zoo all opened.[33] During the twenty-three-year interim, the Detroit Public Library and the Detroit Museum of Art both gained new homes, a cultural center was developed, and a symphony orchestra was established along with a hall in which it could perform. Donald Finlay Davis's book on the auto industry and elites in Detroit, *Conspicuous Produc-*

*tion: Automobiles and Elites in Detroit, 1899–1933*, describes how new money could buy its way into the upper class by donating the capital necessary to build these cultural institutions (Horace Dodge literally bought his way in by supporting the new symphony).[34] Supporting these institutions was an expected responsibility of the elite that "helped to legitimize the social privileges of the local upper class."[35] Early members of The Players participated in this process, as many of them played a significant role in the nascent stages of the auto industry and supported the new or expanded cultural institutions.

Names that only survive at present as car lines within the Big Three automakers were once freestanding companies. Both entrepreneurs and members of the moneyed elite in Detroit built these institutions before being bought out by larger automakers, usually at a significant profit. The money that was invested in the auto industry came from profits made in enterprises that ran the gamut from manufacturing parts to producing seeds. Player Lem W. Bowen was an officer and director (and later president) of the D. M. Ferry Seed Company, one of the largest businesses in Detroit at the turn of the twentieth century. He, along with Player Frank W. Eddy (his fortune was from chemical and rubber manufacturing) and Player William H. Murphy (his father made his millions in the lumber industry) were the three major backers for the Detroit Automobile Company, which was formed in 1900 and dissolved in 1901 to form the Henry Ford Company. (Eddy chose not to be part of the new company.) When Henry Ford left this company because he was not allowed to focus exclusively on race cars, he was allowed to take his name with him, and the company became Cadillac Automobile Company. Cadillac was sold to General Motors in 1909 for $4.75 million, $4 million of which was clear profit. Murphy was the largest stockholder, with Bowen not far behind. The Henry Ford Company started with only $60,000, Cadillac with $300,000.[36]

Player Henry B. Joy followed much the same path. Joy's father had made his money in railroads, making his son a millionaire and allowing him to invest $25,000 in 1901 in Packard when it was still called the Ohio Automobile Company. Joy invited ten friends to invest the same amount. Four of these were later members of The Players: Richard P. Joy, Truman H. Newberry (Henry Joy was married to his sister, Helen), Frederick Alger, and Joseph Boyer. The Detroit investors took over when the company was reincorporated the next year as Packard Motor Company. After disagreements between Henry Joy and James W. Packard, Packard resigned and Joy's friends forced him to take the presidency, which he held until he resigned in 1916. Even after his resignation and the stock's going public in 1910, the families of the Joys, Newberrys, Algers, and a fourth Detroit family, the McMillans, held two-thirds of the voting stock and prominent positions on the board of directors for the company.[37]

Player Roy D. Chapin, former sales manager for Oldsmobile, formed the E. R. Thomas-Detroit Company in 1906 at the behest of Howard E. Coffin, the former chief engineer for Oldsmobile, and two other colleagues from the company to build a four-cylinder car that Coffin had designed, but Oldsmobile did not want to build. In 1907, Chapin brought in Hugh Chalmers (who became a Player in 1915) to take over the presidency of the company, and by 1908, the company name had been changed to the Chalmers-Detroit Motor Company. Chalmers had recently been fired from National Cash Register's (NCR) vice-presidency but had learned a lot about sales techniques while working for NCR. According to Davis, Chalmers "devoted most of his energies to marketing, and under his personal leadership Chalmers-Detroit became celebrated for such promotion as its annual award to baseball's leading batter and for the triumphs of its 'Blue Bird' racing team."[38] By 1909, Chapin had left to form the Hudson Motor Car Company, and Chalmers-Detroit soon fell under the control of Maxwell Motor Company.[39]

Chalmers had stock in Hudson Motor Car (named for department store owner J. L. Hudson, a major investor), but he traded his stock in Hudson for the stock Chapin and the other original investors still had in Chalmers-Detroit. In addition to the stock trade, he paid them a further $788,000 to make up the difference in the value of the stock. Although this gave Chalmers indisputable control over his company, the former investors made millions on Hudson, whereas Chalmers's company eventually folded. Hudson Motor Company merged with Nash Motors in 1954 to become American Motors.[40]

The seven Fisher brothers followed this same pattern. The fourth Fisher brother, Lawrence P. Fisher, was the only one of the seven to become a member of The Players. His two eldest brothers were incorporators of Fisher Body Company. Lawrence started out in the company as a mechanic. He was vice-president of the company by the time it was sold to General Motors (GM) in 1926. The original investment in the company was $142,000, and it was sold to GM for $208 million. Lawrence chose to remain with the new company as president of the Cadillac Motor Car Company division of GM; Cadillac doubled its business during Lawrence's first two years as president.[41]

Player James Couzens outstripped them all for success in the auto industry. Couzens first arrived at Ford Motor Company when his boss, Alexander T. Malcolmson, a coal dealer and an original Ford investor,[42] sent him to "manage the business end of the enterprise."[43] Although Couzens was not overly enthusiastic about the transfer, in 1903 he put up $1,000 of his own money along with a note for an additional $1,500 for twenty-five shares of stock. When he finally sold his stock back to Henry Ford in 1919, he received $29,308,857.[44] Frank Donovan describes his work for Ford Motor in *Wheels for a Nation:* "The Ford Motor Company might not have survived its infancy without James Couzens. He managed, with an iron hand, every aspect of the business except design and production. He was sales manager, advertising manager, office manager, and purchasing agent and performed the actual duties of secretary and treasurer. He signed up dealers and made closely bargained contracts with suppliers."[45]

In addition to his work in the auto industry, Couzens was appointed Detroit police commissioner in 1916 and elected mayor in 1918. In 1922, Governor Alex Groesbeck appointed him to fill Player Truman H. Newberry's vacated United States Senate seat. Couzens remained in office until his death in 1936.

Other members of The Players held various positions in the car companies. Player James G. Heaslet designed a twenty-horsepower engine for the E-M-F Company.[46] Player Sidney T. Miller was a major stockholder for the Reliance Motor Car Company.[47] Players Arthur H. and Theodore D. Buhl's family owned Buhl Sons (wholesale hardware), Buhl Aircraft, Buhl Stamping, and Buhl Malleable Companies and had invested in Maxwell Briscoe in 1903 and in Paige-Detroit in 1909.[48] Both men were involved in various managerial and director positions with the companies. Player Harry W. Ford was president of Saxon Motor Car Company when it formed in 1913 and previously had been general manager for Chalmers-Detroit Motor Company. Within three years of its founding, Saxon was eighth in the industry, and Ford had bought out the other original investors. Unfortunately, money problems plagued the company after 1917.[49] Edsel B. Ford, Henry Ford's son, held various positions at Ford Motor Company, including president, but is best known for the cultural contributions he made to Detroit.

Another Player had close ties to the auto industry but was better known for his political career. Player Edwin Denby was a major investor in Hupp Motor Car Company, but his family had made its name in politics (his grandfather had been a United States senator, and his father was the first United States ambassador to China).[50] With this background, it is not surprising that Denby himself went into politics. He served in the Michigan House of Representatives (1903–5), was a United States representative from Michigan from 1905 to 1911, but gained infamy as the secretary of the navy who had to resign over the Teapot Dome scandal. The scandal involved improperly leasing naval oil reserves at Teapot Dome (Wyoming) to the Mammoth Oil Company and at Elk Hills (California) to Pan-American Petroleum and Transport for drastically below worth and involved bribes paid to various government officials. Denby was not personally involved in the scandal but was asked to resign because he had not overseen the reserves and the actions taken involving them by Secretary of the Interior Albert B. Fall, who was the main conspirator in the case.

The auto industry helped spur on the development of several advertising firms in Detroit. Eric Dregni and Karl Hagstrom Miller in their book *Ads That Put American on Wheels* go so far as to say that "the two industries rode each other's coattails to prominence."[51] Early Players figured prominently in advertising from both within and without the auto industry. Player Lee Anderson began his career as a sportswriter for the *Detroit News* but moved on to become the advertising manager for Chalmers Motor Company and eventually began his own advertising companies, first Advertisers, Inc., and then Lee Anderson Advertising Company, Inc.[52] Advertisers, Inc., had accounts with Dodge and Chrysler, and Anderson lured another Player, Frank G. Kane, away from a Chicago advertising firm to work on the car accounts. Three other Players, Al M. Corrigan, Albert L. "Al" Weeks, and Edward A. "Ned" Batchelor, also worked for the firm.[53] Anderson, who created the slogan "Body by Fisher,"[54] later became vice-president of MacManus, Inc., an advertising firm that remains nationally prominent to this day.

MacManus was the self-titled firm of another Player,

Theodore F. MacManus, who had worked "as director of publicity and advertising counsel at various times for Ford, General Motors, Peerless, Hupmobile, Graham Bros., Goodyear Tires, Fisher Bodies, Chrysler, Dodge Bros., Packard, etc.," an impressive advertising resume by any standard.[55] Player Kirkland Alexander was his treasurer for a time.[56]

MacManus was not the only major advertiser in town. Campbell-Ewald, another nationally prominent firm, was founded in 1911 in part by Player Henry T. Ewald, who became its president in 1917. He also founded the Adcraft Club of Detroit in 1905.[57] Adcraft, still in existence today, describes its current purpose as providing "support and direction for those involved and interested in the advertising industry in metro Detroit."[58] Players Joseph H. Neebe and Walter Boynton were both on the executive staff of the Campbell-Ewald Company. Player George Harrison Phelps was the president of his own firm, George Harrison Phelps, Inc., National Advertising Counselors, and another Player, Maxwell Irving Pitkin, worked as his director of copy.[59] Not every Player in advertising specialized in the auto industry, however. Players founder Guy Brewster Cady specialized first in counter displays and then later in mailers,[60] and Player James Strasburg was the advertising manager for Detroit Theatres, Inc., making his membership in The Players an obvious choice.[61] Appendix C discusses Players' professional lives in more detail.

Detroit put the money generated by the auto industry to good use. When the symphony was established in 1914, future Player William H. Murphy was one of three principal benefactors. Among the eight "prominent" but smaller donors listed by Davis who contributed to the construction of Orchestra Hall, five were members of The Players prior to their donation.[62] One of these, Player Jerome H. Remick, was the president of J. H. Remick and Co., a large Detroit firm that specialized in sheet music, giving him an excellent reason to support a symphony.[63] That same year, the club contributed to the Detroit Museum of Art (now the Detroit Institute of Arts) to help "defray the expense of the exhibit of the Hume Models of Stage Craft."[64] Sam Hume, along with other theatrical designer greats such as Lee Simonson and Robert Edmund Jones, had studied in Europe in the early teens and brought the "new stagecraft" to the United States. This new stagecraft reflected the influence of Adolphe Appia and Gordon Craig on the theoretical purpose of stage design. Hume was later president of the Detroit Society of Arts and Crafts.[65]

Members of The Players had ties to both the Detroit Museum of Art and the Detroit Society of Arts and Crafts. A very early gift from Player and pharmaceutical manufacturer Frederick K. Stearns (his son, Frederick S. Stearns, was a founding member of The Players) in 1890 provided the museum with "16,000 objects from China, Japan, Korea, India, and Persia; the institution's first antiquities."[66] Later, when the institution moved from private hands to public ownership by the city of Detroit, the first Arts Commission was formed, and Player Ralph W. H. Booth was elected president, and Player Clyde H. Burroughs, secretary. Burroughs was also a curator for the museum. The commission saw to the transfer of title of the collections and land from the Museum of Art to the Detroit Institute of Arts and the planning and construction of its current building in the Cultural Center.[67]

Player ties to the Detroit Society of Arts and Crafts were just as close. The society was founded in 1906 but not formally incorporated until 1915. H. J. Maxwell Grylls, a founding member of The Players, became its president in 1911. Even before his election, the Arts and Crafts society had a strong link to the dramatic arts. In 1910 and 1911, the society sponsored masques (dramatic pageants; see chapter 1) and had a costume design department. When the Abbey Players of Dublin (a significant art theatre of the time) were touring America, the Detroit society brought one of the Dublin society's founding members, Lady Augusta Gregory, to Detroit to speak.[68] When the Arts and Crafts society constructed its own building in 1916 at 25 Watson Street (not far from Wayne State University's current Bonstelle Theatre), it became the first Arts and Crafts society in the United States to include a theatre and also the first American society to design and build its own theatre.[69] It was also the first "art organization in the world to publicly acknowledge the automobile as an art form."[70] Grylls designed the Arts and Crafts society building with his fellow Detroit architect and member of the society, William B. Stratton. During its first season, 1916–17, the Arts and Crafts Little Theatre produced nineteen shows, most of them one acts, and several members of The Players appear in the cast lists.[71] The society's involvement in theatre quickly attracted the attention of Sheldon Cheney, who became a member of the society and founded *Theatre Arts Magazine*, one of the first serious publications in America about theatre.[72] He also wrote *The Art Theatre* (1917), one of the earliest American books on the topic. An appendix in the back of the

# The Player

Volume I      Detroit, Michigan, December 1, 1916      No. 1

## New Governors at Work

Tuesday, November 7, 1916, is a date that will go down into history. It was election day. The Players' annual meeting was held at the Hotel Statler and officers for the coming year were chosen.

Four members were retained from last year's Board of Governors and three new men were elected. Players Boynton, Cady and Lerchen, having worked long and earnestly as directors, begged to be relieved of their duties. They were replaced on the board by Players Corbin, Pabst and Reed.

At a meeting of the new Governors which followed the general election, Player J. Theodore Reed was made president. Players Ely and Murphy were made vice-president and treasurer, respectively, while Player Standish was again the unanimous choice for secretary. President Reed immediately appointed committee chairmen, and the season's work was started.

On November 20, Player Corbin announced his intention to move to Petrograd. This made it necessary to appoint a new member to fill the vacancy on the board, so Player A. Laurence Smith, who has always been an enthusiastic and hardworking member of the club, was selected to take Player Corbin's place.

## Among Those Present

Sam Hume, than whom there is no greater luminary in the world of stagecraft, has been invited to our first meeting. Mr. Hume is responsible for the Arts and Crafts stage and all appurtenances thereto and also deserves great credit for the selection and direction of the initial productions given in that theater.

With the man who built the stage in our midst, and acting under his stern scrutiny, the Players must show that their work merits all of the extra care that could be put into the realm behind the curtain, even by such an expert as Mr. Hume.

If some kind soul will show Mr. Hume this item he may feel more kindly disposed toward our organization and give us the manuscript of a couple of plays which we know he has, and which we could produce, as Guy would say, floeently.

## The New Theater

So much has been written and said about the delightful little theater just completed by the Society of Arts and Crafts that no description need be given here. It is sufficient to say that the Players will at last have an ideal place to stage their productions.

The auditorium is of a size that will accommodate our audiences with comfort. The stage has been emphatically and unanimously approved by the Players who investigated its merits. The acoustics are perfect and the location is central. The rental cost per performance will be much greater than we have been accustomed to paying, but this advance will be justified by the increase in attendance.

The Arts and Crafts Theater

Cover page of the first edition of *The Player*

first edition of this book lists the plays and players from that first season at the Arts and Crafts society, in addition to pictures from the productions. Later editions replaced these lists with information from more nationally prominent theatres.

The Arts and Crafts Little Theatre at Watson Street was designed to accommodate the ideals of the Art Theatre movement; thus it was an intimate space with chairs that could be moved around instead of rows of attached seating.[73] This was the perfect atmosphere for The Players, so they chose the Arts and Crafts theatre as their new home when it opened in 1916. That same year, The Players began publishing their newsletter, *The Player*.

To help make the entertainment after the frolics run more smoothly, the club initiated the position of "Toastmaster of the Afterglow." The Afterglow was the party that followed the frolic in the tradition of the opening-night party. There were skits, glee clubs, bands, comedians, talks, minstrel shows (in the early decades), and all manner of other entertainers, both amateur and professional. Because every frolic but the May Show was technically an opening night, that meant a lot of parties. The Toastmaster helped arrange for entertainment and guest performers for The Players and generally helped maintain the convivial atmosphere. At some point this position was dubbed the "Glowworm," a title that first shows up in *The Player* in 1919.[74] The exact origins of this name have been lost to the mists of time, but the title allows an endless stream of Player critics to determine after the evening's entertainment whether the much put-upon Player who occupied this position was more "glow" or worm.

The first mention of a possible permanent home (i.e., bought or built, not rented) shows up in the January 1916 minutes, but the board did not seriously consider the issue until March 1917.[75] The pros and cons were discussed, including the possibility of combining with other theatrical clubs (the Fine Arts Society and the Theatre Arts Club), but this latter idea was not met favorably. Although there was great interest in a permanent space, most members did not think the club was in a position either to outlay the necessary money or to incur the debt.[76] That same month, a discussion regarding a permanent home appeared in *The Player* under the heading "Our Own Playhouse?": "We want a man's playhouse. We want cloak rooms and space for storing our own scenery and the privilege of choosing our own dates for rehearsals and performances. If it is the Players' pleasure to drop lighted things on the floor let's have a place with an iron floor and asbestos upholstered furniture. We want—well, there are many things we want which we might be able to get if we felt at home."[77] This quote broadly hints that The Players incurred the displeasure of the Arts and Crafts society on several occasions by breaking, damaging, or burning various pieces of property, which they definitely did, and that they were frustrated at having to work their frolics around the activities scheduled for the society.

The war in Europe in 1915 impacted the purely social nature of The Players. Although the United States was not yet engaged in the Great War, it was not unusual for Detroit residents to cross the border into Canada to enlist. When Player Charles Stringer left for Europe, the board of governors remitted his dues and gave him a leave of absence from the club. This became standard policy during the war years.[78] The United States declared war on the Central Powers on 6 April 1917, and twelve days later the board of governors decided that the May Show would be held as a benefit for the Red Cross.[79]

In November 1917, the war hit home for The Players as many members were called into service. Although accommodations had been made in the past, the board sent a letter to all members in the service indicating that dues would be remitted upon request and that any who had sent checks could have them returned.[80] There must have been some criticism of the club during that year as being too frivolous in a time of war. In a November 1917 article, *The Player* defended the club on the grounds that "there never was a time when The Players were needed as they are this particular year."[81] A year later, *The Player* again spoke out on the issue: "Many a busy man is finding that he needs The Players as a sort of tonic."[82]

Players were involved in the war effort at home and abroad. Player (and police commissioner) James Couzens had been appointed chairman of the War Entertainment Board (an official position, not a new club committee), and Player president Campbell offered the services of The Players to the war effort. Along with the Fine Arts Society, they donated money to buy a Victrola for the military hospital at Camp Custer.[83] Advertising executive Player Henry T. Ewald was the publicity director of the Liberty Loan Drive for Detroit that raised $5 million.[84] The theatre world in general volunteered time and money to the war effort. Some playwrights had The Players send royalty checks to the Stage Women's War Relief Committee in lieu of personal payment.

Individual members participated in Drama League productions at Fort Wayne, but the impact of The Players was not confined to Michigan. Player Charles M. Steele was sent a makeup kit to use in shows he put on for his fellow soldiers in France.[85] The 1918 May Show was held for the benefit of the Patriotic Fund, and the Saturday matinee of this show was free to anyone involved in military service. By the time the war ended in November 1918, fifty-four Players had served in the military, and Player Harry W. Ford had died in action.

The war was never far from the minds of The Players. An "honor roll" listing members in service appeared in every issue of *The Player* for the duration of the war (a typical practice for most clubs, from bowling leagues to the esteemed Detroit Athletic Club). The most interesting effect of the war on The Players was their choice of plays. For the most part, plays dealing with war were avoided, although some were set aside for production at a later date. "A general discussion as to material for the season followed, Player Weeks reading *Wine O' Dreams*, an anonymous sketch. It was decided inadvisable to produce it this season because of the general feeling on the part of the board that war plays should be dispensed with."[86] This attitude was remembered a few years later when another rejected play, *Whispers*, by Marian Eddy Standish (wife of Player W. Colburn Standish)[87] was once again brought to the attention of the board:

> Governor Phelps Newberry submitted an anonymous script called "Whispers," and read it to the Board. It is an unusual dramatic piece dealing with the war in France. Governor Meadon recollected the same script being submitted to the Board, (and named whom he believed to be the author), in 1919 or '20. At that time it was decided not to produce the sketch, although it had undoubted merit, because too many of the returned service men, and even those at home, had been "fed up" on war plays. It was the opinion of the Governors that such a play should be done on an evening when a good comedy can go on each side of it on the program.[88]

This preference was not unusual. The Players have always produced more comedies, mysteries, and adventures than serious pieces. An occasional melodrama or dramatic piece crops up, but the social nature of the club demands lighter material. No serious piece is performed without being accompanied by less dramatic fare and usually is sandwiched between more humorous pieces as described in the previous quotation. In addition, The Players has always encouraged plays by its own members (or members' wives, as was the case here). This tradition is as old as the club itself, as evidenced by members' coming up with their own skits for the vaudeville nights.

Although this time period brought some hardships to the club, it also brought some of its most admired members. One of the Players most revered by club members to this day, Sam I. Slade, was proposed for membership in January 1915.[89] Sam Slade was one of the best dramatic actors to tread the boards at The Players. He was a voice teacher by trade, but he appeared on the Detroit stage from time to time as well as at The Players.[90] A 1924 article in *The Player* notes some of his professional work: "For a fortnight at the Adams Theatre Player Sam Slade impersonated Lincoln. This week he is doing an imitation of Jackie Coogan at the Capital."[91] His portrait smiles down on the Founders Room at the Players' Playhouse today.

The Players were fortunate to have resident playwrights who provided material that catered to the tastes and needs of the club (witness the early *Hairlooms*). One of the first great Player playwrights was Albert Loren Weeks. Al Weeks joined the club in January 1915 (not long after Slade was proposed) and quickly became a prolific producer of one acts. He had a varied career that emphasized writing. In his early years, he wrote advertising copy while writing plays on the side. He was the coauthor with Seymour Simons of *Her Family Tree*, a Broadway musical in 1920 that starred Nora Bayes and Frank Morgan. Professionally, Weeks was first a reporter for the *Detroit Free Press* and later the drama critic for the *Detroit News*.[92] Following that, he was a writer and narrator for the Metropolitan Motion Picture Company.[93]

During the 1919–20 season, Player C. Hayward Murphy appears as a stage manager/stage director. He had joined earlier in 1911, but he took over a role for The Players that was much akin to that of a technical director—someone who oversees the construction of the set and props plus the implementation of the lighting design. He was very influential in ensuring that Player productions had individually designed sets and a stage crew to run the shows.

This was a massive job, as there were a minimum of five frolics a year plus the May Show. The monthly frolics had an average of three one acts that often had complex sets. Union stagehands were hired to run the actual frolics, with Murphy acting as stage manager. Carpenters and scenic painters were also hired, although the sets were designed and sometimes built by Players. In addition to his responsibilities at The Players, Murphy was also the commissioner of the Detroit Fire Department.

Player Russell H. Legge joined the club that same season, and his caricatures first appeared in the March 1920 edition of *The Player*.[94] Although sketches were a regular part of the magazine, Legge's drawings were to become a standard in *The Player* until his death in 1941. He was a professional illustrator and worked for the *Detroit Free Press*, where he also sketched performers that passed through Detroit. In many instances, Legge's drawings are the only visual record of Player performances. His original sketches of frolics and Player activities still grace the walls of the Players Playhouse.

In addition to the Great War, during its early decades The Players also had to deal with the effects of Prohibition. Prohibition was enacted in the club's home state before it was established nationwide. Michigan voted on 7 November 1916 to become a dry state, with the law taking effect on 1 May 1918. Despite institution of the new regulations, liquor did not stop flowing in Detroit: the location of the Detroit River, which separates the United States and Canada, presented what Prohibition historian Larry Englemann describes as a "natural invitation to smuggling."[95] Englemann's chronicle of the fight to enforce Prohibition in Michigan details the hopelessness of the task in stark detail. Not only did the river pose a keen temptation to smugglers, but also the province of Ontario, located across the river from Detroit, profited from its own liquor taxes and thus had no incentive to enforce America's Prohibition laws.[96] Apparently, officials on the U.S. side of the river also had little incentive. A reporter for the Grand Rapids *Herald* was shocked to discover that liquor was openly served to members of the Michigan legislature in the capital hotels.[97] The lesser officials who were expected to enforce Prohibition on the streets were "ill trained and poorly equipped, disorganized and uncoordinated," in addition to being underpaid and therefore highly susceptible to bribes.[98]

Detroit was a natural entry point for smuggled Canadian alcohol not only because of the strategic location of the Detroit

"Farewell to Bacchus," a 1918 cartoon in response
to Michigan's becoming a dry state

River but also because the Hiram Walker plant is directly across the river. According to an article in *The Player* written by Player James Strasburg, the beer flowed freely during Prohibition, but it arrived over a rather circuitous route:

> Under the regime of President George Harrison Phelps, the Governors would authorize the purchase of three barrels of beer for the next Frolic [these authorizations were never recorded in the minutes]. This authorization was delegated to Player Henry Koch, head beer buyer. Henry then passed it to his assistant beer buyer, another Player, who knew how to get the real stuff but had to keep his knowledge secret, which was in accordance with the ethics of those days. The assistant then passed the order to Harry, maitre d'hotel of the Racquet club [also on Jefferson Avenue, not far from the present day location of the Renaissance Center]. Harry was the key man. He really knew personally the bootlegger who could deliver simon pure alley beer. The loaded barrels were eased surreptitiously into the Little Theatre [the Arts and Crafts theatre] on the Saturday afternoon of the Frolic and Player Olie Standish, then enjoying the first flush of success in his bartending career, would go to work on the barrels with his paraphernalia after which technical process he would don his accouterments for the evening.
> 
> This bootlegger would sneak out his empties early Sunday morning. That was the theory. He couldn't always get into the place, which generally led to pretty embarrassing consequences. Before long the bootlegger would begin to think that he wanted his money. So he would dun Harry of the Racquet club. Harry would dun the assistant beer buyer of the Players. The assistant would dun Henry Koch. Henry would dun the Treasurer. The Treasurer would mail a check made out to Henry. Henry

would mail it to his assistant who would mail it to Harry of the Racquet club. Harry would nip off his bit, which he had ably earned, and would pay off the bootlegger.

That's the way the Players got it. And that's the way big business of all sorts was transacted in the rich and roaring '20s. Those were the days!⁹⁹

Later stories, passed down through generations of Players, recount incidences of bootlegging at the Players Playhouse. These stories point out that the Playhouse faced the river and thus had a clear view of Canada: supposedly, Players could stand at the windows and watch the progress of the boat carrying their liquor to the dock, where two uniformed Detroit city cops would meet the delivery, escort it to the Playhouse, and hand it over to the police commissioner. (It is unclear whether there was ever a truly unobstructed view of the Detroit River, let alone being able to see a little boat in the dark on the river.) One of the present-day Players, John M. Butterfield, points out that the upstage loading dock at the Playhouse is designed to accommodate beer barrels, and other Players have insisted that the grooves worn into the back steps by the stage door are the result of beer kegs being bumped down them.¹⁰⁰

Although it is true that several major Detroit officials have been members of the Players, there is no documented evidence to prove that they were directly involved in the bootlegging or that any members of Detroit's finest had any part in procuring for The Players. In fact, as *The Player* pointed out to members, it was Player Bob Toms's job to prosecute bootleggers: "Graft, alleged vote-frauds, hold-ups, wholesale bootleggings, or Grand Jury investigations, are things of great moment to citizens of Wayne County. Player Prosecuting Attorney Robert M. Toms not only makes a one hundred per cent job of the foregoing, but also finds time, by working between 2:00 to 5:00 A.M. [to rehearse a play]."¹⁰¹ One hopes that he never had to prosecute the bootlegger that supplied the club. As these officials could not have missed the presence of alcohol at the frolics, they could not have been too set against the bootlegging. Beer is, after all, as ubiquitous as tuxes at the frolics.

Conversely, *The Player* published a warning to the membership to keep their less-than-legal activities under wraps around Detroit politicians who were also members of the club:

James Couzens, the Mayor; John Lodge, vice mayor and president of the Common Council; and Edward T. Fitzgerald, the Woolsey of the incoming Government, are all members of The Players. Knowing all three gentlemen, the editor wishes to remind fellow Players that if they contemplate any dirty work in the way of licker *sic*] lugging or starting a stuss game, it might be just as well to see one of this powerful trio before beginning operations. See them and say goodbye, for that will be the last meeting.[102]

Considering the general attitude of The Players and the knowledge that these politicians *must* have known about the alcohol, this may have been a subtle reminder to include them in the goings-on, or face their wrath.

Another interesting indication of Players' position on the social climate of the twenties is the attitude toward the "New Girl." The New Girl was personified by the flapper, a woman far more brazen then the older generation of women brought up under Victorian mores. An indication of this attitude appears in a review of the show *Fair Enough* by Richard Connell, a courtroom drama in which all characters but the defendant were female. "There is no need for Flo Ziegfield to come to Detroit again, ever. We who saw this up-to-date drama and gazed fearfully at its characters, realize that the American girl has been glorified too much—too much!"[103]

The play that is most indicative of their attitude toward both Prohibition and the New Girl is *In the Thousands of Years to Come* by Player Lee Anderson. Written in 1920, the play is set a hundred years into the future in a very different America in which constitutional amendments have "raised the world to the perfection of efficiency."[104] The list of amendments covering everything from what clothing can be worn to what kind of furniture can be used is so extensive that it takes a book the size of a large dictionary to list them all.

The play begins as a scientist and his friends discover a bottle of mysterious liquid that predates the passage of the Eighteenth Amendment, described as the first of the "great laws which, starting with abolition of then-described intoxicating beverages have purified the race of all deleterious habits."[105] During the course of their "scientific exploration" of this bottle, they are constantly interrupted by the women in their lives. One woman enters to request the hand of the scientist's son. As provided by the "great laws," she is an inch taller, two years older, and has sufficient income to support him once they are married.[106] This reversal of traditional gender roles is the future consequence of the idea of the "New Girl," as Anderson sees it. The wives of the scientist and his friends are much worse than this young woman. When the men are caught sampling their find in the name of science (and enjoying its effects), the women order the friends home like small, disobedient children (the Seventy-Sixth Amendment says that husbands must obey their wives). When the men ignore them, their wives threaten to report them to the authorities. When that does not work, the women destroy the remaining alcohol in triumph.[107]

This satire addresses the general dislike among club members of not only the government's attempt to legislate morality but also the changing of social roles that was accelerating at the start of the twenties. As the "guardians of the home," women were a major part of the Prohibition movement. They were, however, not alone in this: most people who voted for the law thought that it would help bring about "social order" and had assumed that wine and beer would still be legal for public consumption.[108] As Lynn Dumenil's chronicle of social life in the twenties records, it was popular to bash Prohibition; *Life* magazine used Prohibition as the butt of their jokes in numerous articles and cartoons.[109] With the attitude of club members and society in general against the government's morality laws, it is hardly surprising that Prohibition failed miserably both in Detroit and across the nation.

Although the image of the Roaring Twenties may lead one to believe that a stag club, particularly a club with a lighthearted attitude, would relax the rules of conduct, quite the opposite was true of The Players. As mentioned in the introduction to this volume, tradition and a certain level of formality were integral to club activities. There was a strict policy that all members attending frolics were to wear tuxedos—although apparently they had to be reminded of this occasionally, as happened in an article that appeared in the March 1922 edition of *The Player*, "Nunquam Renig Tuxedorum."[110] In addition, the minutes record several occasions on which the board of governors felt it necessary to admonish an individual Player's conduct as unbefitting of a member. Although the exact nature of the conduct is seldom detailed, it is often recorded as having been "disruptive" to a frolic.[111] This code of conduct extended to guest performers at the Afterglows. Walter Hiers, a silent film actor best known for his comic roles, participated in an Afterglow, but according to an article in *The Player*, his performance was not up to Players' standards:

Mr. Hiers was very funny and we appreciate his presence. However, he made us wonder. Why do men who should be audience-wise persist in telling smutty stories at stag gatherings? Perhaps there isn't one of us who does not enjoy a deep-hued story in a Pullman smoker or off in a corner. But we all shrink several sizes smaller and look for some hole to crawl into when one is pulled from the stage. The funny part of it is that professional actors are the ones who do it, as witness Leon Errol and Mr. Hiers. Some day some of these folks will learn that such stuff isn't necessary. Furthermore, it isn't funny. Mr. Hiers ['s] stories would have been uproarious to an audience of five.[112]

Another famous and much more appreciated performer brought to the Players' stage was the comedian Bert Williams:

Through the efforts of Player Al Weeks, the inimitable Bert Williams had been prevailed upon to appear. With Player Holliday at the piano, the famous comedian appeared and sang "That's a Plenty." But as he started the second verse, out from the wings came the real Bert Williams, who quickly unmasked (or perhaps unwigged would be a happier word) the singer, and showed him up for the man he was—Al Weeks. The real Bert then told us all about "Martin," and also made us laugh until we cried as we, in delightful imagination, dodged baseballs with him at Coney Island.[113]

Williams was a major comic performer of the day who started out in minstrel shows, worked the vaudeville circuit, and eventually was hired as one of the stars of the *Ziegfield Follies*. In his rise through the ranks, Williams, a black performer, broke several color lines, not the least of which was headlining the *Follies*.[114] Although there is no indication that African Americans were members of The Players in the early twentieth century (there were African American members in the late twentieth century, however), or indeed would have been allowed to join in the early years, the club seems to have welcomed both black and white visiting performers to its Afterglows on an equal basis. The Playhouse also hosted a special event in 1927 when the Detroit Urban League wanted to hold a presentation for the African American poet and playwright Countee Cullen.[115]

The club did perform occasional minstrel shows (variety shows featuring white performers in blackface singing, dancing, and performing comic acts with stereotyped racial humor and caricatures) in its early years, as they were considered part of the vaudeville tradition, were seen on the public stage at the time, and were easily produced by the club. There were occasional minstrel shows as part of the Afterglows in the twenties and thirties, and one rather late Afterglow performance in 1952.[116] Blackface performances (including black performers in blackface—something Bert Williams did) were seen on Broadway into the thirties, and the movies *White Christmas* (1954) and *Holiday Inn* (1942), among others, make reference to minstrel shows, and these performances were therefore common for the time, although they have become distasteful to later generations.

Prior to 1923, the club had had some discussion of building a permanent home. By February of that year, The Players was seriously considering a permanent playhouse and as a first step created a Site Committee. To further the overall effort to build a space, the board established a General Committee "to direct the preliminary operations of various committees looking to the establishment of a Players' home and playhouse, this committee to have power to create sub-committees to carry on any special phases of the work."[117] Player Joseph Meadon, a past president, was elected chairman of the New Playhouse General Committee. By April, the committee was already considering a piece of land near the Detroit Society of Arts and Crafts.[118] Despite this, at the general meeting in May, the membership decided that it would be better to postpone construction until a building fund could be established. The board of trustees, consisting of Players Henry G. Stevens, C. Hayward Murphy, and Lee Anderson, was elected to organize the building of the Playhouse.

At a general meeting in May, the members were shown stereopticon slides of the proposed playhouse and subsequently passed a motion to begin a subscription drive to raise money for it.[119] By the annual meeting on 15 May 1923, $28,240 in subscriptions had been pledged. The members also decided at this meeting to increase the number of active members allowed from 125 to 150 and associate members from 200 to 250. This was done as a means both to generate revenue and to meet the growing demand for admittance to the club. The numbers of nonresident members had no limit, so they were unaffected by the changes.

In the meantime, the Detroit Society of Arts and Crafts and The Players had managed to settle their differences. The 1922–23 season had been spent at the Harmonie Society, and The Players wanted to return to the Arts and Crafts theatre. The exact nature of the rift is not detailed, but it was likely related to admonitions that had appeared periodically in *The Player* advising the members to stop leaving a mess and breaking things (unintentionally) at the Arts and Crafts theatre. The Players still protested their innocence almost twenty years later: "In the course of inhuman events, The Players were ejected, along about 1921 from their erstwhile habitat, the Arts and Crafts Little Theatre on Watson Street. This was through no fault of their own. It was due to those relentless circumstances over which one has no control. Thereupon The Players became a wandering tribe—the 'Strolling Players' they were known as, in those days; and they drifted rather helplessly for a time in what is now recorded as the Harmonie Society era."[120] Part of the new agreement with the Arts and Crafts society stipulated that The Players provide an hour of entertainment at the annual meeting of the Detroit Society of Arts and Crafts and that a Christmas show be produced that would be open to children of the members of the society. The Society of Arts and Crafts probably resented being excluded from all of the productions occurring on its own stage. The society had stopped producing its own shows in 1919 when Sam Hume left to take an assistant professorship at the University of California. Even when Hume had been present, however, the board of the society had sometimes felt excluded from the productions in its theatre and thoroughly resented it.[121] Members of Arts and Crafts probably still remembered this and wanted some involvement on their own stage.

This Christmas show was a joint venture in many ways, using members of both clubs and thus including women. *The Tinder Box* was coauthored by Mr. and Mrs. Weeks (Vera, although *The Player* refers to her as "Mrs. Al") and was a great success. Inspired by a Hans Christian Anderson tale, the story was a "yarn about Peter, the brave young soldier of Narbeth, and how, with the aid of a self-lighting tinder box and three of the hottest of hot dogs, he wooed and won the pretty Princess Paulette, whose post office address was also Narbeth."[122]

"The Ballad of the Player's Daughter"[123]

"What is a Player, Papa?
Little Mary said.

"A Player, child," her papa smiled,
Scratching his hairless head.

> "A Player, dear—well now, I fear—
> "Whatever under the sun
> Caused you to ask?" He filled his flask,
> A beautiful flask and a pleasant task.
> "Whatever under the sun!"
>
> "'Cause Ma just told me—pa, don't scold me—
> "Never to MARRY one."

In addition to Al Weeks and Lee Anderson, Player William F. Holliday was another major Player playwright. Like Weeks and Anderson, Holliday dealt with themes that hit close to home with The Players. One of his productions dealt with people near and dear to the hearts of Detroiters. *If a Little Ford Should Lead 'Em* is a satire on Detroit politicians and industrialists and on a potential presidential run for Henry Ford—an actual possibility Ford considered in 1924. This possible explanation of the play's plot is merely an assumption, however, because the script was lost, and *The Player* that reviewed the show recounts nothing of the storyline. Despite this, the cast of characters includes such political and economic figures as Norval Hawkins (postmaster general in this piece, but he actually worked first for Ford Motor Company and then General Motors), William Livingston (secretary of the treasury), and Henry and Edsel Ford (Edsel did not play himself, and it is unclear if he was in the audience that night).[124] The review for the show joked that Jake Hirschfield's makeup was considered so close to the actual figures being represented that pictures were taken and reproduced in *The Player*. The pictures were stock photographs of the illustrious men, not images taken at the frolic.

Hirschfield was another interesting Player fixture. He was a professional costumer and makeup artist by trade. It was his expertise that turned members of The Players into women and historical figures, but he was not made an honorary member until 1955. He was known as Detroit's "Man of 10,000 Faces" and "kept a collection of character wigs and a scrapbook of pictures of famous people whom he might be asked to imitate." In addition to his work at The Players, his business, Hirschfield's Inc., "served amateur groups through the Detroit area."[125]

The humor on The Players' stage did not always come from the material presented but occasionally from the mishaps that occurred onstage. These were always taken in stride, but a particularly amusing incident occurred during the 1924 May Show. During the piece *His Majesty*,

> Player Jeff Webb was to shoot Player Macklin. Well, the gun only clicked. Instantly Jeff began to club Charlie over the head with the butt of the revolver. He made a thorough job of it; so thorough, in fact, that Charlie, quietly, but very emphatically, cried to Jeff during the struggle—"For God's sake, Jeff, quit, quit! I'll die—I'll die!"
> 
> After that, Jeff's line was—"Your father's friend committed suicide!" But not Jeff—he knew better; he didn't say it. Inspiration under unlooked for and unwelcome circumstances made Jeff an author, as well as acrobat, that night.[126]

Many such incidents crop up in the annals of *The Player*: flaming bass drums, misplaced sound cues, and personal injuries have added a bit of unexpected humor to the frolics, and they are as dutifully recorded as the shows themselves (if not more so).

By April 1924, The Players' subscriptions were up to fifty thousand dollars. The club had also increased both dues and fees that year to help pay for the costs associated with building the Playhouse. In 1920, the initiation fee was raised to twenty-five dollars, with an increase in dues to fifteen dollars for actives and twenty-five dollars for associates.[127] The 1924 increase was far more significant. The initiation fee was doubled to fifty dollars, and by 1925, the initiation fee was increased to one hundred dollars, with dues increasing to fifty dollars for actives and seventy-five dollars for associates.[128]

The club had narrowed their site selections to two locations. One site was on East Grand Boulevard near the Packard Motor Company, and the other was on Jefferson Avenue across from the Michigan Stove Works (the location near the Detroit Society of Arts and Crafts had long since been discarded). The Jefferson Avenue site was actually a choice between two adjoining lots. Mr. Miller owned one of these and was willing to sell for five hundred dollars a square foot, and the other belonged to the Newberry Estate, which was selling for six hundred dollars a foot. Player Phelps Newberry was asked to negotiate with his father. If the Newberry Estate was willing to sell its land at the Miller rate, The Players would take it.[129] The negotiations are not discussed in the extant records, but a settlement was reached with the Newberry Estate for their parcel.

The records do say that the Jefferson Avenue location was preferable to the Grand Boulevard site, but they are unclear as to why the Newberry land was chosen over the Miller land. It may have been better situated, it may have allowed for expansion (the lack of parking space for the club was and continues to be an issue), or it may have been a matter of all things being equal, they wanted to give money to an organization that had Player ties. This was not an unusual practice with The Players. Not only was a Player a partner in the architectural firm that was building the Playhouse, but also The Players had moved its bank account from the First National Bank of Detroit to the National Bank of Commerce in November 1923 "as a courtesy to Player L. H. D. Baker."[130] There is no indication that this transfer was in any way instigated by Player Baker.

To aid the Players in dealing with the financial and legal problems of building their home quarters, the board of governors decided to form a separate company that would "own and control the new playhouse." This company would be "composed of members of The Players who have made subscription and may later subscribe for the building and financing of [the Playhouse]."[131] The following Players were members of the board of The Players Holding Company: Edgar W. Bowen, Edsel B. Ford, C. H. Haberkorn Jr., William G. Lerchen, C. Hayward Murphy, W. H. Murphy, Phelps Newberry, George Harrison Phelps, Martin L. Pulcher, and Henry G. Stevens. Each of the ten signed the note that enabled The Players to borrow the money to proceed with their building. By signing, each agreed to be liable for ten thousand dollars apiece. Anyone who had paid on the subscription to the Playhouse was considered a stockholder. Thus most of the Players were also stockholders in The Players Holding Company.

H. J. Maxwell Grylls, one of the The Players' founders, was a partner in the architectural firm of Smith, Hinchman, and Grylls (still a leading firm in Detroit, today known as the SmithGroup), which had been contracted to build the Players Playhouse. The only detailed description of Grylls's contribution to building the Playhouse (other than cutting checks and showing slides) is an article in *The Player* by Player James Strasburg, written when Player William Kapp was elected president of The Players in 1940, fifteen years after the Playhouse was built. Along with Grylls, Kapp figured prominently in the building of the Playhouse, although he was not a Player at the time:

Max Grylls stepped forth into the quandary and quietly, modestly and generously proffered his talents and equipment as an architect to design and erect a suitable building for us at a minimum cost, his services as architect to be free, gratis, for nothing.

Shortly thereafter we became aware of a long-legged, lithe, likable, dark-haired enthusiastic young gentleman with the gleam of the zealot in his friendly eye, his hair and coat tails flying as he dashed about with a roll of blue prints under one arm and a sheaf of sketches under the other. He could always be stopped quite easily, whereupon he would show and explain carefully the blue prints and the attractive sketches which he had made of the proposed Playhouse. This was Max Grylls's bright young man, Bill Kapp. Max supervised Bill. Bill supervised design, constructions, contractors, materials, work and workmen. And—*mirabile dictu!* When the place was done it looked just like the sketches, inside and outside, only better, and it had cost just what Max Grylls and Bill had said that it would, only more. And there it stands today.[132]

Due to his hard work on the design and construction of the Playhouse, the club invited Bill Kapp to join The Players in 1923. He would become one of their best set designers: Player minutes record 198 sets designed by him for the club.[133] Kapp is also known for designing the Detroit Historical Museum in the Cultural Center and the Dossin Museum of Great Lakes History on Belle Isle.[134]

The New Playhouse General Committee had formed subcommittees that dealt with the kitchen and kitchen equipment; audience reception and decoration; and stage, stage equipment, and dressing rooms. In the search for new equipment to furnish their future home, President Phelps Newberry's most important contribution is probably the *Nunquam Renig* steins.[135] From the description in the minutes, they probably bore The Players' crest and motto. A later permutation of this mug, a stein on which was emblazoned the member's name and the year he joined, became a Player tradition. These steins are kept at the Playhouse in specially made cases in the Founders Room. When a Player dies, a black ribbon is placed across his mug, and it is placed on a ledge with those of other Players who have taken their last bow.

Player Phelps Newberry was able to report at the annual meeting on 19 May 1925 that the architects and contractors had promised that the new Playhouse would be ready by the opening of the 1925–26 season. It had been a good season for The Players. The Playhouse was fast becoming a reality, and a new high of 103 members of active status had participated in the frolics. With such successes in mind, Player Bill Holliday put forth a motion, supported by Players Jefferson B. Webb (of pistol-whipping Player Macklin fame) and William G. Lerchen (one of the board members of The Players Holding Company), that the board of governors be reelected as a whole. Because they "had been successful in accomplishing the initial stages for the securing of a new Playhouse for Players, . . . it would be advisable to keep the same Board in Harness so as to finish up the work they had begun." This motion carried unanimously.[136]

The Players decided that they would open their first season in the new Playhouse with *Doing Stratford*, a "musical sketch" written by Players Al Weeks and Bill Holliday: "The germ of the notion was to frame some sort of entertainment (we hoped it would be entertainment) that would permit several Players to impersonate characters from the plays of Shakespeare. ... Through June, July and August the team of collaborators labored in their collaboratory, pounding out the tunes that frequently could not be recognized and lyrics that occasionally scanned."[137] In October, Weeks shared what they had with the board: "Player Weeks read the lyrics and book, and gave explanations of this very amusing sketch. He croaked the music and described how good it was when Bill played it. Members of the Board had previously heard the music played by Bill, himself, so that Player Weeks' efforts were not prejudicial."[138] Weeks and Holliday described the rehearsal process: "The play was put into rehearsal the middle of November, and by the first week in December most of the cast of twenty-three Players (the largest that had ever been assembled in the Club), had met the author and composer and learned the title of the show."[139]

The Playhouse would open 10 December 1925 with a performance for members only, and performances for family and friends to show off their new home were scheduled for 11 and 12 December. Everyone pitched in. The Detroit Society of Arts and Crafts donated materials from their own stage,[140] and wives of the board of governors presented the curtain and the valance for the new theatre.[141]

*Doing Stratford* was so popular that copies of the music were sold at the following May Show. Player C. Hayward Murphy underwrote the cost of printing, and Weeks and Holliday agreed to donate any profits back to The Players. One of the songs from the score, "When the Day Is Done," with lyrics by Weeks and music by Holliday, later became the official Players' Song in January 1952 (see chorus that follows).[142] Bill Holliday passed away in June 1926 of "intestinal influenza," barely six months after the Playhouse opened, but his song is sung at the start of every frolic, so he lives on at The Players.[143]

"When the Day Is Done"
*by Players Al Weeks and Bill Holliday*

When the Day is done, with the setting sun,
For a friendly pipe then we long.
All of us gather here and we make good cheer,
With a mug of beer and a rousing song.

Though, the cold winds blow over drifting snow,
All our troubles disappear.
Sorrows make an end when you toast a friend,
In a mug of foaming beer.

The Players Playhouse is located at 3321 East Jefferson Avenue in Detroit. The structure, as it turns out, was built on a historical site. Before it was stolen, a plaque on the exterior of the Playhouse recorded the location of Parents Creek and the "Battle of Bloody Run," in which the British were ambushed by Chief Pontiac and his men. According to an article in the *Bulletin of the Detroit Historical Society*, when excavations began for the Players Playhouse, "bulldozers kept turning up Indian arrowheads, shining buttons that long years prior to this had adorned the scarlet coats of his Majesty's soldiers, metal parts of muskets and other memorabilia of battle."[144] Jefferson Avenue parallels the Detroit River, and the Playroom in the Playhouse may once have had a view of the river (and supposedly the kegs of beer being brought in from Canada), though this is unlikely, as the location is too far from the river, and the Detroit Stoveworks probably blocked the view in any case. The Playhouse is built in the style of the sixteenth-century English Renaissance as indicated by the Michigan historical marker on the exterior of the building. According to the program for the Fiftieth Anniversary Frolic, the building "is the world's first major structure to be built of cinder block."[145] The stone sculptor Corrado Parducci created the

Exterior of the Playhouse

ten gargoyles that line the front of the building below the roofline and may have created the Players' crest above the entrance.

Even to this day, the structure has been altered very little, and much of the stage machinery is still the same as it was in 1925. Although the lighting equipment has been updated and sound equipment has been added, the stage still has a wooden grid (the structure at the top of the stage house that holds all the curtains and hanging scenery) forty-nine feet above the stage and a pinrail with hemp ropes. (The pinrail is a wooden rail with pegs to which the ropes that control the curtains and any flying scenery are tied—much like the rigging on a wooden sailing ship.) The pinrail is operated from the fly deck, roughly twenty feet above the stage floor to allow for storage of flats below the deck and to keep some of the stagehands out of the way in the limited wing space. The stage house

Interior of the Playhouse (Stage): This picture is from the souvenir booklet for the opening of the Playhouse. This is the interior of the Playhouse looking toward the stage with DiLorenzo's "Seven Stages of Man" clearly visible above the proscenium arch.

is eighty-seven feet high.[146]

The stage is thirty-five feet deep and forty-one feet wide. The original travelers (the curtains that open and close during the performance, not the formal act drop) were donated by Phelps Newberry and were called "The Newberrys" for years afterward. Originally, the stage was flanked by two tall art deco statues, but C. C. Winningham quickly replaced these with large papier-maché urns, also sculpted by Parducci. These are still known as the "Winningham jugs" (or vases). When the mortgage was burned on 22 May 1945, the ashes were placed in the stage right vase. There have also been at least two Players, John Owen and Bill Rohloff, whose ashes were both interred in this vase.[147] Above the stage's proscenium arch is a mural of Shakespeare's "Seven Stages of Man" painted by Thomas Di

Interior of the Playhouse (Auditorium): Also from the souvenir booklet, this photograph is looking toward the back of the auditorium. The balcony to the left is now used for the sound and light boards.

Lorenzo, who also painted the decorations on the ceiling timbers of the auditorium and the lobby.[148] J. L. Hudson Company vice-president and general manager Oscar Webber provided furniture for the playroom and lobby.[149]

The auditorium is tiered to allow for tables and chairs instead of rows of seats so that Players may socialize during the frolics (something undoubtedly learned from the Arts and Crafts society). C. Hayward Murphy purchased iron grillwork and lamps in London, and the railings, chandeliers, and some of the decorative elements were salvaged from the old Ritz Hotel in New York, "which fortunately was razed while the Playhouse was being built."[150] The six tapestries that line the walls were donated by Players Henry T. Ewald, [most likely Frank Scott] Clark, Charles W. Matheson, and Walter C. Piper and were painted by Paul Honoré.[151] Honoré was a painter and a member of the Scarab Club, where he painted a "fireplace mural depicting different levels of club membership."[152] According to Player Bill Rohloff, there were supposed to be two more tapestries, but Honoré passed away before they could be completed.[153] Player Kapp painted the banners that hang from the eight gargoyles in the auditorium that represent the different professions of those who work in theatre. Interestingly, there is one that represents the box office, or more accurately, the producers who provide the money for the productions. For a club that had more theatre supporters than theatre professionals, the inclusion of this banner in effect incorporated all members into the theatrical process. *The Player* described the all-nighter during which Kapp produced these:

> It appears that Player William had worked for about thirty-six hours straight at the Playhouse and had done everything that should or could be done. He sat himself down to rest a few minutes, cast his critical eye around the auditorium—and then rushed for his car. He bought dyes, brushes, silks, spear heads and frames, and then made a zig-zag line for home; swallowed his supper (or breakfast) and then commandeered Mrs. Kapp to help him.
>
> After twelve hours' work, the associated Kapps gave us the symbolism of a Playhouse—starting with the Box Office, then the Artist, followed by the Author; then develops Comedy, represented by a laughing mask and about twenty-five smiling lips; but Tragedy stalks closely and takes the place of Laughter. Then follows the Costumier, and Music, and finally Light—or electricity and power.[154]

The Playhouse and its contents are as much a tradition at The Players as tuxedos and frolics. The Players today refer with pride to the structure as the "Great Lady," a term coined by Player Willard A. Rohloff during the club's seventy-fifth year, and they believe it is one of the organization's most unique elements.[155]

With a successful season in their new home under their belts, the Players set about dealing with their debt. The first thing the board did was to verify that the bank considered the note good so that the ten signers would not be called upon to pay for it while The Players raised the necessary funds. Player Harry Sanger worked for the bank that issued the loan, and he assured vice-president New-

One of six Paul Honoré murals that depict a troupe of players

Detail of the auditorium: This shot of the auditorium shows it set up with tables for a frolic and also gives a clear view of Kapp's banners and one of the Honoré murals.

Lobby of the Playhouse: This is a modern photograph of the lobby, but little of the original architecture has changed. A corner of the most recent Coppin nude is visible above the bar.

berry "that the bank considered it one of its best pieces of paper and that The Players need have no apprehension regarding it while ways and means were being devised to liquidate The Players' obligation."[156]

By December, the Finance Committee had come up with a possible solution. Its first plan was to collect $14,000 due from unpaid pledges. Then it would borrow $18,000 from the National Bank of Commerce. Those sums would allow The Players to pay off its land contract. Once they had the deed, it could be mortgaged for $65,000, which could then be used to repay the note.[157] During the next season, they continued to collect on subscriptions and outfit their theatre. Because both the Fine Arts Society and the Theatre Arts Club used the space, these groups also contributed. When the Theatre Arts Club donated electric chimes for the theatre, the board was so touched by the gesture that they insisted that the Theatre

Arts Club be the first group to use the chimes and that The Players would put on a performance for their benefit at that time.[158] The chimes were formally presented on 16 January 1928.

Members of The Players did their part also. Player Joseph B. Mills, who worked for the J. L. Hudson Company, donated an original drawing by Ferriss of the interior of the Playhouse.[159] This drawing is hung above the fireplace in the Playroom. Several Players donated books to flesh out their theatre library, which soon numbered more than four hundred volumes.

By May 1928, The Players had 422 members with assets totaling $188,995.49, with a mortgage of $74,100.00. As they were doing quite well, they felt secure enough to engage in some philanthropy. The first action taken by the board was to discount the rental of the Playhouse by charitable organizations. The Theatre Arts Club and the Fine Arts Society received (and still do to this day) a standard discount for their use of the Playhouse. In addition, The Players continued to do a children's Christmas show, and they soon added a morning performance for the residents of the Protestant Children's Home next door to the Playhouse. Because some of the Christmas entertainment consisted of hired performers, individual Players would donate the additional cost of having them perform for the orphans.[160]

That same year The Players had a collection of the best one acts written by their members published by Walter V. McKee, Incorporated. Walter McKee was a Player who had moved to New York to start a publishing firm that specialized in rare and limited edition books. McKee negotiated with Samuel French, Incorporated, to "take care of the acting rights" for the plays in *The Players Book of One Act Plays*.[161]

The Players established most of its significant traditions between its founding in 1910 and the end of 1929. This was also the time period during which many of its most beloved and esteemed members joined. During this era, the organization thrived enough to contribute to charities, build itself a permanent home, and inspire present-day members. By 1929, The Players was in its prime. Membership was close to four hundred, and there was a waiting list to join. Unfortunately, that would all change as the Great Depression settled over the country.

# 3

# The Players during the Depression and World War II

The Great Depression descended heavily upon Michigan. The automotive industry that had propelled the prosperity of the twenties now led the rising unemployment rate. Although only 4.5 million people were unemployed throughout the United States by 1930 (8.9 percent), that number would reach 13 million by 1932.[1] Large industrial cities faced a much higher unemployment rate of almost 50 percent. By 1932, General Motors had laid off around one hundred thousand employees, while Ford had cut almost two-thirds of its workforce.[2] In 1929, American investments totaled $16.2 billion. By 1932, this number was $800 million.[3] Historian William E. Leuchtenberg estimated that by that year, an average of one hundred thousand people in the United States were losing their jobs every week.[4]

In the fall of 1930, resignations trickled into The Players and were the first signs of the greater effect of the Depression on the organization. The Players were loath to lose these men, many of whom were members in good standing who had been actively participating in club life for years. The club quickly took several measures to help accommodate the changing circumstances in member finances. Although the bylaws did not allow the rescinding of dues, one of the first accommodations made was to give those in arrears a season's grace period to come up with the money. If they could not pay their dues after that time, their resignations would be accepted retroactively. In addition, the board cut dues from $50 to $40 for actives and from $75 to $57.50 for associates (the initiation fee of $100 was not lowered to $50 until 1932),[5] eliminated the Junior Capers (entertainments for Players' children), and negotiated with the National Bank of Commerce to lower the mortgage payments.[6]

Even with these measures, resignations soon outpaced applications, but applications still continued to come in, despite the uncertain times. Although many people cut back on expensive leisure activities during the Depression, membership must have been valued as evidenced by the continuing submission of applications. Unfortunately, however, applications numbers were still greatly reduced, and the club could not balance out the rate of resignations and suspensions, severely affecting its ability to pay the bills.

Normally, total unpaid dues might be a few hundred dollars by the end of the season. By March 1931, unpaid dues almost totaled five thousand dollars.[7] In spite of the problems, the club still contributed one acts to a benefit performance given by the Civic Theatre and also to the Mayor's Committee on Unemployment's benefit at the Masonic Auditorium in January 1932.[8] In addition to contributing to the community and pitching in to keep things running at The Players (discussed later), they maintained the reduced rental fee for charity groups.[9]

As the Depression deepened resignations increased, and the club had to cancel memberships because of nonpayment of dues. Exceptions were not made for those who did not resign willingly, and former mayor of Detroit John C. Lodge was suspended under this policy.[10] This was especially poignant because Lodge was an institution in Detroit politics. The citizens of Detroit loved him so much that he was elected mayor without ever having campaigned for the office.[11]

No one was safe from the repercussions of the Depression, and declining memberships were typical for clubs during its early years. The venerable Detroit Athletic Club (DAC) lost 30 percent of its membership in a single year (roughly one thousand members), although it was back up to full membership by 1936.[12] The DAC had a membership of 2,800 in 1930, down to 1,881 by 1933, but rebounded to 2,800 by 1934.[13] The somewhat smaller Detroit Club took a similar hit. It had grown steadily to a resident membership of 796 in 1929, having recently raised its cap to 800 members. The Detroit Club lost roughly 25 percent of its membership, reaching its lowest point in 1933 with 595 resident members. Its recovery was slower and took well over a decade to regain its pre-Depression numbers.[14]

Those who tried to resign officially from The Players were usually given a grace period of a year or two. If they were still compelled to resign, the board decided that they could be reinstated at a later date without having to pay the initiation fee. W. Colburn Standish and H. J. Maxwell Grylls, both very active in club activities, tried to resign, but the board refused their resignations.[15] Walter C. Boynton, one of the founding members, resigned on 25 October 1932, but the board reinstated him with a grace period less than a month later. These men were apparently too important to give up without a fight.

With all of the budget cuts made to maintain membership, The Players could no longer afford a stage crew. *Nunquam Renig* intervened, coveralls were purchased, and Players rolled up their sleeves and crewed their own shows.[16] The tradition begun of necessity continues to this day. It is interesting that even positions of manual labor are prized as long as they are part of putting on a show at The Players. After World War II, the club returned to a financial position that made it possible to hire stagehands, but it never reverted to the practice of hiring professionals except for an occasional carpenter to help with the sets.

Throughout their history, Players have always been able to laugh at themselves, even when times were difficult. A good example is a brief quotation about an upcoming frolic in the 13 February 1932 edition of *The Player*. The show was *Outside Looking In*, a "tramp play" by Maxwell Anderson adapted from Jim Tully's *Beggars of Life*: "Upwards of sixteen actors, so-called, have been busily rehearsing this play ever since they were relieved of more important duties by the crash of '29. Not that this is important, for gentlemen, this play is directed by Player Vice-President Michael Todd and that means the actors are as nothing compared to the offstage noises."[17] The "offstage noises" must have been quite good because the play was repeated not long after the frolic as an invitational so that friends and family could see it (or hear it). The club periodically calls an invitational for an exceptionally well-produced show so that friends and family may attend. This is usually done within a month of the performance. This may be due to interest or to the knowledge that the show would be difficult to produce as part of the May Show.

The addition of a Player crew helped ease the club's financial difficulties, but production values still had to be cut. Members of the board suggested that shows with few technical requirements be produced, such as vaudeville. One show that fit this bill was *Bardell vs. Pickwick*, an adaptation of Dickens's *Pickwick Papers*, performed at the April 1933 frolic. It was produced in modern dress, with Players' wives preparing the food for the frolic instead of having it catered. In addition, each Player attending the frolic was charged a small fee to help defray the cost.[18]

Even with the problems facing The Players, frolics were produced and business continued to be transacted. In March 1932, the board set about securing the consent of all the contributors to the building fund who were also stockholders in The Players Holding Company. Members quickly gave their consent, and the property was transferred from The Players Holding Company to the club.[19] Although there are no records of the dissolution of The Players Holding Company after the title was transferred, records from 1926 discuss "liquidating the obligations" of the company, and further discussion in records from 1928 indicate that the company needed to be placed in a "position where it could function properly, or [to] effect a dissolution thereof with an assignment of its rights and assets to The Players."[20] As it did transfer its asset (the Players Playhouse) to the club, it can be assumed that the holding company was also dissolved at that time. The club was still in a precarious position, and the banking crisis that hit Michigan early in 1933 did nothing to improve this, as it struggled over the next two years to keep the Playhouse.

By 1935, the board was able to propose ways to keep from defaulting on the mortgage. Players offered several possible changes to the payment schedule to the bank—that the interest on the mortgage be reduced and that this reduction be backdated to May 1933, that payments be made on the interest and not the principal, that any profits garnered from rentals of the Playhouse would be applied to the principal, and that the taxes be kept current. The Guardian Depositors Corporation that held the mortgage readily agreed to these terms, allowing The Players to keep the Players Playhouse.[21]

The club had abolished honorary membership in 1928, but at the annual meeting in 1933 it instituted a new classification. Although Sam Slade's tender of resignation never shows up in the minutes, it may have been offered to the board. In a letter that was read at the meeting, Al Weeks suggested to the board that it offer

> a new classification of membership, to be know as Life Membership—
> an honor to be conferred on Players whom the Board of Governors
> found merited such recognition because of their long and faithful ser-

vice to The Players. This suggestion was put to a motion and carried unanimously, with the amendment that no member under fifty years of age be considered eligible; and that Player Sam Slade be made the first life member. Life membership in The Players is to carry full privileges without dues.[22]

Player lore says that life membership was instituted specifically to keep Sam in the club, but it developed into a way to reward long-standing members for their years of service to The Players.[23] In 1954, the board decided that honorary life membership would be given to a Player who had faithfully served for thirty-five years.[24]

Like Lodge, though, not every Player was saved from having to cancel his membership. Edsel Ford resigned from The Players in 1933, but this was not the only membership he had to give up. Ford had been hit hard by the bank crisis in Detroit and had been forced to lay off most of his estate employees and to receive help from his father to deal with his shaky position with the banks.[25] In all, he resigned from twenty clubs and associations in March 1933, ranging from country and sports clubs to the American Federation of the Arts.[26]

Other than the introduction of life membership, the other happy note in 1933 was the repeal of Prohibition. The move for repeal was lead by several prominent members of The Players, most notably Henry B. Joy, Emory Clark, and Frederick Alger. Joy and Clark originally had been avid "drys," but years of open flouting of the law coupled with the possibility of revenue generated by taxes on liquor changed their minds. Joy had an additional reason for despising the enforcement of Prohibition. His Grosse Pointe estate was right on the water, and his boathouse and grounds were frequently raided by police searching for rumrunners. Frequently, rumrunners used the boathouses along Lake St. Clair and the Detroit River for temporary storage as they transported Canadian liquor, and even the posting of guards did not guarantee the safety of one's property.[27]

The general dislike of Prohibition ran high. Michigan was the first state to vote for repeal, and the national vote ran close to 73 percent.[28] Players celebrated the end of Prohibition with *The Cabinet Meeting* by Player Al Weeks, depicting Franklin Delano Roosevelt's first meeting with his cabinet officials. The play ends with FDR demonstrating the New Deal to the "forgotten man" (named simply

A New Deal: Players celebrate the end of Prohibition.

Table 1. Effect of the Depression on membership at The Players

| | 1927–28 | 1928–29 | 1929–30 | 1930–31 | 1931–32 | 1932–33 | 1933–34 | 1934–35 | 1935–36 |
|---|---|---|---|---|---|---|---|---|---|
| Resigned | N/A | 6 | 22 | 56 | 32 | 77 | 19 | 9 | N/A |
| Suspended[a] | N/A | N/A | N/A | N/A | N/A | 16 | 31 | 18 | N/A |
| Reinstated[b] | N/A | N/A | N/A | N/A | N/A | N/A | 5 | 13 | 6 |
| New Active | — | 11 | 3 | 3 | 6 | 7 | 14 | 7 | 8 |
| New Associate | — | 20 | 23 | 31 | 19 | 27 | 12 | 17 | 28 |
| Deaths | N/A | N/A | N/A | N/A | N/A | N/A | 4 | 3 | 3 |
| Total lost | — | 6 | 22 | 56 | 32 | 93 | 54 | 30 | 18 |
| Total gained | — | 31 | 26 | 34 | 25 | 34 | 31 | 37 | 42 |
| Life Members[c] | N/A | N/A | N/A | | | | 7 | 6 | 6 |
| Active | 151 | 158 | 159 | | | | 140 | 149 | 157 |
| Associate | 246 | 254 | 247 | No numbers were reported | | | 116 | 115 | 133 |
| Non-res. | 25 | 31 | 30 | for these seasons. | | | 28 | 28 | 26 |
| Delinquent[d] | (21) | (21) | (27) | | | | (29) | (23) | (34) |
| Total | 422 | 443 | 436 | | | | 291 | 298 | 322 |

[a] Suspensions were not recorded until the 1932–33 season.
[b] Reinstatements were not recorded until the 1933–34 season.
[c] Life membership was not established until the end of the 1932–33 season.
[d] Deliquents were not included in the total membership.

"Laborer" in the script) by telling him that not only will there be more jobs, but there will also be 5 percent beer, and to prove it the entire cast (and probably the audience) is served a round.[29]

The board decreased membership dues again in 1933 to thirty dollars for active members and forty-five dollars for associate members, and The Players had to omit the children's Christmas show in 1934. By May 1935, Player membership was down to 298 (see table 1).[30] As 1935 progressed and some Players were able to get back on their feet and pay their back dues, they were reinstated without having to pay the initiation fee (prior to the Great Depression, the club's normal practice was to require someone returning to the club after resigning to pay the initiation fee). Despite a slightly better outlook and the ability to deal with the mortgage, the children's Christmas party was once again canceled in 1935. Although the Depression was still omnipresent (national unemployment was at 20.3 percent), 1935 was the year that saw some happy news for Detroit. Bob-Lo (an island amusement park) resumed operation, and the various Detroit sports teams swept their respective leagues: The Tigers won their first World Series, the Lions won the National Football League championship, and in 1936, the Red Wings won the Stanley Cup.[31]

The plays produced at The Players reflected a sense that they had weathered the worst, even if they were not yet clear of trouble. Player Sheldon R. Noble's *Portrait of a Man* depicted J. B. Hart, president of the Universal Appliance Company, who is about to take his first vacation in years now that he has finally been able to return his company to a sound financial footing. His early lines in the play are clearly representative of the attitudes of those who were responsible for keeping a business open in such times of turmoil:

> Things happen, circumstances beyond our control, but given these as the tools to work with, we can mold other developments to our liking. A man likes to talk of his achievements, but today I have reached the conclusion of a phase begun five years ago—and I was broke. In fact most of the world has been broke sometime during the past five years. It's just a question of who admitted it and who didn't. I'm still broke but the company is back on its feet. I have finally reached the point where I can open my eyes in the morning and not begin cataloging the grief for the day. It wasn't much fun eating snowballs and living in a two by four cave dwellers apartment, but it's paid dividends. Mrs. Hart and I are moving back again to a home instead of a hole in the wall and we're having a vacation first.[32]

Regrettably, all is not well with our protagonist, for there are still forces at work trying to take away his fragile stability. For Hart, the problem is in his own house. He discovers that his son has undermined his company's position by embezzling the company's stock to use as collateral so that the son can speculate on other stock. This practice was fairly widespread in banks up until the Great Depression. Bankers would use the stock of their own bank in risky investments, thus jeopardizing the savings of those unsuspecting customers who thought their money was safe. Hart's son tries to justify his actions, but his father is unimpressed and refuses to let his son deny responsibility: "But stealing isn't a mistake. It's a basic fault. You can't confuse the difference between what's yours and what's someone else's you know. Then it's a question of whether, knowing, you're strong enough to stand by what you know. ... You're a moral coward."[33] The son later commits suicide rather than face the consequences of his actions, and Hart sets aside his dreams of a vacation and a home of his own to devote himself to once again returning the company to a sound footing.

The overriding tone of the play is that of an honorable, long-suffering man who is cleaning up a mess that is not of his making. He has denied himself and his family many of the basic comforts so that he could do what is right for his company and employees. The sense of betrayal is also profound, made even more so because it is Hart's son that perpetrates the treachery. This may well have been how many of the Players felt during the Depression, as they struggled to keep their businesses viable.

Notwithstanding the financial problems still facing the club, certain Player traditions (such as the previously mentioned round of beer at the end of *The Cabinet Meeting*) still remained. The Players loved a party, particularly if theatre professionals were involved. Their sense of fellowship encompassed anyone who shared their love of theatre. In March 1935, The Players threw a party for the D'Oyly Carte Opera Company that was passing through Detroit. This British company was formed originally in 1878 by Richard and Helen D'Oyly Carte to produce British comic opera, specifically the works of W. S. Gilbert and Arthur Sullivan. The D'Oyly Carte Company owned the performance rights to Gilbert and Sullivan works and was the premiere company for years. When Richard and Helen's son Rupert took over the company in 1913, he launched a company tour of America. Several successful American tours followed.[34] When the company came to visit The Players, members presented several pieces from Gilbert and Sullivan operettas as entertainment for their professional guests. The company loved the performance and repaid their hosts by performing a few pieces themselves.[35]

In 1936, The Players produced what was presumably the American premiere of *The Rose of Auvernge or Spoiling the Broth*, an operetta by Jacques Offenbach. The piece was unearthed at the Congressional Library by Player Ray Jacobs, who said that despite some early performances in Paris and London during the 1850s, it had never been published in the United States, and there is no record of it having been produced here.[36] Even by Player standards, the piece was considered frivolous with an obvious plot, mildly pleasant music, and somewhat strained comedy.[37] Despite this, it must have been considered good enough for the May Show, as it was the closing act for that performance.

While reviewing the May Show for the *Detroit News*, Cecil Betron waxed poetic about The Players: "There is something so indescribably jolly about a Players' annual performance that it is equally impossible to refrain from shouting its praises from the chimney tops to a world a bit weary of itself. One could, but one won't for lack of space, preach a sermon on the Players' work for civic good. Likewise it seems lamentable that the entire community, man and boy, woman and child, cannot at some time or other have the opportunity to point with as much pardonable pride."[38]

Beginning in March 1936, the board began actively trying to recruit ex-Players back into the fold. The board appointed a committee to set up a complementary dinner for the ex-Players that the club wanted to recruit, and the board agreed that any who were interested would be welcomed back without having to pay either the initiation fee or that year's dues.[39] By that year's annual meeting, the membership numbers finally began to increase. Membership rolls showed a total of 322 Players, an increase of 24 over the previous year. The Finance Committee must have felt that people's fortunes were improving because it recommended that a subscription drive be started to raise enough money to pay down the principal on the mortgage to $25,000 so that it could be refinanced for a longer term. The current terms of the mortgage had it maturing in 1940, and the club was in no condition to have it paid off by that year, although by the following year the club felt secure enough to raise the initiation fee to seventy-five dollars.[40]

*Roller Skates Must Be Mended* (1937): Written by Al Weeks, this rare Player drama was a vehicle for Sam Slade.

One enduring informal Player tradition of sorts is the revival of past popular shows, often with as many of the original cast members as possible. The January 1937 frolic was an all-revival bill, even down to some of the Afterglow acts. One of these pieces was *Roller Skates Must Be Mended*, a Player original written by Al Weeks for Sam Slade and Edgar Bowen. Bowen had recently passed away, but Slade was able to reprise his original role. This piece is characteristic of The Players' more dramatic fare:

> It's about an old, broken down harness maker, cheated out of a living by motors, and his attempt to shelter and guard and nourish his ward, a lad too backward to make his way as other boys do. When little Joey is killed by one of the iron devilments that cost him his trade, the old fellow has nothing to live for. Even the affection of his friend Louis scarcely seems a sufficient incentive—but a pair of roller skates must be mended for a cranky customer's little boy, and the closing picture is one to make you fog your cheaters, with Onkel Heinrich (Slade) priming the pumps.[41]

There is a certain amount of nostalgia at The Players for times gone by. This feeds directly into their love of traditions and formality. The story of how *Roller Skates* came into being is indicative of the soft spot Players have for the past:

> Many years ago Player Al Weeks, a writer of recognized ability, and a fine actor as well, got an idea for a play while waiting for a streetcar. This was before the horse became extinct as a beast of burden and horses, being the motive power for many vehicles, required harness. It was, therefore, not unusual to find at least one harness shop in every community. It was in such a shop that Weeks, as he stood gazing through the window, saw a harness-maker busily at work. This craftsman was sitting astride a buck used to facilitate the sewing of leather; a most fascinating apparatus. It had stirrups much like a saddle except they were connected to a wooden vise. Pressure exerted on the stirrups caused the vise to close tightly on the harness to be sewn. The body of the buck was covered with leather and had a high polish from constant use. It was not unlike the common gymnasium buck except for the stirrups and the vise at its head.[42]

Because this show was a popular one and showed regularly, Weeks had to convince the old harness maker to loan this piece of equipment on more than one occasion. It appears that a few tickets to the May Show were considered a fair trade, and The Players got the buck.[43]

D'Oyly Carte was once again in town in 1937, this time for a performance of *H.M.S. Pinafore* at the Cass Theatre. The Players threw another party for the company, but this time the members of D'Oyly Carte were treated to a full-blown Player production of *The Book of Etiquette*, by Mark Connelly. In the announcement, the Players call the piece a "marine masterpiece," obviously a play on the maritime theme of *Pinafore*.[44] What no one outside of The Players realized was that this was an example of American humor at the expense of their British guests. The protagonist of *Etiquette* is a "distressed American" among a group of Brits who is trying to find a discrete way to ask directions to the nearest lavatory.[45] Luckily, the visiting performers found it hilarious and once again sang for their supper.

This was typical of the humor displayed by the Players through their creative work. The late 1930s and early 1940s saw the introduction of a new playwriting team, Sheldon Noble and Ray Jacobs. By day, Noble was the president of an investment securities

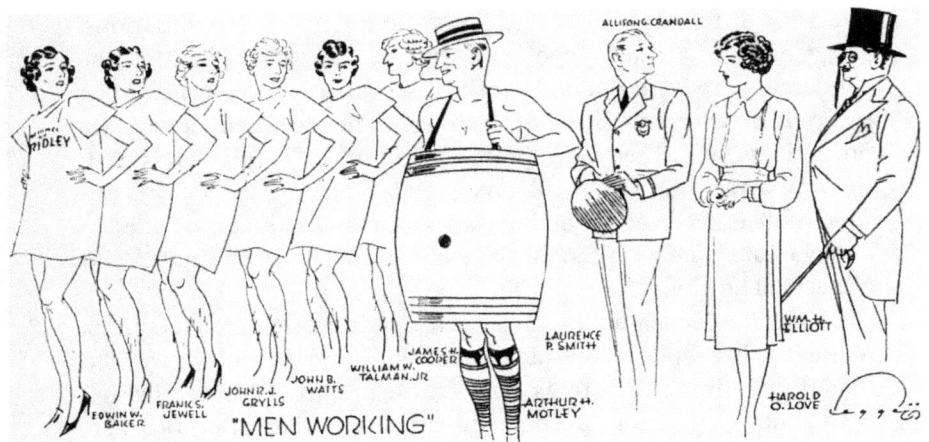

*Men Working* (1937) is a Noble and Jacobs musical comedy satire on WPA projects.

firm, H. W. Noble and Co., Inc., and Jacobs was the vice-president of the First National Bank of Detroit.[46] By night, Noble and Jacobs were known to the club as the resident Gilbert and Sullivan. This was the first time since Weeks and Holliday that The Players had a musical comedy team. Together, they wrote several pieces: *All Aboard, Men Working, It's a Buoy,* and *Who, Me?* These shows had been made possible not only by their writing but also by the introduction of an all-Player orchestra. An orchestra had been a common feature at the frolics since the beginning of the 1920s, when many of the orchestra members had been hired from the outside, much like the backstage crew. With the budget cuts of the Great Depression, however, Players stepped into the breach left by the necessity of having to let go most of the regular outside help, and by the 1940s they had assembled an impressive all-member orchestra that accompanied most of the frolics.

In *Men Working*, produced in 1937, Noble and Jacobs explore the Works Progress Administration's (WPA) means of creating jobs in a uniquely Player way. The play is set in an older gentlemen's home, with a WPA project being built next to it—a nudist camp. Following the tradition of the situation comedy, putting together two very different devices sets the stage for humorous situations. The main plot actually involves a romance between a maid at the gentlemen's home and a police officer sent to shut down the nudist camp by outraged members of the town. (The older gentlemen have no problem with their new, pretty neighbors.) The play ends with the couple marrying (they call it consolidating), and the idea of consolidation is received so enthusiastically that the home decides to amalgamate itself with the camp next door, becoming a single WPA project: "The Home for Aged Nudists."[47]

As the 1930s waned, The Players slowly pulled out of its slump. Membership numbers continued to increase, and the club was able to hold the children's Christmas party for the first time in several years, with a morning performance for the orphans and an afternoon performance for the children of the Players.[48] That same year, membership was further stabilized by making William G. Lerchen (who had been one of the ten signers of the note on the Playhouse), C. Hayward Murphy, and founder Frederick S. Stearns life members.[49] There were still occasional resignations due to inability to pay dues, but these were sporadic and nowhere near the exodus of 1931–33. New members were also being elected in larger numbers (sixteen were elected in November 1937 alone).[50] Another sign of vitality was the January 1938 article in *Life* magazine that included a two-page photo spread on The Players' 150th frolic. Neither *The Player* nor the minutes record how the club warranted the national attention garnered by this article. It is possible that Players such as McKee who worked in publishing in New York and others who had moved out to New York to work in advertising and other fields knew someone who worked at *Life*. The Scarab Club had been featured in an article in 1937, so there may very well have been some sort of Detroit–New York connection.

Sam Slade celebrated his seventy-fifth birthday in February 1938. In recognition of the occasion, he was asked to present the Gettysburg Address at the February frolic.[51] Abraham Lincoln was by far the most famous role that he performed at The Players. Slade had first performed the role in 1927, and he had given repeat performances on a regular basis. Hirschfield's makeup was so effective that a portrait was taken of Slade and published in the *Detroit News*.[52] A print of the portrait is located in The Players' archives.

The frequency with which Sam Slade was singled out for various honors by The Players confirms his popularity at the club.

Player Henry T. Ewald presented to the club a portrait of Slade painted by Player John S. Coppin in 1940.[53] (Later Player lore claims that it was Slade who actually commissioned this portrait and presented it to the club.)[54] Coppin had also provided a nude to the club, which hung above the bar (a tradition in many Detroit clubs, including the Detroit Athletic Club). Slade's portrait not only memorializes one of the most beloved Players but also boasts an interesting history. It, along with what was probably the Nastfogel nude (a replacement for the Coppin nude that went missing in the 1960s), was stolen from the Players Playhouse during August 1976 (not by an adoring fan), only to turn up much later in the windows of Edward Hickey's art emporium on East Grand Boulevard and Gratiot Avenue. Although the portrait displayed in the window was identified as the industrialist C. S. Mott, one of the Players recognized Sam. He notified the police, they succeeded in tracing the nude, and both were returned to their rightful places in the Playhouse.[55]

By 1940, trouble was stirring in Europe once again, and the Players' stage reflected the unrest. Despite the fact that Hitler had already invaded Poland, he is still painted mostly as a figure of fun in a contemporary piece by Sheldon Noble, *What the Heil*, performed at the January 1940 frolic. Player Harry W. Kerr described the show in an article in *The Player*:

> "What the Heil," which to begin with snapped with Player Noble's best dialogue disclosed Players Granse as Der Fuehrer and Forsyth as Goering, who get their heads together in the hall at the Berchtesgaden to work out some more effective plan of chastising the hated English. Nothing seems to be going right. Granse, very Fuehrer, with mustache and Teutonic gutterals, and Forsyth, resplendent in several changes of swank uniforms with enough medals to cover even his expansive front, advance with very witty and well-delivered lines through the various difficulties to a conclusion. Where can they get some help from someone who knows the English "backvards undt forvards?" By some sort of witchcraft known only to Fuehrers, Alexandrina Victoria (Player Hayward S. Thompson), once a visiting Queen of England but really citizen of Saxe-Coburg Gotha, is conjured from her grave and a lively old body she is. She takes command of the situation and evolves a plan to bombard the hungry English with frankfurthers and sauerkraut. Dot's it. Ve vill do it. And they all sing an amusing song with excellent music by Player Jacobs.[56]

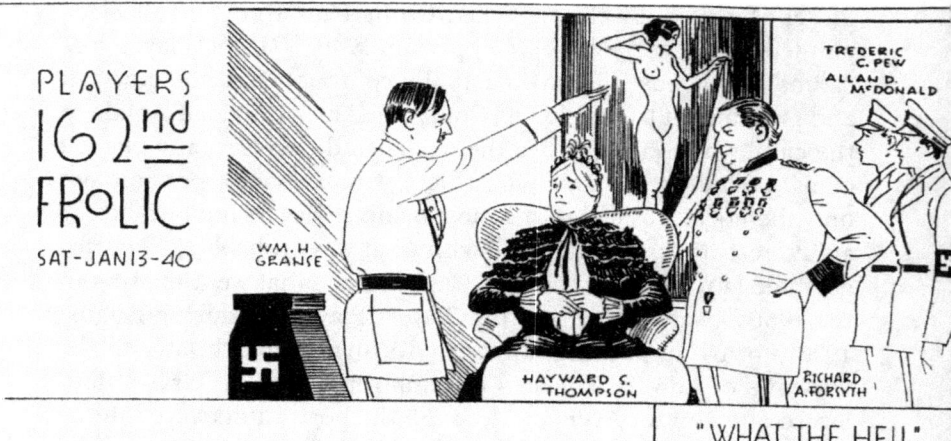

*What the Heil* (1940): A solo piece by Sheldon Noble, this comedy offered an otherworldly take on both the London blitz and Hitler.

Strangely enough, this was performed on a bill with Eugene O'Neill's *Ah, Wilderness*.

War was once again encroaching on the serenity of The Players. Unlike during World War I, during this time war plays were frequent and welcomed by the membership. Even though the United States was not yet in the war, Americans definitely knew which side they wanted to win. Player Alan H. Pearson wrote a play for the March 1940 frolic called *Tonight's the Night*. Unlike the spoof, *What the Heil*, the mood of this piece was a little more menacing, with a German spy taking over an English lighthouse as a means to aid German submarines. In the play, the lighthouse keeper's son discovers the plot and kills the spy.[57]

This thriller was on the same bill as a rather large Player-written musical most likely inspired (with a twist) by *Anything Goes*. The musical comedy, *All Aboard*, had music by Ray Jacobs, lyrics by Sheldon Noble (of *What the Heil* fame), and book by Franklin M. Reck and Albert D. Conkey. The show is set in Union Station where several members of the Potwhistle family are trying to surreptitiously meet up with significant others that they are hiding from the rest of the Potwhistle clan. With the help of the man at the information desk, young loves are brought together, marriages are mended, and everyone makes it to the train on time. The show was quite large by Players' standards, with a cast of twenty-one and a music director.[58] This was a lot of effort for a show that was intended for a single performance, but it was a rousing success and returned as the final number of the 1940 May Show.

Aside from their many shows that dealt with war issues, the Players were already being asked to contribute to the war effort before the United States officially entered the global conflict. The British War Relief Society asked that The Players contribute one play to their benefit performance in February 1941 at the Scottish Rite Cathedral in the Masonic Temple. The Players try to avoid benefit performances (it is supposedly against a long-standing club policy, but they violate it frequently in times of great need), but they agreed in this case.[59] The Theatre Arts Club was also asked to help, and The Players donated the use of the Playhouse for their rehearsals.[60]

Although the war added an unhappy note to the proceedings, the 1940–41 season marked the thirtieth anniversary of The Players. The club had been unable to celebrate its twenty-fifth anniversary in 1935 due to the effects of the Great Depression. One of the ways that they marked the thirtieth anniversary was to include articles on snippets of The Players' early history in *The Player*. These articles are invaluable now, because they preserve several events in the words of the members who participated in them. Founder Alexander K. Gage reminisced about the years leading up to the club's beginnings with Guy Brewster Cady.[61] James Strasburg described The Players' association with bootleggers during Prohibition.[62] Strasburg also recorded Grylls's and Kapp's contributions to building the Players Playhouse.[63]

February brought both Presidents' Day and Sam Slade's performance as Lincoln at The Players. Since his first appearance as the revered president, the Gettysburg address or a play involving Lincoln had become standard February fare. This year the board memorialized the moment permanently and secured the rights from Samuel French to record the final act of *Nor Long Remember*, which featured Slade as Lincoln performing the Gettysburg address.[64] Player Frank V. Martin recalled the experience for *The Player:* "As Sam Slade arose to deliver Lincoln's immortal Gettysburg speech you could have heard a pin drop. He delivered that eloquent address with a spiritual understanding that is part of his character. Sam seems the perfect reincarnation of Lincoln. He does not appear to be speaking Lincoln's words, but rather his own. Sam has the same spiritual understanding of men, the same charitable viewpoint, the same tolerance of all. To The Players Sam Slade is Lincoln and Lincoln is Sam."[65]

As to Slade as a person, Martin had an even stronger sentiment: "I've always maintained that if a guy wanted to commit suicide he could dispense with the purchase of a gun or any other lethal device, and simply stroll into the Playhouse on the night of our Frolic and say something derogatory of Sam Slade. Of course the said guy would be a somewhat messy corpse, but a thoroughly dead one."[66]

From that high point, 1941 began to go downhill. On Easter Sunday, 13 April 1941, C. Hayward Murphy, a past president, the person that made all the backstage magic work at The Players and the man who had given so much time and effort to the continuation of The Players, died.[67] Russell Legge, longtime recorder of Player events, also died that year. Player George W. Stark recorded his contributions in the November 1941 edition of *The Player:*

> Russ became a Player in 1920 and his great contributions to this club, outside of his never-failing presence in his first-row chair on the evening of every Frolic, was the series of sketches he made of plays and Players. In this capacity his fancy has captured the face and form of more Detroit men of affairs than any other artist. That he did this with such accuracy and grace was the constant amazement of his subjects.
>
> Not many knew that in the last years of his life he worked with a handicap that would have stopped most men. He was blind in one eye and he saw out of the other only by placing a magnifying glass over the powerful lens of his eye-glasses.
>
> His newspaper friends say that he drew pictures in shorthand. That is to say, he took notes, employing a dot, dash and line system all his own. He depended on these and on his own amazing memory for detail. What emerged on his drawing board was a constant source of wonderment.[68]

In addition to these losses to The Players, America's involvement in the war was impending. The board passed a resolution in June that anyone in military service whose duties took him from Detroit did not have to pay dues during his absence.[69] The board made another change that year to the bylaws allowing everyone but nonresident members a vote. These changes may have been made to keep associate numbers from dropping further. Their ranks had plummeted throughout the season, and for the first time in the club's records, actives (158) outnumbered associates (138). Club numbers were also down in general. The rolls record only 363 Players in May 1941.

December witnessed the attack on Pearl Harbor, and America was catapulted into the war. Player Harry Mitchell recorded the event in *The Player* with some particularly nationalist and very prophetic words:

> While we quipped and quaffed and had fun generally at the 173rd Frolic on the night of December 6 the Japs were sneaking up on Pearl Harbor and Manila to strike the first blow with planes and bombs.
>
> The toothy little gangsters struck treacherously and hard. They don't like us because we have in this country everything they and their fellow gangsters would sell their souls to have. We have a way of life they don't even understand. We get what we want by working for it. They're trying to get what they want by ganging up and stabbing others in the back.
>
> In the first coup they seemed daring and clever, but they're scared and desperate. They've picked a scrap that will bust them three ways across the middle.[70]

Once again the country was at war, and The Players felt the need to remind people that there was a place for the club even in trying times. Franklin M. Reck dug through the records to find that it had been business as usual for The Players during the First World War and decided that it should be the same during the Second World War:

> And as men work harder they play harder, too, because private worries go by the board, men are better able to forget everything for a few hours, and have a good time.
>
> And maybe that's the safety valve in times like these. That, we suspect, is what happened in the last war. Men gathered on Players' night and forgot things more completely, laughed harder, and relaxed more thoroughly than ever before. So now we're engaged in another war, and The Players will become more rich and meaningful to the men who come here, one Saturday night a month, to refresh their spirit in our cockeyed, highly original, somewhat insane form of amateur dramatics.
>
> So here's a toast in foaming Bock to Players' health in the second World War.[71]

Yet again, *Nunquam Renig* interceded, and The Players pulled together, cut costs, and volunteered to keep the club going. Several of the Players donated gifts, entertainment, and time to make sure that the children's Christmas party was special that year.[72] The House Committee that ran the party found ways to cut costs in half, which meant more work for them, but happy children. All food and gifts that were left over were sent to the participating orphanages.[73] Player W. Colburn (Olie) Standish was head of this committee and was praised for his efforts. Olie ran the House Committee that had served the late-night supper at the frolics for years. He was best known as the unofficial Players bartender. He would spend most of the frolic night behind the bar in the lobby dressed as an 1890s bartender complete with sleeve garters and handlebar mustache.[74] By day, Olie was an executive at Walker and Co., an outdoor advertising firm.[75]

May 1942 saw numbers at The Players drop further to 334 members. One accommodation had already been made to try to stop this descent: in May 1941, the board had changed the terms of associate membership to allow them to participate in whatever club activities they so chose, but would not force them to do anything. Even if they participated in club activities, they could still retain the title of associate if they wished, but the board could recommend a transfer if their contribution warranted it.[76] Despite these changes, including the modification in 1941 that allowed associates a vote on club activities, associate numbers still continued to drop. In desperation, the board took two additional steps to keep the club numbers up. For the upcoming season, the board decided that any former member could be reinstated by paying a small fee of fifteen dollars, and the initiation fee was lowered from seventy-five dollars to twenty-five dollars for that season to encourage recruitment.[77] Declining numbers were not the only unhappy note that year. Founder H. J. Maxwell Grylls, whose business had built the Players Playhouse, died 21 June 1942.

With the war on, The Players made accommodations in order to adapt the life of the club to a different social climate. The club purchased war damage insurance to cover the Playhouse, and they made the building available gratis to the United Service Organization (USO) for rehearsals.[78] In addition, the board instituted a new class of membership for the duration of the war. Temporary membership was created for "temporary residents of Detroit serving in the Armed Forces or in other departments of the Government. Such members to be exempt from the payment of initiation fees."[79] Only a few men appear to have taken advantage of this new class of membership, so it had minimal impact on the club. Also during this time one Player tradition was temporarily suspended. Conspicuous consumption was frowned upon during the war, so Players were allowed to come to the frolics in business suits. Although many thought that tradition was more important, the change was accepted with little grumbling.[80]

For the November frolic the board made another major concession by allowing the performance to be repeated for the benefit of the USO and other war charities.[81] Furthermore, The Players broke with its long-standing tradition and made this a public performance to which tickets were sold. Mary Ellen Menard, a reporter for the *Detroit Free Press*, was impressed with the size of the audience: "Perhaps the fact that proceeds from the show are to be turned over to various war charities had something to do with the tremendous turnout, and we're sure that Detroit's ever-growing war consciousness was a direct cause for the lack of dressiness on the part of the ladies."[82] The show was an abridged version of John Osborn's *On Borrowed Time* and featured Player Bill Elliot and young Sandy Forsyth, Player Richard Forsyth's son. The elder Forsyth directed the piece. Sandy Forsyth garnered rave reviews, and even his parents were surprised at his "sheer talent."[83]

In November 1942, a severe blow was dealt to The Players when Sam Slade died. At his funeral, all of the club members were named honorary pallbearers and six Players performed this last service for him.[84] At the December frolic, Slade was singled out for his final honor. The Barrymore dressing room was renamed "Slade," and it remains so to this day.

By May 1943, Player numbers had once again increased, bringing the number to 377 members: 35 new active and 45 new associate members had been added. By May 1944, the membership at The Players was once again over the 400 mark. The club was slowly paying down its mortgage, and it had more than two thousand dollars cash on hand. By February 1945, the board felt confident enough to increase the initiation fee to fifty dollars, still twenty-five dollars less than it was before the war.[85]

The summer of 1944 witnessed an interesting event in Player history. After the former office secretary left the position, the board hired Leona Carroll to replace her.[86] Lee, as she was known, was to mark a new Player tradition. She worked for The Players until her retirement in 1991. At her retirement, a special frolic was held to commemorate the event. Thus Lee is the only woman to ever be invited to attend one of the Players' noninvitational frolics.

The Players continued to produce war-related plays during World War II. The war even crept into the Afterglows, when troops from the Romulus Air Base performed *These Doggoned Elections* in addition to several musical numbers.[87] War references also showed up in other manifestations. In one instance, a reviewer felt the need to explain what a maid was to the more youthful Players. "For the benefit of our younger readers, we will state that a maid is a type of domestic servant that used to be fairly plentiful before war plants began to pay women better than a dollar an hour but now has entirely disappeared."[88] Another indication was a curfew that had been instituted because of the war. As a result, the March 1945 frolic was probably the shortest in The Players' history. March also saw the passing of Founder Alexander K. Gage.

During the 1944–45 season, the board began actively soliciting contributions to the mortgage fund to pay off The Players' debt. By 24 January 1945, $10,020 had been contributed toward the mortgage fund.[89] In less than a year, The Players had raised almost $18,000 to pay off the mortgage. By the following May, after the new board had been elected at the annual meeting, Player Harvey Campbell climbed onstage with a rod, stuck the mortgage on it, and Player Dick Harfst (the man with the unhappy task of soliciting the money for the mortgage) lit a match and burned it.[90] The ashes now lie in the stage right Winningham vase.

What is particularly striking about this period, from the onset of the Depression until the end of World War II, is that it was business as usual. Despite the social and economic upheaval of these two wide-reaching international events, the club continued to function in much the same way that it had since its early years. All of the frolics were held, even if some were performed on a shoestring and others ended early because of curfews. New members were joining even as the board struggled to pay the bills and to retain the club's many treasured older members. In addition, some changes had to be made to accommodate the pressures of the time, such as providing the crew for their own shows during the Depression and setting aside the beloved tuxedo when such displays of wealth were considered improper during World War II.

One of the most interesting departures from tradition is the amount of community service activities The Players engaged in as an institution during this time, even though they repeatedly claim (and reaffirm) that the club has a policy against participating in charity events. The charitable works may be just a reflection of the national attitude during these years that everyone had to pull together and do their part, superseding any minor long-standing club practice. The Players went so far as to go against its commitment to amateur theatre to open its doors to a paying audience to raise money for war charities. *Nunquam Renig* had always ruled at the club in times of crisis; it was now just being expanded outside exclusive Player benefit.

As with the rest of the nation, the conclusion of World War II thrust The Players out of its economic crisis and commenced an era of prosperity. The Players began the new season in 1945 with an incredible sense of stability, both financially and socially. The hard times were over, and The Players was about to enter its second golden age.

# 4

# The Long Run

## Postwar Prosperity

At the end of World War II, The Players, like the rest of the country, sought to return to a sense of normalcy. Detroit had served as the "arsenal of democracy," with the auto industry manufacturing "92 per cent of American military vehicles, 87 per cent of its aircraft engines and 56 per cent of its tanks."[1] As mass employment in the war effort had finally defeated the economic woes of the Depression, the industry quickly retooled its function to provide cars to the public, who had had few products to purchase during the war years and who were now ready to buy. Urban historian Thomas J. Sugrue notes that although there were fears of a recession caused by the downtime necessary to refit for civilian production, the period was "so mild and short-lived [that it] quelled many lingering uncertainties about the city's future." The resulting demand for consumer goods kept unemployment levels to the same low levels experienced during the war. Sugrue explains that if "Detroit had an economic golden age, the decade of the 1940s seems as likely a candidate if any."[2] According to David M. Kennedy's chronicle of the Depression and World War II, "Within less than a generation of the war's end, the middle class ... more than doubled. By 1960 the middle class included almost two-thirds of all Americans, most of whom owned their own homes, unprecedented achievements for any modern society."[3]

*The Player* reminded members once again that tuxedos were the rule, not the exception, and the November 1945 frolic played to a full house. The season opened with a series of comedies. Not a single one dealt with war in any sense, a welcome change from standard fare, but this did not last long. The war still held a distinctive place both in the minds of the Players and onstage. The January 1946 frolic featured *On High* by Player Albert D. Conkey. Set in heaven, the play opens with King George III of England, Louis XIV of

France, and Julius Caesar drifting on a cloud. They spot an approaching cloud with Frederick the Great of Prussia, who is quickly welcomed into this select group. The men grouse about the boredom of being dead and the vagaries of history. Caesar is particularly miffed that his image for posterity has been shaped by Shakespeare, which leads to Frederick's horror "that a weakling dramatist is of more importance than a great general," and he inquires if they will have to tolerate this upstart in heaven. Louis quickly reassures him that "he chose to go the other way—always a fellow to play to the pit."[4] The recent war in Europe quickly becomes a topic of conversation among the quartet, revealing more about the playwright's views than an accurate historical portrait. Frederick laments his lack of involvement in any kind of fight, and Louis comments that "you are consistently Germanic, Frederick, *any* fight has always suited Germany."[5] Caesar chimes in about the Huns being the "only race our culture did not touch and humanize."[6] Frederick is nonplussed, because he believes that "Prussia" will be able to dominate the world in a way that Rome never did, "even though a funny little mustachioed corporal may grasp the credit."[7]

The other men quickly realize that Frederick has not checked on the progress of the war in several months. They try to break the news to him gently, but he misunderstands their hints and thinks they are discussing World War I and blames that loss on the fact that the Germans "had forgotten those Yankees—the damned mechanics."[8] The three gleefully tell him that it has happened again, while each tries to give credit for the victory to his home country. Frederick blames the loss on "leaving military decisions to that schweinhund corporal" and peevishly tells George that it is a "pity England couldn't win a war without calling on her rich relations."[9] They settle down to grumbling and making jokes at each other's expense, until they finally admit that they are bored because there are no women in heaven (thanks to original sin, they all automatically go "below"). As men appear to be able to choose where they go, and because after glancing down at Nuremberg, where the trials of the Nazis are progressing, they realize that "in a little time some very scurrilous rats are going to head for eternity," the men decide that they would rather join the ladies, and they end the show by trooping down into a red glow.[10] As in earlier plays, Hitler seems to be mostly a figure of fun, although he is never referred to by name in the script.

Although the original three characters pick on Frederick and the combative nature of his people, he is still welcome as part of their group, everything forgotten in the pursuit of fun and women.

The February frolic featured a patriotic piece, *The Flame* by Player Gordon H. Miller, set during the American Revolution. This was a serious piece completely different from the previous frolic's satirical *On High*. Miller's play examines the last night of Captain Carter, who is about to be executed for treason. Carter spoke out against what he saw as the waste of men dying in the fight against the British and encouraged the men to desert to save themselves. His wife and father-in-law have devised an escape for him, but before he can get away, General Washington visits him. Washington has come to offer his condolences and his reasons for insisting on the sentence even though he claims to love Carter like a son. Carter is angry because he believes that his actions were only common sense: "You know—I know and the men know that the ideal of American independence is a lost cause. That's why when in your stubbornness you refused to surrender—when you insist on continuing this useless slaughter of men—I not only permitted but actually encouraged my men to desert—to go home and save what they could. God knows, at best that can be little enough."[11] Washington asks him what has happened to the idealist he once was. Carter insists that he still is an idealist: "But I also believe that we are a defeated Army and in God's name we should surrender. The cause is not defeated, General. The flame of liberty will continue to burn in our hearts. And perhaps, who knows, some day we may gather strength to strike again."[12] Washington is not won over by this argument: "If I surrender now the flame of liberty will be stamped out of this land forever. This land may not be destined to be great, but it is destined to be free. I believe that as I believe in my God. It will be *free.*"[13] Carter believes the general's zeal has become madness, but Washington insists that his way is the only way to ensure freedom for the fledgling country: "I believe that this nation must be free. It won't be an easy victory, but it will be a victory. And our freedom, once won, may not be an easy thing to hold in the centuries to come. We may have to fight and bleed again to guard it. But it will be ours to have and to hold high. … If I can't have discipline through faith, then, by God, I'll have discipline through fear. If that's the price of liberty—then that price will be paid."[14]

He further clarifies that this is the only way to win the fight. He would love to let Carter go free, but then he too would be guilty of desertion. That he must let this man die and have Carter's son suffer the ignominy of being the son of a traitor is the price that must be paid for freedom. Carter refuses to shake Washington's hand before he leaves, but when given the chance to escape, he decides he is willing to die for liberty. This is a much more somber piece, conscious of the toll of war, but insisting that freedom is worth the price of the lives spent earning it. For an audience that had not yet enjoyed a full year of peace, this play also cautioned that wars would continue to be fought over freedom and paid for in blood, but the price, though horrible, was worth the alternative.

The other piece dealing with war at the same frolic was also somewhat dark, *The Lights of the Apocalypse* by Louis N. Ridenour. Player Ned Batchelor described it in his review for *The Player* as showing "how wars of the future will be fought by soldiers in bombproof shelters pushing buttons and pulling levers, instead of by those in hand-to-hand combat on the ground, in the air and on the sea."[15] Even knowing what had happened at Hiroshima and Nagasaki, Batchelor could not possibly appreciate how accurately this predicted the nature of future combat.

During the 1946–47 season, the club established the Photographic Committee to record Player events.[16] As Legge had died in 1941, only sporadic sketches of frolics had appeared in *The Player*. This committee hoped to pick up the slack and leave a record of the activities at the Playhouse for future Players. Even with the new committee, Players clung to its traditions, and tradition in this case meant publishing caricatures of the frolics in *The Player*. In keeping with this, Verne Minge, a *Detroit News* staff cartoonist, stepped forward to record frolics for *The Player* in October 1946.[17]

That season opened with what was to become a new Player tradition, a full-length play. The long summer hiatus allowed for the time needed to prepare such a long work. *The Hasty Heart*, by John Patrick, was set in a military convalescent hospital, a tearjerker with a young soldier near death from a shrapnel wound.[18] The play was so well received that an invitational was given so that Player family and friends could see the show.[19] In particular, the show was also noted for an exceptional performance of a female character. Because it is often perceived that a man playing a woman will be comic at best,

First Minge caricature (1946): This was also a great example of the Players' ability to play female roles.

this show was an example of what Players could accomplish at their finest:

> In the role of the nurse, Player William W. Merrill was asked to assume a task hardly less demanding than that of the principal male character. Speaking personally, Player Merrill achieved the previously impossible of making us forget that a man was impersonating a young woman on our stage. Not that we haven't seen some fine jobs of female impersonation on the Players' stage. We have seen some fine comedy, and some very convincing simulations of glamor and some excellent portrayals of

middle-aged to elderly ladies. But here was a case wherein Player Merrill carried the illusion so far that, to us, he wasn't merely playing Nurse Margaret, he was Nurse Margaret. Even in the brief and tender love passages, the illusion held, and that is a real test, for so frequently there is an inclination to laugh at the very idea of a man's trying to interpret a woman in love. We can well understand how all the patients succumbed to the charms of this efficient, cheerful, thoroughly lovable nurse.[20]

A brief reminder of the war that had just passed and the related political clout of some of its members appear in this same edition of *The Player*. Player Robert L. Toms, who was a judge by profession, was leaving for Germany to serve on the American judicial staff dealing with the war criminal trials.[21] This was a fairly rare occurrence in the newsletter, for in the main only the heroic aspects of war were mentioned at The Players; they chose not to dwell on the more horrific details. Toms returned in November 1947 after having tried two cases: Erhard Milch, Goering's chief lieutenant in charge of aircraft production, and eighteen men who were charged with running concentration camps. In an interview with the *Detroit News*, he said his biggest surprise was that "neither the defendants nor spectators at the trials had any sense of guilt or shame over the enormity or the crimes that had been committed by them and in their names."[22]

The 1948–49 season was good to The Players. May 1948 finally saw a stabilization of Player membership. The numbers stood at 405, with 36 new members and 32 having resigned that season.[23] The opening show, *Room Service*, a door-slamming farce about life in the theatre, was well enough received to warrant an invitational performance, and that season also saw yet another new playwright for The Players. The multitalented Daniel C. Beattie, a writer by day for the WXYZ studio on the popular *Lone Ranger* radio program, wrote the book, lyrics, and the music for *Down to Rio* for The Players.[24] The show is a musical comedy, an homage to *Anything Goes* complete with boat trip (to Rio, not England), singing sailors, drunk millionaires, a rich debutante falling in love with a stowaway, gangsters, and dancing girls. The Players loved it so much that not only did it make the May Show, but also a record of the music was made and sold to the membership.[25]

This season also included a significant amount of philanthropic work by The Players. In addition to the standard Christmas party for orphans, members collected 100 pounds of clothing for "blind German children" in January 1949.²⁶ Although there is no mention of it in the minutes, this is the same time that the Berlin airlift was taking place. In February, the board agreed to present a show at the Marine Hospital.²⁷ In March, it allowed the Playhouse to be used for scholarship tryouts for the Clara Tree Major Studio of New York, provided that the studio would pay for electricity and heat for the time it was there. Although in general The Players' boards staunchly insist that the organization does not do charitable work, this last action was justified because "this was a project in line with our efforts to promote training and education in the field of dramatics."²⁸

Years after the war was over, the Players continued to perform military subject matter. The 1949–50 season opened with William Wister Haines's *Command Decision*. This show is a military drama about an officer torn between executing a bombing raid in the way that experience has taught him is most effective or one that is pleasing to high-ranking officers more concerned with politics than practicalities. As in previous years, the opening frolic was repeated as an invitational. A play such as *Command Decision* is perfect for The Players' stage, as it has an all-male cast:

> I presume the content of this play would date more heavily if it did not have in it most of the seeds of the currently publicized military services unification effort. This prevents its absolute dependence upon historical interest.
> A long New York run and brilliant road success had attested to the soundness of this all-man show before Players could secure rights to perform what seemed, and surely has now been proved, a "natural" for us. The spontaneous standing Player tribute to the final curtain call makes this review anti-climactic and merely a matter of pleasant record.²⁹

The year 1950 saw an enormous production of a Player musical revue. *Inside Detroit*, book and music by Player W. Howard T. Snyder, set its skits everywhere from Belle Isle to the Detroit Club. One particularly clever skit, "Love's Labor Won" is a "Labor relations conference at Bored Motor Company." This thinly veiled satire about the Ford Motor Company featured "Walter Toother" (Walter Reuther) as the United Auto Workers (UAW) boss and his "Labor henchmen," Mugs, Lugs, and Bugs. The audience is first treated to a brief street scene where "Forth-Worth Scrapin, a Parke-Davis research chemist" (a reference to Player Dallas Chapin, who did indeed work for Parke-Davis) tells Joe the paperboy that there has been an accident at the plant and a new drug has been tossed into the incinerator by mistake. The fumes of this drug cause anyone inhaling them to completely change his or her mind. The only antidote to the drug (as this is a show at The Players, after all) is drinking some kind of alcohol.

Next we see the conference where the labor relations director for Bored Motor Company, John Bugle (the actual labor relations manager was named John Bugas), is informing the "management henchmen" that their word for the day is "no." When Toother and his cronies arrive, they immediately begin threatening to strike if their terms are not met. Bugle is just about to tell them "no" when he gets a whiff of a strange odor coming from the Parke-Davis plant. Toother had been asking for a "four day week with eight days pay," but Bugle ups the ante and offers him a "one day week with a month's pay."[30] By this point, Toother has gotten a healthy dose of the fumes himself, and he counters with an offer to work "eighteen hours a day, six days a week. And, we'll put in an escalator clause— the higher your profits go the lower our wage rate goes."[31] The pair continues to top each other until Bugle finally offers Toother the keys to the kingdom:

> Listen, Walter—we've got the perfect solution at last. We are going to turn over to you the keys and deeds to every Bored property and plant we own. They're going to be yours, all yours. The CIO will become the sole owner of Ford! *sic*] *Well*! Now, what do you say. Oh, wait until Henry and Ernie hear this![32] [Henry Ford II was the president of the company at the time, and "Ernie" referred to Ernest R. Breech, executive vice president of Ford, a man Henry had recruited from General Motors to turn the ailing Ford Motor Company around.][33]

Toother likes the idea so much that he offers Bugle the union. Bugle gives him the deeds and keys, and Toother has his henchmen turn over their assets (according to the stage notes, these included "guns, black-jacks, stink bombs, [and] brass knuckles").[34] They all celebrate the transfer with a shot of Scotch, reversing the effects of the drug. Bugle is horrified when he realizes what has just happened. He demands the return of the deeds, but Toother refuses to give up the signed documents. Bugle counters with a demand that "if you're the management now and we're the CIO we want more wages, more time off, more pensions, more portals, more—."³⁵ Toother chases them out as Bugle threatens a strike. When Toother counters with a threat to shut down the factory for inventory (a common means of thwarting a strike), Bugle decides to go over to General Motors to call a strike there.³⁶ For a club whose members would have most likely sided with industry over labor in most disputes, the parody of both sides is actually evenhanded.

Another skit in the revue, "On the Birmingham 8:05," is set on the commuter train to Detroit from Birmingham, one of the wealthier Detroit suburbs. In it, Snyder mocks the manufacturers and advertisers that are overcharging "Venerable Motors" (General Motors) for their products. However, the advertisers get in an extra dig, as so many of them were members of The Players at the time. When the manufacturer asks the advertising man the name of the advertising club, he replies, "Adcraft," the actual industry club for members of advertising firms. The manufacturer comes back with "No—the other one, oh, yes—Players."³⁷ They banter back and forth about how they bilk "VM" out of money for their services until another gentleman on the train asks them for their business cards. Once they hand them over, he hands them his card, introducing himself as the president of Venerable Motors, at which point they both faint.³⁸ Thus, at least one of the car companies came out on top in *Inside Detroit*. Chrysler, the last of the Big Three, does not get a mention in this revue, probably reflecting its status as the smallest of the trio.

Snyder pokes fun at yet another august Detroit institution, the Detroit Club. The humor in "Lunch at the Detroit Club" primarily focuses on the advanced age of this club's members. One of the characters is actually determined to be dead during the course of the piece, but this is such a common occurrence that they do not even worry about removing him for a day or two. There have been so many deaths that one of the waiters has calluses on his hands from running the flag down to half-mast so frequently. In fact, the flag moves so often that one of the members reports that a military plane landed nearby because it thought it was Selfridge Field.³⁹

Player Verne W. Tucker's review in *The Player* raved about both the performance and the author:

> This quiet, unobtrusive gentleman, modest almost to the point of shyness, has been a Player for eleven years. He has appeared in a number of

roles, mostly inconspicuous ones, nicely interpreted. If he ever wrote anything, it missed these eyes. So, what happened in April—and, of course, again in May? Jackpot. The guy turns out to be another Momma Dionne. Gives birth to an entire musical revue: book AND score! And to make it still more preposterous, the son-of-a-gun produces quintuple sketches all geared into Detroit life, each a little gem and just as playable and amusing as they ever come.[40]

Tucker also complimented the choreographer of the piece, Miss Ruth Haidt, who used to work at Radio City Music Hall.[41] There is no mention of how Haidt came to be associated with the club, but she later appears as the choreographer on other Player musicals and eventually marries a member of The Players, Robert T. Hughes, who joined the club in 1955.

The Players was thriving. By 1951, membership was up to 426, yet it did not technically exceed the limit of 425 set by the bylaws because the almost 50 nonresident members were not factored into this limit.[42] Despite the hearty numbers, the board wanted to make sure that everyone was getting the most out of the club. The summer of 1951 brought the introduction of the Twenty Year Club as a means to "recapture the older members who have dropped by the wayside. There are quite a few of these elder statesmen who, while continuing to pay their dues, don't come to the Frolics regularly."[43] All Players who have been members for twenty years or more are invited to a special dinner before the November frolic, in addition to other activities. In 1955 the board of governors went to particular trouble to make sure that each new member would feel welcome. Each member of the board was assigned seven new members to contact to discover their interests, to get them involved in club activities, and to determine why they had joined in the first place.[44]

January 1952 saw the advent of a new tradition: the members sang "When the Day Is Done" by Weeks and Holliday to open the frolic. Player John L. Thornhill reported on this event for *The Player*:

> Every tradition must have a beginning, and Players lucky enough to enjoy the really wonderful 234th Frolic midwifed the latest in a long line of Player traditions.
>
> There's no better way to break the ice (if not the rafters) in any gathering than with a good song, which to be specific, is exactly what happened. The thing I can't understand is how we overlooked such a good thing for so long a time, particularly since the words and music were

authored in 1925. Anyhow, everyone had a chance to exercise the musical side of his vocal chords other than in the privacy of his bathroom.[45]

Also that January the board determined to create a memorial plaque for the chair nameplates of deceased members.[46] This may have been prompted by the passing of Founder Charles Pierpont Larned earlier that month. The board searched for an appropriate inscription for the plaque, but it was not until October that Player W. Howard T. Snyder's suggestion of the quote "Our Play Is Done" from *Twelfth Night* was accepted.[47]

That year several Players asked if their wives could attend dress rehearsals. With their strict adherence to tradition and male camaraderie at The Players, the general feeling was that the presence of women would change the atmosphere of the club. Because the board felt that their presence at dress rehearsals would compromise the nature of the club, they regretfully refused, but they did agree that "little stags' of an understanding age" would be allowed at the discretion of the parents.[48] The admittance of "little stags" was most likely a way of indoctrinating future Players at an early age. The success of this strategy can be viewed in the multiple cross-generational Player families, most notably the Guests, Standishes, and Robinsons. Another board decision made that year was to eliminate the classification of associate membership, as granting associates a vote on club matters left little distinction between this group and actives. The vote passed at the annual meeting, leaving the designations of active, nonresident, and honorary life members.[49]

About this time, sound finally came to the Playhouse. Player Al Shelden Jr. was instrumental in this innovation. When he joined in 1950, he was shocked that such an excellently equipped theatre was still using rudimentary sound techniques. When a thunder-storm was needed, sheets of tin were rattled and paper bags blown up and popped. Shelden complained to the board about these deficiencies, and the board suggested that he fix the problem himself:

> Soon we received a script called "Minus Zero." This science fiction show was a tough one. At the time we had not yet sent John Glenn off into space. Players was not equipped to handle such a show. So they, the powers that be, came to me. "OK," they said, "here's your chance to prove that we need sound at Players. We have decided to produce it. Good Luck!" And prove it we did! At the time I was working at Channel 4

Detroit TV [the local NBC affiliate]. Also, I had a recording studio in my parent's basement which a group of us built. So I got my crew together and we recorded all the sound for "Minus Zero." I rented a complete sound system which was brought into the theatre, and we certainly did blast our guy off into space. The audience loved it and the show was picked for the "May Show."

Shelden also had to convince the board to allow him to take over half of the balcony for a sound booth. It was not until he and other like-minded Players were elected to the board of governors that they were finally able to set up the sound booth in the balcony. Eventually, when computerized lighting boards came in, the lights were also controlled from the balcony, making a huge difference in the quality of the technical elements in Player shows.[50]

During the 1953–54 season, Player Bob Toms got the chance to experience the luxury available to few playwrights when he was able to "revise" his work *There Once Lived a King*, written nine years earlier. It is described as a spoof of drawing room comedies meant to be played completely straight. The only thing altered between the "original" and the "rewrite" is the addition of two actors. The characters were mentioned in the original, but never seen. The Narrator explains at the beginning of the piece that they were added "to soothe the feelings of a couple of Players who always feel slighted when they are not cast, that their names appear on the program and that they will take a curtain call, but that otherwise they will not be seen or heard."[51] The two actors listed in the program were Albert D. Conkey and Richard A. Forsyth, two Player workhorses who spent a significant amount of time on the stage of the Playhouse.

In February, the board once again affirmed their oft-broken policy on charity performances. The Starr Commonwealth, a children's home in Albion, Michigan, had asked The Players to repeat their May Show as a charity performance, but the board wrote a letter to them saying that "it is contrary to a forty year policy of Players to play for charity."[52] It is quite possible that the board did not realize how often this policy had been ignored. Although it is equally possible that the policy is kept as a handy way out of obligations that the board does not feel are in the best interest of The Players. They tend to favor any theatrical endeavors, wartime support, and charities that support the arts and children, but they avoid entanglements that could cost them too much time, effort, or money or that could put them in the position of consistently providing entertainment at charity functions, which would quickly become burdensome.

On 21 February 1954, Guy Brewster Cady, father of The Players and the last of the original five who had met at Richter's to create the club, died in Los Angeles. He was seventy-eight years old and had retired from active business, but he still kept in touch with the club, and his passing was mourned by the Players.[53]

That March saw one of the most ambitious productions ever to grace The Players' stage. *The Trial of Anne Boleyn*, adapted from Maxwell Anderson's *Anne of the Thousand Days*, was directed by Player Dallas Chapin and designed by Player William E. Kapp. Player sets were often composed mostly of two-dimensional scenery with three-dimensional pieces of furniture. This was as much for ease of changing sets (since it was usually a three-show bill) as it was to keep down costs. The set for *The Trial of Anne Boleyn* was enormous, with a large, three-dimensional stone-columned courtroom, dramatically lit so that the columns seemed to disappear into the rafters. The costumes were appropriate to the period (although Anne was wearing magenta and blue, somewhat out of place for the gravity of the subject, in this author's opinion). Player Harry Guest (author Edgar Guest's son), a long-standing pick for female roles, was made up so well by Hirschfield that one of the audience members was heard to seriously remark, "Who's the blond?" Henry VIII appeared to have stepped straight out of a Holbein painting, and even the guards' costumes were given the same amount of attention as those of the lead roles. In the words of one reviewer, it was "as professional a presentation as an amateur audience has any right to expect."[54] Needless to say, it made the May Show that year.

The next frolic packed an even bigger surprise and ended the 1953–54 season on a high note. Without any prior warning, Vice-President Richard Nixon showed up at the 3 April frolic:

> Taken completely by surprise at his entrance, the Players rose as a body and gave our guest such an ovation as the old Playhouse has never heard before. Players Allen Crow, Alan Canty and Wilber Brucker engineered this happy event, which also gave us an opportunity of welcoming Senator Homer Ferguson, Roscoe Bonistell and Rudy Reichert. Mr. Nixon was just as at home on-stage as in the informal elbow-rubbing reception in the foyer, where he met and chatted with all comers. His gracious remarks made you feel that Players was really his kind of club.[55]

*The Trial of Anne Boleyn* (1954): This is an example of one of the more elaborate set designs by William Kapp, one of The Players' most prolific designers.

Nixon was in town for two reasons. He was officially there to speak at a dinner in Senator Homer Ferguson's honor, but he was also there to be an "administration spokesman on the hydrogen bomb," according to a *Detroit News* article on his visit.[56] Bill Rohloff was performing in a show that evening, and he remembers being impressed at Nixon's friendly personality. Nixon later sent an autographed photo that hung for years outside the office of the Playhouse until Nixon fell into "ill-repute" and it disappeared. Rohloff later found it on the floor of a dusty storeroom, but it has since disappeared again.[57]

This frolic was also indicative of standard Player fare during this time period. It contained a bill of frothy comedies of manners including a show called *Red Peppers* by Noel Coward, which recounts the

> alternately hilarious and stormy personal life of a second-rate song and dance team, played to perfection by Harry Moock and Bob Garrison.

Vice-President Nixon's visit to The Players (1954): Player Wilber Brucker is on the left and Senator Homer Ferguson is on the right.

Scene I opened with George and Lilly Pepper doing a very trite routine, with the orchestra conducted by Harry Turrell in white tie and tails. The next scene shifted back-stage, with the Peppers making a quick change amid charges and counter charges of missed cues and bungled exits. The give and take banter was salty and witty, and finally involved the orchestra leader, the theatre manager, played by Loren Robinson and the leading star Mabel Grace, played in his usual expansive way by John Peters. ... The final scene brought the Peppers back on-stage, all sweetness and light, with a song and soft-shoe dance routine that brought down the house. Its professional smoothness was an eye-opener and reflected the training of choreographer Ruth Haidt Hughes.[58]

The May Show that year featured *Red Peppers* along with *The Trial of Anne Boleyn* and Gilbert and Sullivan's *Trial by Jury*. In many ways this is the most representative of Players' productions. *Anne Boleyn* shows that members can do drama, although the set and costumes had an equal part in getting this show chosen for the May performance. *Peppers* has the witty (and fluffy) comedy that was always a hit at The Players, while *Jury* allowed the glee club and the orchestra to show off during yet another light comedy of manners. The only thing that was missing from this show was some sort of adventure or war play that allowed one of the Players to get injured during the performance.

Although members of the club sometimes claim to be confused about how May Shows are chosen (one older member remarked, "I've been a member for twenty-five years and I'm damned if I know"[59]), the board is actually responsible for picking the bill. Several things have to be taken into consideration, including staging, length, and the presence of cast members in May. A fairly representative example of the kinds of performances held at the end of the season would be an elaborately designed drama, a musical, followed by a rollicking comedy.

Enjoying such successes and wanting to reward longtime members, it was decided at the 1954 annual meeting that those Players who "have completed 35 years of continuous active membership" would be granted honorary life membership.[60] The transfer was automatic, although the board could bestow this honor at their discretion, even if the Player had not had thirty-five continuous years at the club.

In the forty-fifth year of the club, the board of governors decided that it was time to start compiling their history. The Historical Committee was formed with Player Bob M. Toms as chairman and included some of the pillars of The Players, Olie Standish and Bill Kapp, among its members. The board hoped that they could "outline and collect material for an eventual history of The Players."[61] That same year, in the summer of 1955, the board convinced Olie Standish to undertake the writing of the history.[62]

In addition, the club honored Player Edgar A. Guest that

year. Guest had been a Player since 1913 and was a nationally recognized poet. His poetry, like the productions of The Players, celebrated friendship and the simpler joys of life.[63] In contrast to this happy event, the following summer the Players lost esteemed member Lee Anderson. Anderson had been one of the early Player playwrights, and like Al Weeks, he saw some professional success thanks to his start at The Players.[64] Anderson authored twelve one-act plays, three of which were published in *The Players Book of One Act Plays;* only Al Weeks shared that many plays in the compilation. Anderson's profession had been advertising, working first at Chalmers Motor Car, then later at Hupp Motor Car. He then went on to become vice-president of the advertising firm MacManus, Inc. Obituaries in both the *Detroit News* and the *Free Press* described him as a pioneer in the field of automobile advertising and credited him with the slogan, "Body by Fisher."[65] This reminder of the passing of the old guard should have made apparent the need for a written account of their shared history, but this project never made it into the club's archives.

The Players as a club was comfortably settling into "middle age." They continued to hold the monthly frolics, give occasional receptions for visiting performers, hold the children's Christmas party, and give sporadic community outreach programs such as putting on shows for hospital patients and orphans.[66] The board of governors was not complacent in their enjoyment of the successful organization. Not only did they seek out individuals to make sure they felt welcome as new members, but also they invited the presidents of other local amateur theatrical groups to the frolics as a means of connecting The Players with other like-minded groups (and potential members). These efforts were successful, and May 1956 saw another jump in membership to 483. Seventy of these members were non-residents, but they evidently felt a close enough connection to the club that they maintained their membership despite being unable to attend most or all of the frolics.[67]

The next season continued the trend in membership numbers. It is not recorded which of the three groups first had the idea, but for the first time since the joint Christmas show with the Detroit Society of Arts and Crafts in 1924, The Players teamed up with the Theatre Arts Club and the Fine Arts Society in putting together a Drama Festival that consisted of three separate acts (one for each group) that was held at the Players Playhouse in October for semi-public performances.[68] The Fine Arts Society chose Noel Coward's

*Ways and Means*, the Theatre Arts Club chose the recognition scene from *Anastasia*, and The Players chose the old Arthur Sullivan standby, *Cox and Box*. Tickets were sold to members of the three organizations plus the presidents of local amateur theatres.

The show was quite a success and was written up in both the society and theatre columns in the local newspapers. The board was pleased with the outcome but decided that if the festival was repeated in the future, it should consist of a single three-act play with a cast comprised of members from all three groups.[69] The profits from the festival ($1,300) were put into a joint account that was earmarked for lighting improvements that would benefit the productions of all three groups.[70]

The board tackled some serious house cleaning that season, repairing windows, scrubbing the walls, and making improvements. Also that season, the club was approaching its resident membership limit of 425. President Harry Guest (known for his talents playing female roles) warned Players to propose any new members soon or they would be placed on a waiting list.[71] That season ended with the high-water mark for Players members: 496, 78 of whom were non-residents.[72] Reaching the membership limit was also experienced by other Detroit clubs, such as the Detroit Athletic Club, which stayed at its maximum membership for the 1950s (2,800 for that time period), and the Detroit Club, which hovered around its 750-resident-member limit set during the 1950s, although the numbers slipped a little during the 1960s.[73]

In 1957, the board yet again reconfirmed its much-disregarded policy of not giving benefit performances by refusing to put on a show for the Senior Center, although they virtually undermined their pronouncement by their assertion that "this decision, however, [will] not … affect our annual Christmas party or other established traditional activities."[74] It was also decided to hold another Drama Festival with the Fine Arts and the Theatre Arts clubs, with the funds earmarked for the purchase of a new cyclorama.[75] That year, a single show called *Glad Tidings* was performed with a cast from all three organizations:

> It provided a wonderfully wacky evening's fare for enthusiastic audiences, a lush oasis of relief from the Russians [this was the year Sputnik was launched], the Asian flu and all the other woes of the world.
> As Players we were outnumbered, five to four, but it was a battle happily lost. Edward Mabley's script concerning the bachelor who thought

he had no children to speak of, his fiancee, his old flame and a brace of precocious youngsters gave plenty of room for laughs with much of the juicier lines saved for the ladies. And how well they did with them!

As the actress-flame from Steve Whitney's past, Isabelle Pearse as Maud Abbott had herself a gorgeous time. She was forgetful, provocative, maddening, witty and always decorative. The lobster-for-breakfast bit in the last act was sheer joy and no mean feat of gastronomy and articulation combined.

Our own Harry Guest as Whitney, the bachelor who is suddenly presented with a 20-year-old bundle of joy in the form of Karen Putnam as Claire Abbott, was a perfect picture of frustration and confusion. The recognition scene between Whitney and the daughter he didn't know he had was certainly not out of *"Anastasia,"* but it was charmingly underplayed by both.[76]

Once again, the show was a great success.

If there is any doubt that the membership of The Players had a serious dedication to their productions despite their amateur status, the November 1957 frolic dispels it. When faced with the possibility of a lousy show, the cast rebelled:

The November Frolic was originally to have been *I Killed the Count*, an Alfred Hitchcock thing seen lately on Broadway and television. After a few spiritless rehearsals, however, the cast united in silent revolt and not only killed the Count but the entire play. Script Chairman Walker Graham's committee rose to this crisis by swiftly substituting *Reclining Figure*, which the cast readily accepted as being at least three times better than the first choice. Trouble was not at an end, however. At the first rehearsal of the new play Director Bill Deneen fell ill and was quickly removed to the hospital. Player Jim Hughes nunquammed as substitute director until Bill returned, and then the two of them brought the play to the perfection that will be exhibited on Saturday next.[77]

All was not fun and games, however. Once their house was in order, Players set about cleaning up their finances and started looking at long-range planning instead of merely living year to year. The board instituted the Long-Range Planning Committee, but also asked the Budget and Finance, Building and Property, and Ways and Means committees to start making suggestions for ways to ensure the perpetuation of the club. The board also began discussing their fiftieth anniversary, and a temporary committee was established to deal with planning the celebration.[78]

As part of the suggestions made by the Long-Range Planning Committee, the Players Foundation was formed to "be used as a recipient of capital gifts and bequests, and will be administered by a Board of Trustees made up of past presidents and members of the Twenty Year Club."[79] The board hoped that the foundation would be able to "solicit contributions from the membership for the perpetuation of the Playhouse, the possible expansion of the property at some later date, the offering of scholarships to deserving dramatic students or for such other purposes as may be later decided."[80] In addition, the board hoped that Players who had written original plays would be willing to sign over their rights to the Players Foundation.[81] Past Player presidents Albert D. Conkey, Richard A. Forsyth, and Leslie C. Putnam were elected as incorporators of the foundation.[82]

The year 1958 was something of a watershed for The Players. Just when everything seemed to be golden, the first inklings of the problems to come began to appear. The season had started out with a warning that membership was about to close, but by January, the board notified the membership that new members were not being proposed in the usual numbers (only seven by January).[83] This was to become a gradual problem for the next several years, but both declining numbers and a lack of new members are serious problems today. The board gave a gentle reminder to current members that new Players could still be added. Membership hardly seemed to be a problem at the March frolic, which boasted seventy-two Players directly involved in the performance (not counting stage crew or orchestra, which added at least another twenty Players).[84] Nonetheless, discussions appear in the minutes as to how to increase membership, including ensuring that Membership Committee members were all from different professions and forming two campus groups, Wayne State University and University of Detroit.[85]

Little did the Players suspect how severe the problems were in Detroit's development. Sugrue's book *The Origins of the Urban Crisis: Race and Inequality in Postwar Detroit* chronicles the problems that were to plague Detroit for decades:

> The 1950s marked a decisive turning point in the development of the city—a systematic restructuring of the local economy from which the city never fully recovered. Detroit's economy experienced enormous fluctuations in the 1950s. Between 1949 and 1960, the city suffered four major recessions. Because the auto industry was tremendously sensitive to shifts in consumer demand it weathered recessions badly. The unpre-

dictability of demand for automobiles, especially in times of economic uncertainty, had serious ramifications for Detroit's working class. A slight shift in interest rates or a small drop in car sales resulted in immediate layoffs. ... What was new in the 1950s was that auto manufactures and suppliers permanently reduced their Detroit-area work forces, closed plants, and relocated to other parts of the country.

... More important than the periodic downswings that plagued the city's economy was the beginning of a long-term and steady decline in manufacturing employment that affected Detroit and almost all other major northeastern and Midwestern industrial cities. Between 1947 and 1963, Detroit lost 134,000 manufacturing jobs, while its population of working-aged men and women actually increased.[86]

The process of deindustrialization, "the closing, downsizing, and relocation of plant and sometimes whole industries," devastated the people and the landscape of Detroit.[87] The combination of relocating plants to avoid the powerful labor unions, to control labor costs, and to avoid integration of the workforce; the increased use of automation that reduced personnel and put small independent automakers out of business; and the increased use of overtime allowed for the decreasing size of the labor force.[88] The 1950s may have been prosperous for the nation, but Detroit did not share in this affluence. The city's frustration in not participating in the national success combined with job loss and economic hardship inequitably experienced by the African American population in Detroit set the stage for a massive riot in 1967.[89] Sugrue provides some grim numbers: "Between 1953 and 1960, the area [Detroit's east side] had lost ten plants and 71,137 jobs."[90] The departing jobs took with them a significant amount of the white population:

> As jobs left the city, so too did white workers with the means to move to suburbs or small towns where factories relocated. Wealthier whites also followed investments outward. As a result, Detroit's population began an unbroken downward fall in the 1950s. As Detroit's population shrank, it also grew poorer and blacker. Increasingly, the city became the home for the dispossessed, those marginalized in the housing market, in greater peril of unemployment, most subject to the vagaries of a troubled economy.[91]

What was most disturbing about this trend was that, like those unemployed by the Great Depression, the people who needed the most help were blamed for their predicament despite underlying causes completely out of their control. Various agencies and activists groped for solutions that never seemed to address the needs of displaced workers.[92]

The fifties were also a time of anxiety. The Cold War and the potential use of the nuclear bomb were constant sources of unease. Player Gordon H. Miller's *The Day We Captured the Devil* is set at the army testing ground at White Sands, New Mexico. During the test of a nuclear bomb (the characters say it is the largest in their history), the Devil showed up to observe the blast himself. Unfortunately for him, he was knocked out by the blast and found by the base's observation team, who were quite frightened by the fact that they had discovered an unconscious man, completely unscathed, in the blast area. They were even more disturbed when they noticed he had cloven hooves instead of feet. The Devil is now imprisoned in a lead-lined vault fifty feet below the surface, the characters tell us, and since he discovered (much to his chagrin) that he cannot pass through lead, there has been no evil in the world since 4 o'clock that afternoon.[93]

The Devil tries various means of convincing General Stone and Captain Martin (the post's chaplain) that he should be released. His first argument is that without his work, the entire military and clergy will be out of a job. Martin is not worried by this, and Stone insists that an end to war is "the hope of every civilized man."[94] This argument shot down, the Devil then argues that his imprisonment will cause economic havoc. Anyone who has to work fighting evil will now be out of a job, and the advertising industry will not be able to survive when it has to tell the whole truth. This argument begins to sway the general. The Devil moves in for the kill and points out that God has allowed him to exist. He begins to sway the chaplain with the argument that humanity's progress in civilization has come often through combating evil. With no evil, humanity will not progress. Evil is part of the divine plan, according to the Devil: "So, I maintain that the winning—the conquering of the evils of greed, poverty, filth, sickness and pain—one step at a time—I say, is part of the divine plan for the salvation of mankind."[95]

The general is not impressed with this hypothesis: "As a soldier, why should I be satisfied with winning a few skirmishes or even an occasional battle when suddenly I find I can win the whole war?" This only angers the Devil: "Because, you damned fool, you're not ready to win the war—mankind isn't ready."[96] The chaplain leaves the decision up to the general and departs. It is a small thing that finally decides the case for the general. Stone has requested air conditioning for the base, and he stretched the truth somewhat in his case to Washington. Nothing is an outright lie, but it is also not an accurate representation of the situation. The general is going to correct his report, but a sergeant stops him by reminding him that he has lied before in pursuit of justice for a court-martialed private: "You and I both know that was a lie. But the result was justice in the true sense of the word." The general acknowledges that "sometimes a little evil has to be exchanged for a lot of good."[97] The Devil counsels him that if he signs the paperwork as is, he will be "morally bound" to let him go. Knowing this, the general does it anyway, and the play ends with life returning to normal as one of the sergeants is once again able to lie to his girlfriend.

The ending may seem a little less than satisfying, but it was an honest one. The general cannot imagine a world without the small evils, even if that means that there will be larger evils with which humanity will have to struggle. The obvious parallel seems to be the testing of the nuclear bomb. It is a terrible evil, but it is perceived to be a necessary one that will ensure "a lot of good."

The 1958–59 season did not get off to an auspicious start. Breaking with tradition, the opening show, Howard Teichmann and George S. Kaufmann's *The Solid Gold Cadillac*, was not repeated as an invitational. The board of governors' minutes say that it was not up to the usual Player standards,[98] although Player Conkey reviewed it for *The Player* and gave it a glowing review:

> In this hilarious script, the afore-mentioned duo [the authors, Teichmann and Kaufmann], with an assist from acid-tongued Fred Allen, wedded farce to fantasy while poking a sharp finger at corporate ethics and antics. It was played by Players, as it was written, for laughs and it seemed to me that the Player audience responded somewhat less fully than the working Players deserved, or were they implying that all does not glitter that is gold.
> ... I hope the reluctant reception was not due to the thin-skinned reaction to a script that is a very thinly-veiled Detroit story.[99]

The show must have been bad enough to remain in the minds of the membership, because it was brought up years later in a 1975 review in *The Player*, when Player Robert L. Greene used it to contrast the previous frolic's outstanding performance, calling *The Solid Gold Cadillac* a "monumental turkey."[100]

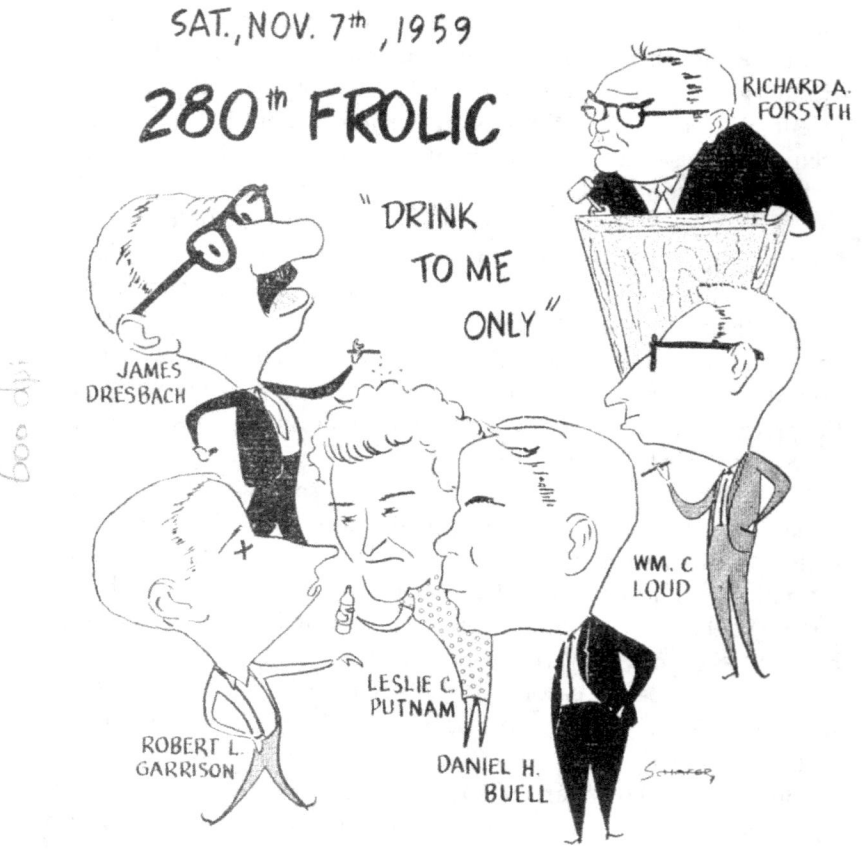

First Schafer caricature (1959)

To make things worse in an already bad year, Player Bill Elliot, a member since 1918, passed away on 19 October. Bill was a dentist by trade, and he had been appearing onstage regularly at Players since he became a member and had served as president during the rough years of 1934–35. Like Sam Slade, Bill's name graces one of the dressing room doors. At the time of his death, only Sam and Bill shared this honor, although other Player names have joined them since.[101] On a lighter note, a replacement for Minge as caricaturist for *The Player* was finally found after two years of searching, and Bob

Schafer took over in the 28 November 1959 issue. When Minge returned a few years later, he took over the caricatures until he resigned in 1973.

Membership numbers were steadily dropping. By May 1959, The Players were down to 459, 82 of whom were nonresidents.[102] A note of anxiety crept into the president's letter in *The Player* the following season. Player Walker Graham could feel that something intangible was slipping away from The Players: "I'd like to see our club be just what it was to me in '42 and '47. I want The Players always to be somewhat unattainable, to continue as "Detroit's 400," to be a goal that is thrilling to earn. I want each of us to be proud of belonging to the greatest club of its kind in the world, and to introduce new members in the light of that pride."[103]

In a January 1960 meeting, the Membership Committee submitted a report to the board outlining their major concern and some solutions:

1. A concern over loss of members.
2. A suggestion to the Board of Governors that a booklet be prepared which would explain The Players, committee structure, and committee functions.
3. A suggestion that two members of the Membership Committee be assigned each Frolic to greet members and prospective members, one to be stationed at the door of the Playhouse and one at the bar. Then, one of these members would see to it that prospective members were brought to the Playroom to meet the Board of Governors.
4. A suggestion that Membership Committee members "on duty" wear badges similar to those worn by the House Committee, identifying them as members of the Membership Committee.
5. A suggestion that the Board of Governors emphasize Junior membership [cheaper dues for members younger than thirty years old].[104]

Despite these concerns, the Players were already looking forward to the next season and their celebration of their fiftieth anniversary. It was only February, and their celebration would not occur until 10 December, but they energetically set about making plans. The birth date was debated, and at least two sets of minutes that year mention the issue, but the board finally settled on the December date, when the five men gathered at Richter's, rather than the January date when the Articles of Association were signed.[105] Tying into the membership problem, it was soon after decided that the initiation fee would be waived for any former Players that wanted to return to the club.[106]

The board established a formal anniversary committee (it appears that the earlier committee established in 1957 did not last) and made several suggestions as to how the club should celebrate. Many of the proposals were not unusual for any organization marking an important occasion. Commemorative jewelry was commissioned (a tux stud), and a publicity campaign was put into place. The committee also attempted to initiate a one-act play competition (a suggestion that had appeared off and on for years, but one on which no action had been taken up to this point). The committee also suggested that the club try to bring back some of the more famous guests of The Players for the celebration. It also sent a request to nonresident Player William Talman that he participate in the anniversary celebration. Talman was the son of a founder and was playing the prosecutor on the *Perry Mason* television show at the time.[107] Due to the festivities, The Players elected not to participate in the Drama Festival with Fine Arts and Theatre Arts clubs.[108]

Even members of The Players were a little shocked that they had survived fifty years. At the end of the 1959–60 season, *The Player* marveled that this "little 'gentleman's acting club' should have survived, and so well for so long."[109]

Although major plans were underway, the true business of The Players was still continuing. January 1960 got underway with a bang:

> The opener was a hair-raiser titled *"The Hitchhiker."* Written by Lucille Fletcher for Orson Welles during his heyday on radio with the Mercury Players, it is a haunting story of a young man's nightmarish encounter with death on a lonely, transcontinental auto trip. Adapted for the stage it lost none of its ghostly grip. Director Bill Rohloff pulled out all of the spine-tingling stops with his imaginative opening scene and his use of a combo of sound technicians in full view. Although sound effects played a big part, they were never allowed to be overpowering or distracting. This is quite a trick when your stage is a clutter of mikes, cables, tape recorder, record player, life-size door slam and miscellaneous studio sound gadgets. The cast played it absolutely dead-pan without gestures or undue vocal emphasis, nor movement, except for the necessary steps

to and from the mikes. Voices, piano and sound melded perfectly to create a monotonous eeriness.[110]

The occasion of The Players' fiftieth anniversary was recorded not only in the *Detroit Historical Society Bulletin* by Player George W. Stark but also in the *New York Times*. In addition, The Players found other ways to mark the celebration. Like members during the thirtieth anniversary celebration, the Players celebrating the fiftieth anniversary wanted to memorialize their history. Unlike the earlier Players, this involved writing articles in *The Player* on famous stage accidents on the stage of the Playhouse instead of significant events in Player history. Two of these events deserve recounting:

> President Walker Graham's accident during the November Frolic recalled to Players Eldredge, Fellows and Dresbach an earlier incident of accidental mayhem. Years ago Player Bill Lerchen was starring in Lee Anderson's *"Is Peculiar"* which required Bill to be stuffed into a wooden box. Between rehearsal and show a stagehand got around to putting handles on the box by means of two inch screws. When Bill was stuffed into the box at the performance the protruding screws shredded his head like cabbage. Bill maintained a stoical silence, emerged from the box and finished the play with head bloodied but unbowed. Maybe that's when the phrase Nunquam Renig was coined![111]

The next installment included this gem:

> Nostalgia: Chapter II. Last month, dear little ones, we told how Player Bill Lerchen was bloodily detopped for Players and Art. This month we shall recall for you how Acting Mayor John C. Lodge lay unconscious on our floor while sanguine members merrily bruited jests: Mr. Lodge entered the auditorium from the stage door and unhappily missed his footing. He fell in the vicinity of the left Winningham jug and struck his head on the cold stone floor. Someone shouted for a doctor and several ambled over. Presuming a bit of Player playfulness, they held a mock consultation over the supine form. It was not until oozing blood was discovered that the then unhappy medicos realized that this was something considerably less than a practical joke. Fortunately for Players, for Detroit and for Mr. Lodge, the patient recovered. We hope that this fragment of Player history will soothe your jangled nerves when next you are stuck in a traffic jam on the John C. Lodge Expressway.[112]

Fortunately, these seem to be the worst of the accidents that ever occurred on The Players' stage, with those that were wounded retaining no lasting harm from the incidents.

The Fiftieth Anniversary Frolic was a celebration of past Player successes. Conveniently enough, even the dates were amenable to The Players, and 10 December 1960 fell on a Saturday. The frolic was a standard three-act bill, and the final piece, *Kaleidoscope 50*, was a montage of big musical numbers from Player favorites. Pieces from such plays as *Hairlooms, Doing Stratford, Men Working,* and *Down to Rio* were resurrected, often with some of the original actors. The members turned out in force for this effort, including a twenty-six-member, all-Player orchestra and a thirteen-man crew.

Apparently, the high-profile anniversary and the membership drive both succeeded. Forty-three new members joined after the frolic, and there were two reinstatements (in all probability far fewer reinstatements than the board would have liked to have seen). The Players marked the passing of the year by recognizing another beloved Player, Richard A. Forsyth, a noted director (*On Borrowed Time*), actor (*What the Heil*), and past president (1931–32), with a dressing room door named after him.[113] Although Slade has gotten more "press" throughout the years (actors are always more visible and prominent than other theatre people), Forsyth was just as important to the club in his capacity as director and board member.[114] The board made the decision to honor the still living Forsyth (Forsyth did not pass away until 1971), rather than waiting until he was gone to recognize the work he had done for the club.

Mindful of the necessity of perpetuating the club, the Endowment Committee prepared a letter to send out to the membership soliciting funds.[115] The board also made another business decision to make the Playhouse more marketable. "It was also agreed that for the purpose of acquiring new renters, the Playroom be henceforth called the Founder's Room."[116] It is most likely that the board found "the Playroom" too frivolous a name to use in selling the space to corporate renters, as it made the room sound like a pool hall instead of the stately room with a stone fireplace that it is in reality. Although it is not listed as a cost-saving measure, it was decided that the Drama Festival be held every two years instead of annually.[117] This change may also have come about for logistical reasons.

Probably prompted by the recent celebration of their anniversary, The Players yet again considered a compilation of their history. Such a task had first been contemplated in 1955 when the Historical Committee was formed, but serious attempts to collect

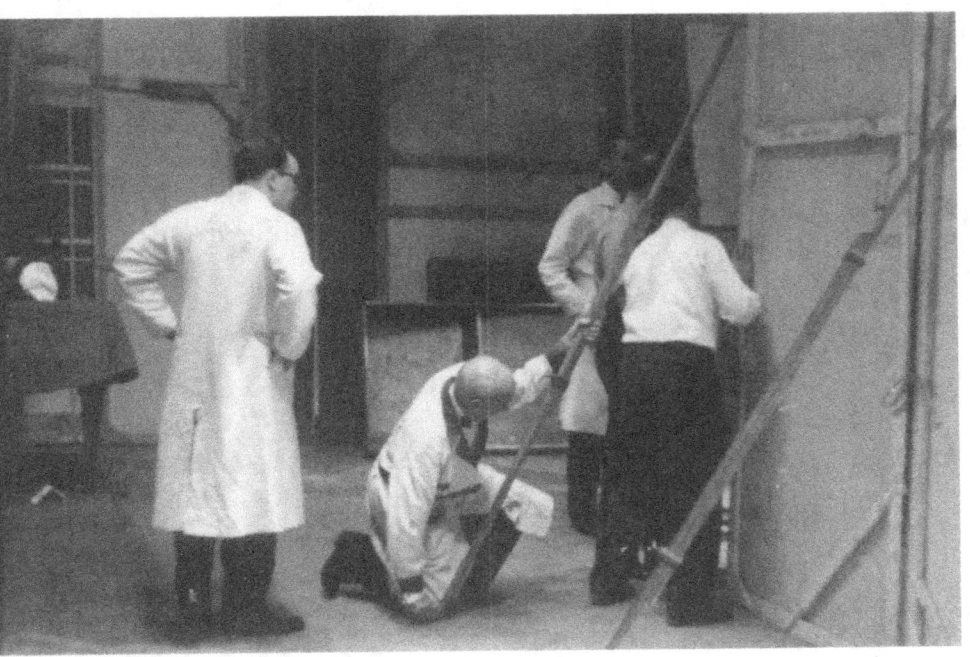

Backstage crew in tuxedos and lab coats

their history did not begin until September 1961. It first took the form of a booklet suggested by President William L. Robinson, with some of the material being used for a new member pamphlet that would outline briefly the "activities, history and traditions of The Players."[118] Not long afterward, Robinson reported that a tentative outline of twenty-three chapters had been written, "each dealing with a different phase of Players and each being assigned to a different Player for research, writing and compilation."[119] By July 1962, nine of the then twenty-four chapters had been submitted, but the cost of typing the material was prohibitive, and the board started looking for a volunteer to type the chapters.[120] Mention of a Players history does not reappear until December 1966, when the Historical, Publicity, and Publications committees planned to meet to resurrect interest in the history of the organization.[121] The outline and completed chapters are currently missing.

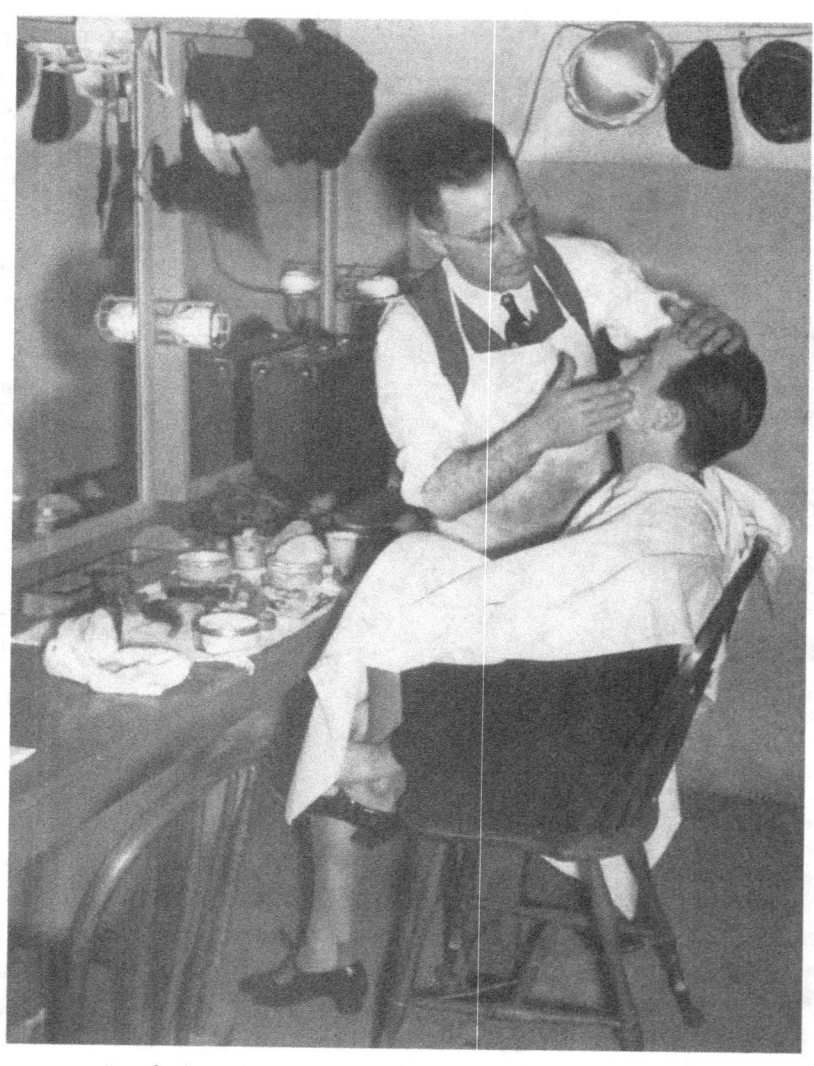

Pre-frolic prep: Unidentified Player getting made up before a frolic (note the heels).

Unfortunately, the 1960s saw the passing of a whole new generation of Player greats. James Strasburg, who had recorded not only frolics but also significant events in Player history, passed in 1961. W. Colburn Standish, affectionately known as "Olie," longtime bartender for The Players, died in 1962, but his son carried on the family tradition at the club. W. Colburn Standish Jr. donated a new act drop in March 1961 on behalf of his family.[122] With little fanfare, the act drop acquired the name "Olie."[123] Jake Hirschfield, whose gender-bending makeup and costumes had turned men into women at The Players for years, and who had been partly responsible for Sam Slade's enduring Lincoln, also died in 1962. He had taken up costuming duties until October 1961 when he retired and asked that a Costume Committee be formed so that he could train them before he hung up his tape measure.[124] Despite his loss to The Players, his wife, Frances, continued to help costume the frolics until 1982.[125] Al Weeks, Player playwright laureate, author of *Roller Skates Must Be Mended* and The Players' Song, and president during the rough years of 1930–31, died in 1963. Loren T. Robinson Sr., historian for The Players and a very active member, died a few months after Weeks, but like Standish, he was survived by a Player son to carry on his work. These men had built The Players from a roving band of drunken miscreants in tuxes to a respected Detroit institution with its own landmark. When they passed, they took some of the spirit of days gone by with them.

The Players embraced a new tradition in 1961 that enhanced one of the already long-standing traditions at the club: drinking beer at the frolics. While pricing china to replace what had been lost over the previous seasons, Governor Arthur V. Diedrich noted that china beer steins with the Player crest and individual Players' names could be sold to the membership. These mugs would be kept in a cabinet in the Founders Room.[126] The steins became a serious topic of discussion for the board. Player Kapp designed cabinets for the mugs, and Player William Walter built them. Secretary Bill Rohloff called for bids on nameplates to be affixed to the cabinets so that Players would always know where to find their mugs.[127] It is an exciting day when a new Player receives his mug. Prior to purchasing the labeled mugs, a lot of beer was wasted at great expense at the frolics. Players would stand around talking, set their mugs down, and then not be able to identify which one was theirs. They would leave the mugs and get fresh ones. The mugs with the Players' names thus actually resulted in significant savings for the club.[128]

Much as there has always been beer at the frolics, there had been a nude hung above the bar in the lobby for many years (the corner of it can be seen in the 1938 *Life* article, and it may have hung there since the Playhouse opened). No record exists as to how the nude left its place above the bar (and should not to be confused with the 1976 theft of the nude along with Slade's portrait), but the "desirability of returning the Coppin Nude to its proper and accustomed place over the bar in the lobby" was discussed in July 1964. Governor Joseph J. Hartigan was given the task of recovering the nude.[129] This task was swiftly completed, and the 5 August 1964 meeting "was called to order by Player President Ray Potter ... amid an air of jubilation and rejoicing as Governor Hartigan announced the forthcoming return of a Coppin nude to the Playhouse. Governor Hartigan read a letter from Player Dean Coffin to Mr. Coppin that had evoked a promise of an unframed painting in time for the first Frolic. Governor Hartigan agreed to have the oil available for a preview at the next meeting of the Governors."[130]

This celebration had a slight hitch. The arrival of the nude was precluded by a few conditions:

> The initial discussion centered quite properly around the eagerly anticipated return of the Coppin nude. A letter from Player Dean Coffin, however, disclosed that Players' ownership of a framed suitable painting was contingent on an award of three years free membership for artist (and one time Player) John Coppin. The proposal evoked a suggestion from Governor Houston that artist (and one time Player) Verne Minge be awarded a free membership during each season that Minge provided sketches for the back page of The Player.[131]

The board greeted Coppin's demands with distaste. Minge had resigned from the club almost a year prior to the time that the suggestion was made that he be reimbursed (he resigned a total of three times), and the board found Coppin's offer unthinkable (remember *Nunquam Renig*). A motion was put forth to decline the offer, but it was tabled until the 30 September meeting when it was passed unanimously.

In the tradition that most proposals that do not involve nudes or beer steins take several years to come to fruition at Players (five years for the history, eight years for the Playhouse), the first playwriting contest finally came into being in late 1964 (the first mention of a contest shows up in the 1928 minutes).[132] The club established a Playwriting Contest Committee (five out of the nine members were to be judges) and discussed its aims: "It was pointed out that the program might be valuable in assuring continuation of our tax-free status as an educational institution and in attracting suitable new members; that the Players Foundation might find it appropriate to pay the cost of the awards; that the cost of the program in its first year—estimated at a minimum of $300—would exceed the budget figure of $300 for scripts and royalties for the entire season."[133]

This contest was to take place between students at the University of Michigan and at Wayne State University. The winners from each school would be showcased at the March and April frolics of 1965, but there is no record in the minutes, scrapbooks, or *The Player* of these plays ever being performed.[134]

Another interesting tradition was established and then abandoned that same year, only to reappear years later. The January frolic was always difficult to plan because of the holidays that precede it. Player Sid Sinclair, chairman of the Special Activities Committee, suggested that a party be held instead, to which Players could invite their wives or lady friends. He further suggested that a Millionaires' Party providing gambling with "play money" would be "both fun and fund raising."[135] A party was held, but not all members were happy about a mixed gathering. If a frolic could not be held, they would rather nothing was held at all than a party with ladies invited.[136] At first the board hoped to have a frolic, thus settling the matter, but by November, it was apparent that a party would have to be held instead.[137] There was such difficulty getting anything done that the party had to be postponed until February, and thus no Player activities were held at all in January.[138] In an odd way, this satisfied both camps, and a February or March party was held for couples for a few years, even when a January frolic was held. The idea of a "Las Vegas" night was once again resurrected in 1967.[139] The nature of the January activity fluctuated for years, but today the club holds a Millionaires' Party in place of the January frolic.

Despite a very active board, numbers were down at the end of the 1964–65 season, and Players' rolls only numbered 397.[140] The fear of losing too many members was quite real, so the board had the resigning members' sponsors contact them to see if they could find a way to make them stay. This was successful in several cases but not foolproof.[141] The board also got involved in productions. In an attempt to ensure quality frolics and thus maintain member interest, members of the board of governors were assigned as producers for each frolic to make sure the productions maintained their standards.[142] Other attempts to maintain membership included instituting a student category of membership so that less expensive dues would allow younger men to participate (and give them a pool from the local universities).[143] Letters were sent out to the membership asking them to recommend possible new members. This netted seventy prospective names, but there is no indication of how many of these became Players.[144]

Very quietly, despite active boards and new initiatives to make The Players a strong institution, numbers were dropping. After reaching their peak in 1957 of 496 members, membership rolls numbered 400 in May 1967. Although this is still a large enough membership to support Player endeavors, the years of declining employment, plus racial tensions caused by segregated housing and job opportunities, finally came to a head in Detroit in the summer of 1967. The resulting problems, coupled with the continued downward spiral of deindustrialization, white flight, racial polarization, and a decaying downtown caused a severe drop in membership and revenue at The Players that made the troubles of the Great Depression seem simple by comparison.

# 5

# The Long Run Ends

## Changing America and Changing Players

The 1960s might have begun with a sense of optimism, but they ended with war, cynicism, and an irrevocably transformed America. With the changing lifestyles brought about by various social movements and the troubles facing Detroit, The Players' membership began to decline, and multiple problems threatened the club's survival. In many ways, the health of the club has always paralleled that of Detroit, even though many members no longer live in the city. The club boomed with the expanding city and auto industry, struggled during the Great Depression, enjoyed the post-World War II prosperity, and began a subtle slide at the end of the fifties that accelerated after the 1967 riot.

In 1967, celebrating its fifty-seventh year, The Players was already an anachronism, a remnant of a bygone era. Nationally, the late 1960s were not a time of peaceful evenings gathered around a table with some friends, drinking beer and trading stories. They were a time of major social changes. Women and minorities were demanding equal treatment. College students protested the Vietnam War. Images from the civil rights movement rocked the nation, which was further shocked by the assassination of a president and civil rights leaders. Popular music and theatre expressed many of the changing attitudes. People were dissatisfied with the roles that had been traditionally assigned to them for decades. Locally, the 1967 riot was the final nail in Detroit's coffin. A culmination of years of racial tensions, declining employment opportunities, and sheer frustration, the riot caused many people to abandon the city and its institutions for good.

On 23 July 1967, police raided a "blind pig" (an illegal bar) in a large African American neighborhood in Detroit. The bar was located at 9125 Twelfth Street near Clairmont and called the United Community League for Civil Action, according to Detroit historians Frank B. and Arthur M. Woodford.[1] Instead of following their typical procedure of arresting a few people and sending the rest on their way, the police arrested everyone. A crowd began assembling, harassing the police and throwing debris. By morning, the crowd had swelled to more than three thousand. The riot lasted five days, involved a combined force of police, National Guardsmen, and federal troops numbering almost 17,000, culminating in 7,231 arrests and 43 deaths (30 of the killings attributed to law enforcement).[2] In Joe Kerr's "Trouble in Motor City," he estimates $50 million in property damage and describes the event as "the worst civil unrest in twentieth-century American history up until that time." The death and damage were indeed significant, but Kerr sees the real blow as the effect the event had on the social climate in Detroit: "Although segregation was already a fact of life there, the riots left an enduring legacy of extreme polarization that further contributed to the community's social collapse. By the 1970s, Detroit had acquired the thoroughly deserved nickname of Murder City."[3] This event, combined with the oil crisis and the 1974 recession in the auto industry, nearly irreparably damaged the city's ability to recover.[4]

The Woodfords choose to interpret the event without its racial implications in *All Our Yesterdays*: "[Detroit] had not endured a battle between white and black like that which had ripped the city in 1943. What they had been a part of was the new litany in rioting, a battle against authority, whatever its skin color."[5] Urban historian Thomas Sugrue disagrees: "The problems of limited housing, racial animosity, and reduced economic opportunity for a segment of the black population in Detroit had led to embitterment."[6] For the most part, "Detroit's rioters were disproportionately young black men, the group most affected by racial and economic dislocations, and the most impatient with the slow pace of civil rights reforms."[7]

After the riot, the recession, and the resulting exodus of people from the city, sections of Detroit remain decimated to this day. The burned out, abandoned buildings make areas of the city look like war zones. There are so many abandoned structures in the city that photographer Camilo José Vergara uses the city as one of the primary examples in his book *American Ruins*. Vergara's work chronicles the rise and fall of buildings in industrial cities. In his introduction to the book, he describes his undertaking as "photographing the ghosts left behind" by the demise of the manufacturing cities in the Rust Belt.[8]

The exodus of a huge portion of the city's population has further depressed the city. From a peak in the 1950s of 1,849,568, Detroit's 2005 population was estimated at 899,387. This is a 5.5 percent decrease from five years earlier, when the 2000 census placed the city's population at 951,270.[9] As of 2005, Detroit had officially fallen out of the top ten largest cities in the United States, supplanted by San Jose, California.[10] A U.S. Census Bureau fact sheet provides further troubling statistics. Out of 375,096 housing units, 38,668 are vacant. Presently, the mean household income in Detroit is $29,526, as compared to the national rate of $41,994. Detroit residents with a bachelor's degree or higher represent only 11 percent of the population, as compared with the national average of 24.4 percent.[11] Poverty has dogged the city as its tax base has fled. According to Sugrue, "Between 1970 and 1980, the number of high-poverty tracts in Detroit doubled, and the population of the city living in these areas nearly doubled as well. In 1970, only about one-tenth of the city's poor lived in high-poverty areas, a figure rising to nearly one-fifth by 1980."[12]

Player Jerry McMechan believes that it was not necessarily the problems of the city, but the general social trends of the 1970s that had the most impact on the club:

> Beginning in the 1970s, Players were severely affected by changes in life styles. Membership began to decrease. In social activities, men and their wives sought recreations they could share—such as ski weekends (obviously detrimental to male-only participating and Saturday Frolics). There was no room for Players in their lives. Also, the dress code almost disappeared in that era of fancy Tuxedos with colored, ruffled shirts and spangled jackets. Other than for Players, there was little or no need for a man to own a formal Tuxedo. We struggled against this kind of dress and with the passing years the formal Tuxedo is now back—though guests are allowed to come in business suits.[13]

The formalities, such as the conservative black tuxedo, are the foundation of The Players. The changes took away from the feeling of tradition that had been so integral to the nature and attraction of the club.

Players of the time were not unaware of this. They recognized that society was changing. This snippet appeared in the October 1971 edition of *The Player:*

> In the sixty years since the founding of Players, an entire way of life has pretty well disappeared from America. We reluctantly concede that much of this change was inevitable and some of it for the good. But taste, good manners and intelligent, rewarding fellowship are never out of date. "Style" survives each first Saturday from November through April with upwards of 200 Players in Black Tie providing a high level of entertainment for themselves and among themselves. It is a worthy survival.[14]

Although the club was a haven from the social upheaval outside its walls, it was not immune to it. The racial problems in the city in addition to the relocation of many of the divisions and factories in the car companies encouraged people to move out of the city, leaving downtown and the city neighborhoods devastated. Within ten years of the 1967 riot, The Players had lost almost half of its membership. Even the hard times of the Depression had not hit the club so severely. As people left the city and demographics changed, the typical Player—a white "gentleman" with some disposable income, who would have lived fairly close to the club—left with them. Player Greg R. Thorn believes that people from the suburbs were no longer as willing to come to downtown Detroit. He also credits the decline in numbers to the lack of new blood in the club:

> The Players' membership consisted of the same group of people for a long, long time. They didn't start a drive to get "younger" members (translation: anyone under 60) until I joined in 1972. So the very fact of retirement, and basic attrition (to put it politely) probably also started to take its toll. Couple this with the fact that people weren't venturing into Downtown as much, and you can surmise that Players had a difficult time replacing members who retired and moved to Florida … or places beyond.[15]

The club was able to stabilize the membership by the end of the 1980s, but they were never able to build it back up to the pre-riot numbers.

The minutes record time and again the efforts to recruit new members as they lost members of the old guard. Player Dick Forsyth died in April 1971. Player James Dresbach wrote his memorial for

*The Player*, citing his forty-five years with the organization and crediting him with helping create the atmosphere at The Players and his many activities on and off the stage. Dresbach reminded members that "he is the only Player who, while still active, had a dressing room named for him; this might seem like a trivial thing to an outsider but Players will understand what this implies."[16]

As numbers dropped and money concerns became paramount, The Players had to cut back on its charitable endeavors. The board voted that only the morning performance of the children's Christmas party would be held and that this performance would be restricted to orphans.[17] At a later meeting, this motion was rescinded so that the afternoon performance could be reinstated, but the board decided to poll the membership to see how they felt about maintaining the party.[18] By 1972, the party was finally abandoned. The official reason was chalked up to the "increasing difficulty of locating orphans or other disadvantaged youngsters to attend the party."[19] Despite this decision, the board asked that the Christmas Party Committee find other ways that The Players could contribute to the community.[20] Eventually, a Christmas party was reestablished, but solely for members' children. Although the children were not charged for admittance, the adults paid a fee of a wrapped gift for an underprivileged child so that some of the original spirit of the party was maintained. Later, some of this spirit was resurrected at a Christmas in July party held by Sammy Lieberman for underprivileged children. Twelve Players and their sons provided entertainment in the form of several clown routines.[21]

The Christmas party was not the only casualty of the financial downspin. In part spurred by the loss of their caterer, Eddie Elliott, whose ill health forced him to forego feeding hungry Players, Governor William G. Buchinger suggested eliminating the supper that took place after the frolics. If this was unacceptable, and the board did not want to dispense entirely with the meal, he suggested substituting coffee and doughnuts or some similarly inexpensive repast. The board took his suggestion into consideration, but determined that the membership would have to be polled before such a measure was taken.[22] Finally, it was decided that Players would once again step into the breach as they had during the Depression, and members of the House Committee were chosen to prepare the food for the dinners to cut costs.[23] Frolic suppers now cover a broad range from a late-night breakfast of scrambled eggs and bacon to chicken cordon bleu. The coffee and doughnuts were included as a snack, though, and became a late-night staple at the after-Afterglow for years.

An interesting event in the 1980s relates to the frolic suppers. *The Last Meeting of the Butler's Club*, a play by Player Jerry McMechan, was the final performance at the frolic that evening:

> It was set in the dining room at the Butler's Club in London. We find five elder butlers gathered around the dinner table for what appears to be an annual meeting and repast. The faire *sic*] of meatloaf is seasoned by each regaling his associates with details of the demise of the master or mistress to which he was steward, events which have left them quite comfortable in their advancing years....
>
> They are well attended by their own butler, Morgan. ... After delighting at their own good fortunes at the expense of their former employers, our famous fivesome gets a dose of their own medicine from Morgan, who, having designs of his own, conveniently taints the meatloaf. But of course, the butler did it! Directed by Past President Bill Rohloff, "The Last Meeting of the Butler's Club" was indeed a success, most entertaining, a delicious finale—until we were served Doug Rohloff's meatloaf for the evening meal. Inspired by Traicoff, this was the same meatloaf served onstage. Clever and delicious and prepared by yet another Past President.[24]

Everyone survived the meatloaf and was able to enjoy the Afterglow.

Afterglows continued to be a major part of a night out at The Players. Although members will perform at these events, outside acts are often invited in, and famous people and professionals are always welcome as guests. In addition to Richard Nixon, explorer Richard E. Byrd, probably invited in by Edsel Ford, who helped support his flight to the North Pole, had been a guest. In addition, various local glee clubs, barbershop quartets, musical groups, and comics have appeared on the stage of the Players Playhouse over the years. Professionals that have been invited as guests are not expected to perform, but they are introduced to the membership. On various occasions performers such as George C. Scott, Edward G. Robinson (who sent the club a signed photo afterward), Bert Lahr (best known as the Cowardly Lion in the movie version of *The Wizard of Oz*), Bert Williams (a comic in the 1920s), and Soupy Sales have been guests at The Players. Eddie Peabody, a banjo player, performed at seven Afterglows and was given an honorary membership for the hours of enjoyment he had given the club.[25] Other guests are more unique. Player Bill Rohloff and his son, Doug, used to be co-glowworms and had a healthy competition going with the glowworm team of Mike Jeffries and Greg Thom. As part of a friendly rivalry, Bill Rohloff tracked down the "King of the Hobos" (Murry Graham), (the King of the Hobos is an elected position, according to Rohloff). Murry "Steam Train" Graham was luckily living nearby in Toledo. With the help of the local fire department there, Rohloff was able to track him down and invited Graham and his wife to Detroit. Bill put them up and had Graham appear at an Afterglow. He was driven onstage through the back loading dock doors in a Model A roadster that Doug owned. The car got hung up on the ramp, so the entrance had a slight hitch, but Graham still made his entrance and proceeded to regale the club with stories of the hobo life.[26]

As the 1970s progressed, and the club tried to maintain its viability, various avenues were explored to increase revenue. The board decided to advertise publicly for rentals (previously, rentals came from members, or businesses that had ties to members).[27] The governors even suggested auctioning off Players' props and memorabilia or performing for a fee for other organizations, but they never pursued this.[28] An additional consideration was the prospect of obtaining grants, but the board was unsure as to whether the organization could qualify for such money and whether it was necessary for the club to be a foundation in its own right. The board decided to seek legal help in the matter.[29] This illustrates a recurring issue at The Players. Without a clear knowledge of what had occurred in the past, Player boards of governors often spend time reinventing the wheel. A Players Foundation had already been established to deal with the endowment fund, proving that a foundation for the club was viable. In addition, the club had been incorporated under what was clearly an educational purpose, thus making it eligible for nonprofit status. Also, during a discussion of the aims behind the play competition, one of the reasons cited by the board had been that it would be "valuable in assuring continuation of our tax-free status as an educational institution."[30] Although this might have been a useful financial avenue (though a difficult one because of the private nature of the club, making it less attractive to grant agencies), the board did not pursue this option.

One of the most visible efforts made was the 1972 creation of a stylish, illustrated brochure, "This Is Players." According to Player Ken Howard, it was created because of the difficulty of describing the club to anyone unfamiliar with it:

> Possibly one of the most difficult questions any of us is asked by our friends and associates amounts to this: "What *is* Players?" OK. Let's try this as an answer: "A male-only club of some three-hundred-plus members who meet for the purpose of viewing amateur theatricals, performed by members, once a month between November and April." That answer, while precise, hardly conveys the inner nature of our group. It lacks much. The fact that we're a sixty year old organization. That beer is served. That we have a small gem of a theatre which we own and use. That we have hosted famous personalities, including the present President of the United States. And on and on.[31]

The seventeen-page brochure contains a few pictures of the club and its activities, defines *Nunquam Renig*, provides a short history, describes what a member does at a frolic and explains some of the traditions. It was reprinted with extensive photographs in 1987 as a glossy, twenty-six-page brochure. This edition does a better job of showing off the Playhouse and provides an accurate portrayal of The Players in even more detail.

Another effort The Players made to encourage new members to remain involved in the club was to mark with an asterisk first-time performers' names in the program. This allowed other members to single them out and congratulate the neophytes for becoming active on the stage. Also, the new board added a new Future Planning Committee, whose goal was to determine what could be done "to make Players more attractive to future, and especially younger, members and to the community."[32] This was a long-range effort, though, and the club continued to struggle in the short term.

Most things take time to come to fruition at The Players. A good example of this is the establishment of an official November Invitational. These invitationals had been held regularly since 1946. Although a few had been cancelled, they had become something of a tradition. The board decided in 1972, twenty-six years after the first November Invitational, to make this event an official part of The Players' annual activities, thus eliminating the necessity (and stress) of having to "evaluate each individual production" before it could be held as an invitational.[33]

*The Tridget of Greva* (year unknown)

In spite of the problems that increasingly became the focus of the board's time, the real work of The Players continued. Players supported the artistic work of its members, but never to the detriment of a good frolic. When Player Jerry McMechan sent a script for consideration, the board roundly turned down the play:

> By unanimous decision of the Board, it was decided to reject the play—NOT because it dealt with a "sensitive area" but simply because the Board felt it lacked merit as a play. Each member of the Board was polled individually by President Pringle, and each stated that he would *not* want to see it performed. Consensus was that it was simply a tract, sermonizing, and that we would be doing Player McMechan a disservice if we permitted it to be played. The Board authorized Governor Shannon to draft a letter to Jerry McMechan outlining the Board's feeling, expressing our appreciation for the two very fine shows he had written for Players in the past (both of which made May) and hoping that Jerry would continue to submit other efforts in the future.[34]

This did not deter McMechan, and later offerings of his became popular Player pieces.

The March 1971 frolic was an all-McMechan bill (there would be another one in March 1978). One of the first of these was *Running the Gamut, or More Than You Ever Wanted to Know about Human Sensitivity Labs*. In this piece, a Dr. E. Victor Stuyvesant-Knowles has come to talk to the ladies and their guests at the Tuesday Drama and Culture Club (probably a slight joke on the Theatre Arts Club). The doctor runs a center that the club president describes as a place where "they help you get more sensitive to yourself and other people."[35] The doctor defines it in more refined terms: "I hope you all agree that what is so vital—so needed in these perilous times—these days of anxiety and tension—is a heightening of our interpersonal relationships. For surely if we cannot relate to one another, how can we stand up to those formidable forces that buffet us on every side?"[36] Stuyvesant-Knowles is really there to sell his book and his clinic, and he runs several exercises with the ladies and their husbands that are designed to make them feel good about their relationships and dispose them toward a stay in the clinic. His plan backfires when the club president is so excited by the exercises that she literally chases him off the stage. The play is a witty satire on the pop psychology and encounter groups of the day.

Another piece at the same frolic (with an equally long title) was *The Way Cousin Kerby Fought the Steamboat Gambler*. The title does not even hint at the plot of this political thriller of sorts. Trying to defuse a volatile relationship with the Chinese, the president of the United States meets with the marshal of Red China in Uruguay. The marshal openly had challenged the president to a fight, and instead of letting the countries go to war over his violent rhetoric, the president has a unique plan to prevent a war. His general wholly supports this alternative. Although risky, the general prefers to take a chance on the president's gamble and avoid war. The Uruguayan president is surprised at his attitude, but the general believes it is the best choice:

> Look, Your Excellency, I've spent thirty years in the Army—West Point, Staff School, a dozen different assignments and half of them in some dirty little shooting war—Korea, Viet Nam, Cambodia, Jordan, the Caribbean—you name it—and not one of them solved a damn thing! We're kids playing games—and the other side writes all the rules. I used

to think an all-out shoot-'em-up was the answer. Strike first and strike hard! But not any more—not now. So why not this? We've tried everything else.[37]

Since the marshal challenged him to a fight, the president has decided to accept and has picked Uruguay as the location for the meeting, because dueling is still legal there. As the marshal issued the challenge, the president gets to pick the manner in which the duel will be carried out. The president has decided that each man will pick two shotguns out of several offered, checked by representatives of both sides. The men are to sit at opposite ends of a ping pong table, aim at each other, and fire at the count of 30. The count makes it just past 28 when the marshal interrupts, saying that he refuses to play this "stupid game" as it will "prove nothing." The president calmly informs him that the marshal has proven that he is a coward and has lost face in front of his generals and the world. The marshal storms out in anger and the title is thus explained: this is the same trick one of the president's ancestors (Cousin Kerby) used to win a bet with a steamboat man.

This is quite different from the other war plays performed at the club. It is not meant to get belly laughs (the duel is played straight), and none of the characters are complete caricatures. There is a sense of relief at the end that the clever ploy has worked for the time being to stop any greater violence. It is possible that, like the general, attitudes toward war had changed, particularly with America's involvement in Vietnam. McMechan's plays range from social satire (he has a play about streaking written in 1974) to political satire, many of which were well received by fellow Players.

*Nunquam Renig* was not alive and well during the 1970s. Although Players still stepped into the breach to fill in for someone who dropped out of a role, and they had taken over preparing the frolic suppers, there were signs that not everyone held the motto as gospel. When the Building and Grounds Committee held a work party at the start of the 1973–74 season to get the Playhouse into shape, no one showed up.[38] The committee never expected that the entire membership would have shown up to help, but the fact that no one showed up at all was a discouraging sign about the state of the club. The Players was also forced to look for a new caricaturist when Verne Minge left the Detroit area.[39] The board decided to ask Player

Bob Greene to fill the position and decided that if he accepted, his dues would be waived "in appreciation for this contribution to The Players." Greene took over the task in April 1975.[40]

With the problems in maintaining membership levels and the club's running in the red on and off for the previous several years, the board broke down and raised dues for the 1973–74 season. They were surprised when there was no discernable loss in membership as a result of this increase.[41] Notwithstanding this brief triumph, membership numbers still continued to be a thorn in the side of the club. The board had discussed a long list of suggestions earlier that year detailing ways to maintain numbers. This broad array of possibilities ranged from establishing a special committee whose job was to follow up with new members, to increasing the number of full-length shows in the season, to getting a stage manager, to establishing training programs or apprenticeships for new members for various frolic activities, to more wife and family involvement, to trying to find new ways to increase participation (double-casting shows was recommended).[42] The board implemented some of the suggestions, but there were still rumblings at The Players. The younger members felt left out. They complained to the board that they tried to participate on committees and other Player functions, but they felt as if more established members ignored their presence and ideas.[43] Another sign that the club was not functioning as in years past was the presence of women at rehearsals.

One of the oldest traditions of The Players is that it is an all-male club. Player McMechan's earlier quote detailed why this rule was becoming a problem for participation in the frolics, and this may have been a grassroots way to make spouses feel involved, or it may have been that the men wanted to share their pride in their work with spouses and female friends. Whatever the reasons, the "stag" nature of the club is one of the things that makes it truly unique and was a founding principle (otherwise these men would have just chosen to be members of the Fine Arts Society). To reaffirm this position and maintain its traditions, the board presented and approved a formal resolution:

> The Players is, by Articles of Incorporation, By-Laws and tradition, a private male club. Attendance at events of The Players, other than events specially designated by the Board of Governors, is limited to members of The Players and adult male guests invited by the Board of Governors at the request of a Player. Player events are not limited to Players Frolics

but include rehearsals and all other events in the Playhouse attended by members of The Players as part of the regular program of activities of The Players.⁴⁴

Governor Robinson clarified the action that would be taken if members broke this rule:

> This policy and tradition of The Players was not observed at The Player events surrounding the November Frolic and Invitational, as I am sure all of you in attendance observed. In the interest of not disrupting the Frolic and Invitational, and out of deference to newer Players who may not have been fully cognizant of these rules and tradition, no action was taken. At any future Player event at which these rules and tradition are not observed, the senior officer of The Players present, or any member of the Board of Governors or the Chairman of the Committee in charge of the event will ask any unauthorized guest to leave.⁴⁵

The resolution did not appear to be tremendously effective, as it was noted in February that women were still present at dress rehearsals, and periodic reminders turn up in the minutes to reaffirm that ladies were not permitted at dress rehearsals.⁴⁶

Despite the problems facing the club, Player Loren T. Robinson urged the members not to lose sight of what was most important about the institution:

> For that, of course, is what this club is all about—having fun. Sometimes I think we are inclined to lose sight of this fundamental purpose, particularly when bogged down in problems of production, finance and the like, and to think of producing shows and balancing the budget as ultimate goals. They aren't. They are simply a necessary means of achieving the real objective—fun. The Players themselves, the camaraderie and good fellowship; these are the things which are really important, the things which have kept this club alive and growing for over half a century, and the things which distinguish The Players from every other amateur theatrical group in the world....
>
> Ours is a great and wonderful organization, unique in its conception, and even more remarkable in having been able to preserve that individuality for over sixty years. Contemplated objectively it is almost incredible that a club founded on such premises, and limited by such traditions, could have survived, much less prospered, for so long a period.⁴⁷

Dues increased yet again for the 1974–75 season, and once more for 1975–76 season, and the board continued trying to find other ways to keep the membership's interest in the club.⁴⁸ To guarantee quality, members of the Script and Casting Committee acted as producers for the frolics. The board believed they would have the best knowledge of the shows and thus be the most efficient producers.[49] A welcome addition during this time was the establishment of a "Happy Hour during which the Playhouse would be open for members, guests and prospective members to drop in for fellowship and refreshments.... It was the opinion of this committee that this would not only promote Players but help to acquaint members with each other."[50] This event soon became known as the Traffic Hour. It was so successful that, by 1976, proceeds went to the purchase of a new beer cooler and a scrim, with money left to spare.[51]

It should be noted that, unlike many other clubs, The Players is not open on a daily basis, and there is no food service other than frolic suppers. Thus, other than committee meetings and rehearsals, the major social opportunities occurred only once a month. The Traffic Hour gave club members the opportunity to socialize after work in a relaxed atmosphere with no formal attire required.

One of the ways that the board had been able to increase interest in the annual meeting was to include the "Willie Awards."[52] These were "spoof" awards named after "Willie" Shakespeare, meant to "honor some significant embarrassment or silly ness sic] that you did throughout the previous year."[53] The awards developed out of the competition between Players Greg Thom and Mike Jefferies and Doug and Bill Rohloff over their Afterglow shows.[54] Originally, the physical award was a copy of Shakespeare's plays. Now recipients receive a trophy of the back half of a horse. A good example of the spirit behind these awards occurred at the third annual Willie Awards, where Players Jeffrey Kurtz and Kenneth Kurtz made the presentations with the help of "F.D.R., Lionel Barrymore, Mark Twain and Will Rogers."[55] Actual winners of Willie Awards include "the worst looking woman on stage ... answering the phone before it rang ... losing their wigs in the middle of a performance to reveal a bald head (which did not match the dress) ... scratching themselves in the most unladylike areas while on stage, etc."[56]

The Players was not the only club facing troubles. During the 1975–76 season, President Diamond Phillips of the Fine Arts Society and President Mrs. Bernard Whitley of the Theatre Arts Club approached the board with three proposals:

> Proposal 1: That the three groups incorporate as a non-profit organiza-

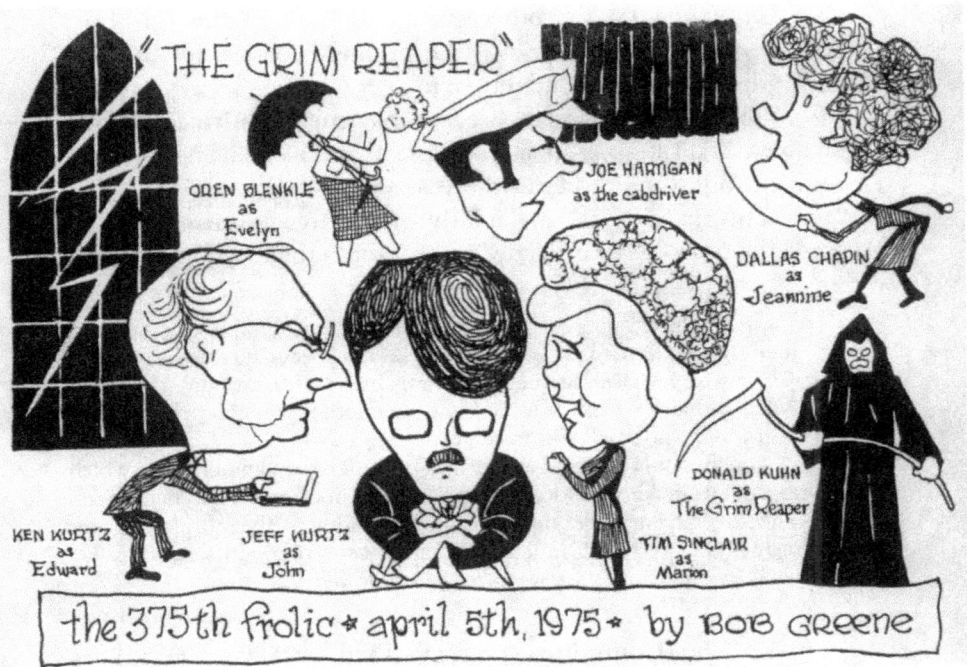

First Greene caricature (1975)

tion, making shares available to members of all three organizations, with Fine Arts and Theatre Arts members each buying a one-third interest in the Playhouse.

President Rohloff was instructed to report that the Player's Board has decided that, for good and sufficient reasons, no action be taken at this time.

Proposal 2: That the Playhouse be made available for Fine Arts and Theatre Arts for the actual cost of opening the building.

President Rohloff was instructed to reply that, for a number of reasons, the standard rental rates established for the two groups must apply.

Proposal 3: That there be a Tri-Effort to produce and present *1776* on November 14, 15, and 16, 1975.

President Rohloff was instructed to reply that The Players would be willing to consider a Tri-Effort [name for the former Drama Festival], but of a different play, and in October rather than November.[57]

Unfortunately, the other groups' interest in the Tri-Effort waned, and the board dropped the proposal for lack of interest, though the Tri-Effort would return in later years.[58]

The 1975–76 season focused on the fiftieth anniversary of the Playhouse and the sixty-fifth anniversary of the club. That season's president, Bill Rohloff, began the year with a call to action in *The Player*. This article was particularly memorable because, in it, he coined the term "beautiful lady" in relation to the Playhouse:

> If gender can be applied to a composition of masonry, wood, and steel, then I would have to say "our Playhouse" is a "beautiful lady."
>
> Now on her 50th birthday she radiates a patina and dignified mellowness that only age, tradition and the motherly instinct of watching over those who dwell within can provide.
>
> One has only to stand at the back of the Theatre and look up, which most of us seldom do, look up from time to time and soak in her charm. The fine hand art work on the beams, the banners, the murals, the ages of man, the very rhythmic design of the construction itself, to realize what a wonderful legacy we have been endowed with.[59]

A "65/50" Committee was established with Player Dick Ross as the chair. Players set about cleaning and refurbishing the Playhouse to get her ready for her anniversary. In keeping with tradition and nostalgia, *Doing Stratford* was performed at the 6 December 1975 frolic, and a dinner and champagne toast were held afterward. This night was only for Players, and no guests were invited to the frolic, although architects Leinweber and Leone of Smith, Hinchman, and Grylls, who had worked with Player Kapp when he was building the Playhouse, were guests at the dinner.[60] A special effort to include nonresident members in the festivities was successful, and twenty-two were able to attend the evening's entertainment. They were picked up from the airport and housed at no expense to themselves at the Parkstone and Parkhurst Apartments in Indian Village (a Player was the manager there). Past presidents and the board of governors hosted a cocktail party at the University Club prior to the frolic, and a double-decker bus transported members to the theatre. That evening, "scarlet garbed Elizabethan trumpeters" stationed on the balcony outside the Founders Room heralded all Players as they entered the Playhouse.[61]

Several Players took the opportunity provided by the anniversary to make various gifts to the club. Some of these were for the building (gold rope for the staircase, a new gas log fixture for the fireplace), but others were intended to perpetuate Player events. Player Harold Love, who had originated the Twenty Year Club, established an endowment fund to host the annual cocktail party for the group (this fund is still active today). Lorraine Nawrocki (wife of Player Henry Nawrocki) gave the club an original drawing of the Playhouse that had already appeared in several issues of *The Player*.[62] Over the previous summer, the board had once again looked into the Coppin nude being returned, and Rohloff went to Florida to see if he could convince Coppin to replace the painting.[63] Because the original nude had been stolen, Coppin did agree to repaint the nude if a "suitable reference" (presumably a picture of the original) could be found.[64] The happy event occurred in time for the December Invitational, and to insure its safety, the nude, also dubbed by Coppin "The Beautiful Lady," was bolted to the wall.[65] (The earlier Coppin painting had been named "In Memory of Happy Times.")[66] The Nastfogel nude that had temporarily taken its place was later raffled off to the membership.[67]

Strangely enough, for a board that upheld a policy that ensured no obligations to charity, it sought out several opportunities to contribute to the community. The board decided to hold a special performance of *Doing Stratford* for members of the senior center next door.[68] This may have been an opportunity, like the original intention behind the children's Christmas parties, to reach out to a neighbor. But this was not the only example of Player generosity. For the 1976 Tri-Effort, in agreement with the other two groups, two weekends of performances would be held, with the proceeds from the second weekend to be given to charity.[69] Tau Beta Association agreed to handle the second weekend's expenses, with all proceeds going to "refurbish a camp for diabetic children."[70] In yet another example, one extra night was added to the 1978 May Invitational to benefit the Boys Club.[71] This worked out so well that the Boys Club asked The Players to repeat the benefit performance at the 1979 May Invitational, with The Players retaining some of the profit. The board approved the proposal unanimously.[72]

The April 1976 frolic featured *Kaleidoscope 76*—"Musical Memories from Previous Players Shows," compiled by Player Bud Pearse, and *Memorable Moments at Players*, written by Jerry McMechan. *Kaleidoscope 76* was modeled on *Kaleidoscope 50*, which had been performed for the Fiftieth Anniversary Frolic. *Memorable*

*Moments* was a tribute to mishaps on the Player stage. Each "Moment" is based on the many, many gaffs at the frolics. "What's Missing, Missing, Missing" recalls troubles with a ringing phone—the ring is there, but the phone is not. Even when the actor finally mimes answering the phone, the ringing continues. "Moment #2" is an encounter between Hamlet and the act drop. As Hamlet attempts to deliver the "To be or not to be" speech, the drop starts to descend "slowly, majestically, without pause." Hamlet manages to get in front of the descending drop, and it does jump up a few feet when he needs to turn upstage, but soon enough, it is falling again. Hamlet first tries to hold it up when it covers his face, but when this does not work, he crouches lower and lower until only his head is seen on the floor as he delivers the last lines. "Moment #3" dramatizes a common event at the Playhouse, the failure of the prop gun. The angry, gun-wielding wife confronts a cheating husband and his mistress, but the gun refuses to fire on cue. The trio stare at one another, unable to figure out how to work around this plot point. Ever versatile, the husband "dies" of a heart attack, and the scene ends. The last "Moment" memorializes the most common problem on the Player stage, the missed line. The offstage Voice, an actual character in this scene, consistently prompts "Charlie" as he forgets his lines and his stage business. As Charlie grows more and more flustered, "Grandma" tries to help feed him lines. After he has been given the same cue five times, Charlie finally turns to the wings in frustration: "We know the line. Whose is it?"[73]

Membership was the most crucial problem facing The Players. Player numbers had dropped roughly 20 percent from 496 to 400, between 1957 and 1967, while by 1977, numbers were down to between 240 and 250. The 1976–77 season had seen only eight new members while thirty-five had been lost.[74] Player Robert L. Greene lamented the decline in Player involvement: "It was almost as if the malaise that has gripped the nation—Watergate and inflation, recession and unemployment, air pollution and the energy crisis—had finally descended on our beloved Players. At 8:30 P.M. the evening of December 4, with the Playhouse barely half filled and a few stragglers drifting in, the picture looked dark indeed."[75]

The Players was in a precarious position. Debts had been staved off only by borrowing from the endowment fund, but budgets were still often exceeded on frolics.[76] This problem had been stemmed in 1976, but still occurred on a regular basis. "An appreciable increase in membership is one of the keystones necessary to increase revenues in the coming year to maintain the operating fund and to provide a means" of paying off the loan made from the endowment fund.[77] Jokes about attempting to balance the budget even appear in *The Player*. Player Thomas F. Burns describes what the club has had to overcome in its past:

> World War I had come and gone and in its wake Empires simply vanished; not us though—we have survived prohibition, Roosevelt, the UAW-CIO, profit-sharing, Vietnam, Nixon, Head-Start, the Republican Party—you name it and we've survived it, outwitted it, or just damn well ignored it. If Jimmy Carter and Arthur Burns have any problems with the budget they can attend our Budget Committee hearings where we wrestled with the longest, largest and oldest surviving continuous budget deficit in the world.[78]

The Future Planning Committee also weighed in and made a series of suggestions to help with the problem. What is probably most notable is how many of these suggestions mirror the ones from four years earlier. The major difference is that the more recent suggestions go into more detail, such as when a season should be announced or when a frolic should be cast.[79]

The club did not reverse the decline in membership by the next season, although there were some cosmetic improvements. The decaying hulk of Deaconness Hospital next door had finally been demolished, largely due to the efforts of Player Bob Hughes.[80] Hughes also made sure that the ten crumbling gargoyles on the exterior of the Playhouse were replaced by Parducci studios, the original sculptors. Reporting on the event, *The Player* denied the rumor that the "grinning devils were carved in the likeness of the current Board of Governors, or that they cast a wicked spell on our thespians, causing fluffed lines and missed cues."[81]

Humor aside, *The Player* warned that the club must have new members: "Though recent administrations have managed to keep operating expenses to a bare minimum, inflation and a declining membership have forced Players into an unsound financial condition. The only real solution to this problem is to increase our membership. Stop-Gap measures such as: Dues increases and Rental Fee increases, are not the answer. If Players, as it is presently constituted, is to survive we must enroll new members."[82]

The warning was not enough. As the membership was less likely to come out for certain efforts, the Singing Players disbanded for lack of interest in 1980.[83] Despite this, there was an attempt to resurrect the group in 1986 by changing the name of the Orchestra Committee to the Music Committee to include the possibility of Singing Players.[84] The year 1980 saw the death of another Player institution, Player Marshall Bruce, who had traditionally sung The Players' Song before each frolic.[85] To do justice to his memory, his taped voice was played to open the November frolic.[86] The club also had to say goodbye to playwright Jerry McMechan as he retired and moved to North Carolina.[87]

Players still loved to host professional performers. When the touring company of *Annie* came through town in 1979, six of the company members joined the Players at an Afterglow, including the conductor and the actors playing Rooster Hannigan and Oliver Warbucks. In the tradition of *The Book of Etiquette*, Players performed their parody of the show, *Fanny*, for their visitors. Just as the D'Oyly Carte members performed in thanks, the visitors performed pieces from the show, and several other musical and dance numbers from other well-known musicals. They enjoyed themselves so much that they asked if they could visit again before their company moved on to the next city.[88]

Another major parody came a few years later in the form of Bud Pearse's *Alice in Playerland*:

> *Alice* was patently a vehicle for bringing back some good old songs, more than once with tongue way into cheek. Among them, "Alice Blue Gown," aptly sung when we first meet Playerland's Alice ... the "Drinking Song," that accompanied the hectic goings-on at the mad tea party ... "Alley Cat," as the Cheshire puss's theme ... "Two Hearts in Three-Quarter Time," Alice and the Jack of Hearts' duet at court... and "Hard-Hearted Hannah," sung by the Queen. Had she realized how well it portrays her, she'd have screamed, "Off with their heads!" right then and there.[89]

On other matters, Players still seemed to be functioning well, but President Douglas F. Rohloff felt the need to remind Players that there was work to be done:

> Players is probably the only exclusive private club in the world where you pay your dues for the privilege of working to keep the club and its theatre successful, economically healthy and to provide for its secure future....

> If you're upset because of all the work that's to be done, *don't be*. That is what Players is all about ... a very exclusive and pleasurable form of labor. A labor of love for the theatre and Players.[90]

Members were willing to make some sacrifices for the sake of the club. Player Jeff Montgomery shaved off his moustache in front of the audience at an Afterglow. "Several Players were heard to comment about the propriety of full frontal nudity on a Players' stage, but that judgment will have to be left to others."[91] Montgomery found a way to outdo his earlier stunt a few years later:

> Glowworm Jeff Montgomery two or three years ago, as part of his Afterglow, shaved off his moustache right before our very eyes! At the February Frolic Jeff again got out shaving cream and razor, with the explanation that Players taking women's roles were often required to remove hirsute adornments. He shook the shaving cream can and brandished the razor. We all expected the regrown moustache to go again, but no! Jeff pulled up his trouser leg and shaved his hairy shin.[92]

He topped this one three years later by shaving his arms.[93]

This was not the only ongoing joke as part of the continuing Afterglow battles: Players Greg Thom and Mike Jefferies presented Bill Rohloff with a door at the May 1981 Willie Awards. According to Player Larry Smith, Thom and Jefferies took the unused shower door off its hinges, stuck a piece of paper with his name on it to the door and gave it to him. They thought they had come up with the ultimate prank on Bill Rohloff, but the joke was on them. Bill believed the presentation to be genuine and was so honored that absolutely no one was going to disabuse this venerable member of that belief.[94] Remember that naming a door after someone was one of the highest honors the club could give to a member. Rohloff may not have realized the prank initially, and he definitely did not know the exact origins of the door. *The Player* described his reaction to discovering that the door led to "our decrepit and disused shower. Undaunted, Bill has completely rebuilt the cubicle into a thing of beauty. Player Sinischo baptized it after the November Frolic. The Board is now considering Rohloff brass plates on the doors of the Furnace Room, Make-up Room, Prop Room, Ticket Office, etc."[95] During his years at the club, Rohloff came to be known as "Mr. Player." He probably earned this name not only because of his varied work at the club but also because he had a cable access home improvement program for a time called "Mr. Project."[96]

Rohloff was not the only one to receive a door that year, although the board made the other presentations. Lee Carroll, The Players' longtime executive secretary/office manager was also presented with one. An interview in the *Detroit Free Press* captured Carroll's reaction: "I am so proud of that.... I was completely unaware they were going to do that. I love my job at Players. This is my second home."[97] The next year, Frances Hirschfield was presented with a door at the April 1982 frolic for her fifty years of service to The Players: "Frances and Jake, her late husband, together and separately have dressed our casts in every conceivable period and theatrical style of haw buck harness to create the illusions of Players play world. The costume room has been named 'Hirschfield.' It is intended as an honor, but with it goes more: each and every member's appreciation and warm affection for the Hirschfields without whom the Players would have been poorer."[98] Both of these ladies got singled out again for thanks in *The Player:*

> Frances Hirschfield is starting *her fifty-second* year with Players. Over all those years she has helped us put on panty hose, bras and sewn our costumes. Without her able assistance, many of us who play ugly women on stage would be playing ugly and poorly dressed women on stage. I would strongly suggest that at November's Frolic, you stop by her room and say hello and thank you. Frances means a lot to us all and we greatly appreciate her.
>
> The other lady who keeps us going is Mrs. Player herself, Lee Carroll. For the newer members of Players I would like to stress to you that Mrs. Player has been running the organization for thirty-seven years. She started two years before I was born. The Board of Governors each year will take charge and handle their appointed tasks and responsibilities, however, deep in each governor's soul they know who really is in charge. There isn't a past president who won't admit that Mrs. Player has made their job extremely easy. Players, past, present and future owe her a great deal of thanks.[99]

There was a feeling that things were finally turning around for The Players. There was a marketing plan in place, and the board of governors implemented an operational plan to ease the transition for committee chairmen from year to year. The plan defined the purpose of each individual committee, its goals, and expected completion dates.[100] The board also started sending out "Dream Sheets" at the beginning of each season asking members how they would like to be involved at the club. This was a means to make sure every

Player had a chance to participate in whatever activities interested him and addressed earlier problems when Players (particularly younger members) felt like they were not being encouraged to get involved.

A new group was formed at Players in 1981, the Gourmet Group. "Informally organized" by Bill Rohloff, the group consisted of twelve Players who catered Fine Arts Society dinners for a fee. All of the money made by this group is used to benefit the Playhouse in some way. In 1985, they had already contributed fifteen thousand dollars to purchase an intercom system, various china and serving items for the kitchen, and even drapes for the stage.[101] They continue to cater four shows (eight performances) a year for the Fine Arts Society, allowing the Gourmet Group to continuously make improvements to the Playhouse. J. J. Jorgensen, 2005–6 president, estimates that the group has served almost three thousand meals since its inception. He also reports that "Bill is fond of saying, and we haven't killed anyone yet!'"[102]

The torch passed rather quickly between three caricaturists in the succeeding two years. Bob Greene's last caricature for the Players was for the November 1982 frolic, but there is no indication of why he stopped doing the drawings. He even welcomed Player Glenn Scoles to the job in his monthly column in *The Player*, "Here's Your Cue …": "Welcome, Glenn. This month's issue of *The Player* marks the introduction of a new cartoonist for our back page. A big hand, please, for Glenn Scoles, who has volunteered to take on the job of preserving Player casts for posterity. Caricatures are brand new to Glenn, as they were for this ink-stained scribe over six years ago. So wish him well, guys. The framed Frolic sketches add décor to our lobby and are conversation pieces for Player generations to come."[103] Scoles took over for the next frolic and continued through the end of the 1982–83 season.[104] When the succeeding caricaturist was unable to do them, Greene recorded the November and December 1985 frolics, and Scoles took the February and March 1986 frolics. New Player Chris Monley took over the caricatures in November 1983.[105] The board so appreciated his work that after a few seasons they made a motion to pay him for his drawings: "The reasoning was that this was his profession, he was much better than any of the alternatives and we felt the quality of this art was important to the club." The motion passed unanimously.[106] Monley later responded to this by informing the board that he would accept the board's "proposed

First Monley caricature (1983)

$50 for each sketch done during the course of this season, but only to reimburse him for material cost only for work done in the past. In following years he will accept only his cost of materials."[107] *Nunquam Renig* was not dead after all.

The mid-1980s at The Players saw some interesting play choices. In 1984, Player Peter J. Bellanca directed Robert Anderson's *The Shock of Recognition*. According to *The Player*, the play "asked the burning question of the day [in 1967], 'should full frontal nudity be presented on the stage?' Seventeen years later an all-male Player audience reacted to the dated question as if it had some relevance, probably less because of the currency of the situation and more because of the excellent Player production."[108] This begs the question of how nudity in 1984 could be truly shocking to members of the same gender. Perhaps this is just indicative of an older generation of values and traditions and a love for lighter fare without burning social (and theatrical) issues.

Some plays remained more traditional fare. The 1984–85 season opened with *The Bowery Burlicue Moves Uptown*, a large revue-style musical written by Bud Pearse. The play resurrected such old favorites as Abbott and Costello and several old vaudeville routines, including barbershop quartets, a "Groucho Marxian" doctor-patient act, and a soft-shoe dance.[109] Another Bud Pearse musical, *Players Diamond Review*, was arranged to celebrate the club's seventy-fifth anniversary. Featuring songs performed on the Players' stage from the 1960s to the 1980s, the show was interspersed with favorite Afterglow acts and ended with the cast singing The Players' Song. This invitational performance was followed by an elaborate buffet and dancing. To top off the celebration, the Playhouse was officially declared a Michigan historic site.[110]

In March 1986, the Players performed a play that was downright eerie. Player Cameron Cross's *The Last Flight of the Columbia* is about a space shuttle disaster. It was written prior to the Challenger tragedy on 28 January 1986. Player John L. Daly remembers how Cross found out about the accident: "On the day that rehearsals were to start, Cameron was having lunch in a bar when they showed a space shuttle picture on TV. He remarked to the bartender that he had written a space shuttle play to which the bartender told him what had happened that morning: The space shuttle Challenger had exploded on take-off. The show went on as planned with an explanation of the irony of the situation."[111] Not surprisingly, the play generated a lot of discussion about whether it should be performed as scheduled:

> Life sometimes comes uncomfortably close to imitating art, as this original script by Player Cam Cross and the Challenger disaster demonstrated. The result was much discussion among Player nabobs about the wisdom of presenting this show. However, as director Allan Dick explained before the curtains parted, eventually it was decided that the show should go on.

> Good decision. We may not need such vivid reminders of the perils of space, but that's no reason to hide from them. Certainly it shouldn't be in questionable taste to consider the human dimension of a tragedy, even when similar events are so recent.
>
> And so the drama, originally conceived months ago, began with the radio transmission of the voices of Mission Control in Houston and astronaut Jack Armstrong in space.
>
> It's Mayday for the Columbia. The craft has been severely damaged by a meteor and one of its three astronauts is already dead. In Houston Mission Control, Captain Ted Brock, played by author Cam Cross, and staff are at their posts in a set that boasts a computer and printer that spits out data.
>
> As the story unfolds it becomes clear that the Columbia is beyond the help of all the technology and skill of the men on the ground. The craft is doomed. Nothing works, neither the attempts at sophisticated planetary loops, nor the blustering orders to Brock by General Barrett, nicely played by Warren Couger.
>
> Finally, with all hope of reentry into the earth's atmosphere gone, Armstrong chooses a course directly into the sun instead of away from it and the men of Mission Control have only to report that three angels have fallen.[112]

The Challenger space shuttle was actually mentioned in the original script as a shuttle that might be able to be scrambled in time for a rescue mission. The name is scratched out and replaced with the Enterprise.[113] A family invitational performance had been planned for the morning of the frolic, and Players were reminded in February about the play and its subject matter, so that they could decide if it was appropriate for their children.[114] The situation becomes even more uncanny with the disaster involving the actual Columbia space shuttle on 1 February 2003.

Not to ignore an anniversary year at the Playhouse, *Last Flight* was on the same bill as *Re-Doing Stratford—1986*. No script remains in the archives to detail what changes might have been made to the script, only that director Peter Bellanca "sharpened and shined that venerable script."[115] The 1975 performance review noted that some of the humor in the piece was dated, so the "sharpening" very well might have related to this issue.[116]

Another unique performance occurred at the November 1986 Invitational. Long before the Broadway musical of Mel Brooks's *The Producers* (2001) was a hit in New York, it was a play (with some music) on the Player stage. Authorized by Mel Brooks, the show took years to make it to the stage at the Players Playhouse:

> In the show's years-long progress to our stage, Co-Directors Greg Thom and Peter Bellanca never lost the faith. They were doggedly determined to make it work—through proposal, acceptance, adaptation, performance rights and exhaustive rehearsal. If now they wallow in their personal achievement, they have ample justifications....
>
> Without the inspired hard work of Maestro Eric Knudson in transcribing, scoring and performing the music from the original tapes of Mel Brooks's 1968 movie, *The Producers* would not have approached anything like the success it was.[117]

In Player Ken Howard's review (titled "Eine Grosse Nachtmusik"), the show gets high praise, particularly one scene: "The tryout scene for the 'play within a play' was (to be crude and because I'm running short of adjectives) a gut-buster. Oren Blenkle as the Mikado drop-out, Arnei Kummerow as the German oompah man and Rick Edgett who never got a chance (except for the wig bit) brought down the house in a few short minutes."[118]

Player Henry Nelson joined the club in April 1986 and got his start in this show, where the director impressed him into service. Player Lew Davies (his father's accountant) had gotten him interested in the club and was trying to make sure he got involved. Davies invited him to the first Traffic Hour of the 1986–87 season:

> Not being one to ever refuse a free beer, I accompanied Lew to the playhouse. After the prompt and friendly service at the bar, Lew led me into the house to watch a rehearsal of the opening offering, a stage adaptation of the Mel Brooks film, *The Producers*.... On the stage were roughly a dozen Players running through the choreography of "Springtime for Hitler," led by director and leading man, Player Peter Bellanca. During a break in the rehearsal, Lew took me on the stage to introduce me to Peter. After introductions were made, Lew facetiously asked Peter if there were any roles in the show that needed filling by someone roughly my size and age. Peter paused, looked at me and replied, "Actually, I do need one more dancing girl to complete the chorus line." Peter then grabbed me by the arm, walked me to a spot on the stage, and gave me my first direction on the Players stage: "Stay there, and hurry up and finish you beer."
>
> Two weeks later I made my Players debut, resplendent in opaque, flesh-toned body stocking under silver streamers (with matching wig), spike pump heels, and ten pound Busby Berkley headpiece replete with ostrich feathers. I was a Player. As I approach my twentieth year as a member, I look back at the experience as one of the highlights of my life, not because of the costuming (ugh!), but because it represented my initiation in a club that helped me discover my love for the stage.[119]

Unidentified society "ladies"

Regrettably, all was not well with The Players; production standards were dropping and membership dropped to its lowest recorded number: 166.[120] On top of this, Player Francis E. Brossy III felt it necessary to admonish the membership after what he considered to be a very poor frolic:

> Unfortunately, the shortcomings of the last Frolic aren't limited to the last Frolic. There's been a steady erosion in responsibility, and quality, over the past few years—actors and directors "too busy" to accept assignments ... members of the stage crew not showing up when they're counted on ... last minute scrounging for props that are "good enough" ... sets barely dressed ... no regular production meetings ... etcetera ... etcetera ... Players, of whatever committee are starting too little, too late.[121]

The year 1986 saw the same problems that had haunted The Players for at least twenty years: "Ron Austin advised all members of the Board to consider the reasons for our diminishing membership as it is the single most important goal. Board member Austin stated that he believed the safety of Players and their guests when at the Playhouse is one major reason for membership apprehension. Suggested was a special task force to look into reasons and solutions to the membership problem."[122] The board made increasing membership the primary goal of that season.[123]

New members still complained that they were not actively used both in activities and in decision making, and this seemed to be the major reason that the newest Players were resigning. One of the governors suggested that a board member be appointed to shepherd the new members and follow up with committee chairmen to make sure the new members were involved with Player activities. The rest of the board declined the motion.[124]

Another idea to help boost the standing of The Players was to reinstate honorary memberships (differentiated from honorary life status for members who had been members for at least thirty-five years). The board would decide the recipients of these memberships, and honorary members would be chosen from the Detroit theatrical community. "It was hoped that this individual would be an active member allowing us to utilize his talents for better productions and to reach out for new members through this new active member."[125] The board never pursued this idea.[126]

Membership was the root problem, but consequently finances were in trouble. Frolics still did not adhere strictly to the budget. For example, the November frolic budget in 1985 was nineteen hundred dollars, but the production cost the club three thousand dollars. To defray costs, the board also considered canceling the Christmas party for Player families.[127] If possible, the board did not want to reach outside of Players for support, although they were willing to accept some help from the Theatre Arts and Fine Arts clubs because of their shared history and membership between the groups.[128]

The 1980s were tough for The Players, as they were for many clubs. The Detroit Athletic Club saw its lowest modern membership in 1983, 2,211, where a membership of 2,200 was considered the break-even point.[129] The Detroit Club followed the same pattern as The Players, recovering from the Great Depression, gaining membership in the 1950s, then showing steady decline in membership from the 1970s through the 1980s. From a resident membership of 746 in 1955, it was down to 428 by 1987. By 1996, the club was disbanded and reorganized. The total membership in the reorganized club is fewer than one hundred today. Detroit historian Arthur M. Woodford cites many of the same reasons for the decline in membership mentioned earlier, but he also adds the additional expense caused when the federal income tax laws changed, no longer allowing for the deduction of club dues.[130] At The Players, the records for the 1980s are incomplete. For the most part, reports of the board of governors have been lost. They resurface briefly during the 1986–87 season, possibly prompted by the seventy-fifth anniversary of The Players, but then they disappear again until the present, with some scattered notes in the 1990s. This may not have been due necessarily to problems at The Players. In 1991, the executive secretary, Lee Carroll, retired after forty-six years of service to The Players. For her retirement, the club hosted a frolic in her honor, making her the only woman to be invited to a regular frolic at The Players. Although the board attempted to staff the position after her retirement, no permanent replacement could be found, and records were not kept as assiduously by several of the succeeding office managers. In her absence, information that she would maintain either has gone unrecorded or has "walked off," along with some of the Player memorabilia such as Nixon's photo and a signed picture of Admiral Byrd. This situation appears to have stabilized at present, and some records have been recovered; currently the board and the office manager maintain club information.

The position of the club remained perilous as the 1980s ended, but the 1990s saw several changes in leadership styles and activities. For example, President Phil Gillis (1989–90) sent out a reminder in *The Player* about the quality and effort necessary to sustain the club:

> Are you satisfied with The Players? I certainly am not. Let's hope that none of you are satisfied or ever will be. Satisfaction turns into complacency, the dry rot which will destroy any organization which depends upon the fellowship of its members for its existence. We can strengthen our fellowship; we can hone our theatrical skills, and we can improve our production values. As long as there is room for improvement, we dare not be satisfied; we must not be complacent.

Lee Carroll caricature: Known as Mrs. Player, Carroll was the office manager for The Players from 1944 until 1991 and was the only woman to have a frolic thrown in her honor.

> But if you ask if I am proud of Players, then the answer, without hesitation, is yes. Our most important asset is our membership.[131]

Gillis is not the only Player president to sound the call to action. Three years later, President William L. Robinson Jr., a third-generation Player, sent out a familiar warning:

> As it is often said, the key to The Players is participation. It is important to the success of our ventures to be sure. More importantly, however, it is the key to any member's enjoyment and full appreciation for The Players experience. Too often we call for your participation in the guise of a chore to be fulfilled. We fail to mention that the best times at the Playhouse do not necessarily come from sitting in the Frolic audience. They can come from peering out over the stage from the fly deck; poising in the glow of the footlights waiting for Jim Turnbull to deliver something even close to your cue; or standing with a beer in hand at 2:00 a.m. after the dress rehearsal, helping Mark Habel select "the best drapes to dress this set." ...
>
> Full participation requires members. Unfortunately, this commodity always seems to be in short supply. Disinterest, transfers and the recession have all taken their toll. Despite the most vigilant efforts of our Membership Committee, we only seem to maintain membership levels. Once again, therefore, we are imploring you to bring your friends, neighbors and even relatives to The Players.[132]

It still was not enough.

Despite the best of intentions, there was a severe drop in numbers within the first few years of the nineties. Player Chuck Steltenkamp explained the decline as the result of several situations that were out of the club's control. In addition to those members lost to the great playhouse in the sky,

> the club also fell somewhat a victim to members who were transferred to other cities and for reasons out of our control. Just as a snowball effect can happen in a positive way, it can happen in a negative way too. ... So, in terms of the early nineties, different members were sort of staying away because they saw other members staying away.
>
> But then that began to change by the mid to late nineties where we experienced some infusion of new blood and sort of a renaissance of energy from some of the older members. And like any volunteer organization, you can devote as much time as you want to it, and it can also suck you dry. You can put your heart and soul into it, and then after awhile, realize, "Wow, I've been spending a lot of time on this, and it gets tiresome." ...

> [During the] late nineties, we've been fortunate to add some members who were very energetic and very positive, and that positive energy sort of begat a more positive snowball effect so by the end of the nineties and into the twenty-first century where we are right now beginning an upswing in terms of replenishing the membership, in terms of having younger clientele to replace some of the older members who just simply died away.'[133]

Steltenkamp's use of the term *renaissance* is not random. It has specific meaning to people familiar with the city of Detroit. In 1970, "26 business, industrial, and civic leaders dedicated to stimulating an economic boom in Detroit" founded Detroit Renaissance, Inc. Originally headed by Henry Ford II, one of its major endeavors was the construction of a five-tower complex that included office, retail, and hotel spaces. The developers named the $500 million, privately financed project through a contest. They broke ground in 1973, and some occupants were able to move into the building in 1976. The seventy-story central tower is the tallest building in Michigan. The Renaissance Center was not enough to combat the abandonment of Detroit's downtown in the 1980s, however. General Motors purchased the building in 1996 for $73 million and spent another $500 million renovating it.[134]

The real renaissance in Detroit happened long after the Renaissance Center was built. Detroit historian Arthur M. Woodford dates the turnaround to 1991:

> For Detroit this era of prosperity really began in 1991 with real estate developer Chuck Forbes, the Gem Theatre, and the development of the city's new theatre district. Detroit probably had more grand historic theatres and concert halls than any other major U.S. city—partly because downtown collapsed so quickly in the 1960s and stayed down so long. In other cities, historic stages fell to the wrecking ball to make way for new development. In Detroit, however, the curtain came down, the doors were padlocked—and there the theatres sat, the seats rotting, the plaster friezes crumbling. Forbes was one of the first to realize what a popular draw the restored old theatres could be.[135]

There were other projects that year. The fifty-story One Detroit Center office building opened, Chrysler Corporation built a new assembly plant on Jefferson Avenue, and "residential projects worth $1.5 to $2 billion" were slated for construction.[136] In addition, there had been some reconstruction prior to this. The historic Fox Theatre, a former movie palace, was restored to its gold-and-red velvet splendor in 1988, and a renovated Orchestra Hall reopened as the home of the Detroit Symphony Orchestra in 1989. In addition to the restored Gem Theatre (1991), the Detroit Opera House (1996) and the Century Theatre (1999) also reopened. In 1997, the spate of construction concentrated in the new theatre district necessitated moving the Gem and Century theatres (the buildings are connected) to Madison and Brush streets to make way for a new baseball stadium for the Tigers (Comerica Park).[137] A new football stadium (Ford Field—site of the 2006 Superbowl) was started behind the ballpark not long after. Following approval by a state referendum, three casinos were also added to the downtown area.

This spirit of renewal pervaded both Detroit and the Players. A children's theatre became a permanent renter at the Players Playhouse in 1990, providing a steady stream of revenue. Peanut Butter Players had only one season at The Players before the troupe's founder left for Colorado. The music director, C. J. Nodus, reconstituted the troupe as Paper Bag Players and took Peanut Butter's place in 1991.[138] Unfortunately, problems with the group resulted in terminating the relationship in 1999.[139] The Players considered founding their own children's theatre, but the start-up costs proved prohibitive.[140]

There were instances of Players returning to the club, as is evidenced by a letter to the board of governors from Michael T. Maurer during the 1991–92 season:

> Dear Gentlemen,
> As a former member of The Players, I find that I miss the bard, the boards, and the beer. Beyond that, I also miss the camaraderie to be found at a gentlemen's club such as Players. As such, I hereby humbly request reinstatement by the board of governors.
> To my benefit, I still remember all the words to the Players song and have a tuxedo that fits. And, as I recall, there was no one chasing me when I left the club, a sure sign that I left in good standing.[141]

The Players implemented a strategic plan in 1994 with the objective of "preserving and improving Players status as a gentlemen's club for presenting amateur theatricals." The committee members charged with enacting the plan examined everything from the location of the club to gender to race. They decided that the club should remain in much its same form and that various activities already allowed for the involvement of women. They affirmed that the club did not discriminate and would welcome any race, religion, or ethnic group, but they did not want to institute a formal affirmative action policy. The 2005–6 president, J. J. Jorgensen, states the club's membership qualifications in his own terms: "Qualifications to join The Players are quite simple and straightforward, i.e., one must be a gentleman and ... as we often joke ... have a check for $450 which doesn't 'bounce.' ... We don't care about the race of a member and don't categorize, pigeon hole or classify members, or prospective members according to race."[142]

The club currently includes minority members, as well as people of various religions and socioeconomic statuses. The club has no wish to identify people on these terms, however. As Player Peter Dawson describes it, "We define ourselves only as gentlemen (or at least try to obtain that goal). When one enters the door in his tuxedo, one ceases being a plumber, a doctor, a lawyer, a carpenter, an artist, a musician, a CPA, a newspaperman, a restaurateur or even unemployed and you are merely part of (and this is a term we overuse but still true) our 'band of brothers.'"[143] The club wants to recruit people based on their love of theatre—nothing else.

On the question of being an all-male establishment, the aforementioned strategic plan stated: "Players is not for everyone. It is not a community theatre. We should consider the fact of being an all-male club as an asset, and promote it accordingly"[144]

Members of The Players have a clear idea of what their club is and how it can be viewed by outsiders:

> For those who haven't attended a frolic lately, and there are many of you, it just might be possible that, viewed objectively, a bunch of guys hanging out in a dark old building, watching a bunch of other guys dress like women and pretend to act, all the while slugging down beers and chomping on pretzels and peanuts until well past midnight, doesn't sound like a very productive use of your time. Maybe that's true, viewed objectively; but *Players, like all the activities that make life really worth living, shouldn't be viewed objectively.* Quality of life is strictly subjective, and Players truly contributes to the quality of our lives.
>
> ... Especially now, when we're all so very busy, it is all the more important to step away from our lives, to step back in time, to step through the front door of Players the first Saturday Night of every month. **Players needs you, and what is more important, you need Players!**[145]

In 1998, the historical documents at Players were gathered together by Player Thomas Brunk, an architectural historian. The club purchased cabinets and folders, and Brunk organized and archived various materials. Prior to this action, Brunk had also had a hand in establishing a permanent historical exhibit in the Founders Room in 1983, the declaration of the Players Playhouse as a Michigan historic site in 1985, and a national historic site in 1987. Not only was he trying to preserve Players documents, drawings, blueprints, and photographs for future researchers, but also he was looking for information to confirm that the club was actually tax exempt.[146] Although the club needed confirmation that they were a 501(c)3 organization (the official IRS nonprofit designation), and the board believed it qualified, this was a huge risk. If they alerted the IRS to their search, and it was determined that the club was *not* tax exempt, it could be held liable for decades of back taxes. The IRS matter came to a head in March 1999:

> Governor [John L.] Owen reported that he had spent countless hours of his business time and commanded special favors to work behind the scenes to determine our actual IRS status. His contact at the IRS said that we are a 501(c)4 organization. Governor Owen told the agent that we have documentation from the IRS indicating that we are a 501(c)3 dated 1973 and 1974. Because the IRS is computerized, these older records cannot be easily accessed and Governor Owen was asked to fax copies to the IRS. While perhaps a risk, Governor Owen is taking the tact that it is the responsibility of the IRS to show when and why our status changed.[147]

The matter was finalized days later:

> John Owen spoke with IRS Agent John Shafer on March 8, 1999, requesting a letter confirming the status of The Players as either a 501(c)3 or a 501(c)4 organization. He was asked to fax the 1974 correspondence indicating our exemption under 501 (c)3 of the Code.... C. Ashley Bullard, IRS District Director, issued a response on March 10, 1999, that "Our records indicated that a determination letter issued in July 1943 granted your organization exemption from federal income tax under section 501 (c)3 of the Internal Revenue Code. That letter is still in effect." Resolving this issue is a major accomplishment.[148]

The serious business of the club finally settled, it was possible to concentrate on its main purpose, producing theatre. There are two particularly interesting performances during the 1990s at The

Michigan historical marker for the Players Playhouse

Players: Jane Martin's *Coup/Clucks* and Bud Pearse's *The Players Take Manhattan*. Martin's piece brought up both social and theatrical questions:

> This pair of one acts presents an interesting dilemma for Players and society in general.
>
> The script, written in 1982 and first presented in 1984, deals with small town [S]outh attitudes and the still resident antipathy for African Americans as represented by the KKK and their supporters.
>
> Both plays seem to be an apology piece where the whites, perhaps more aptly termed white trash, come off as bigoted and moronic while the African Americans come off as wise and tolerant.
>
> The most difficult question, however, in this day and age, is whether or not white actors can portray African Americans in black face and not come off as insulting, insensitive and insufferable?
>
> I was uncomfortable with that notion as well as the notions of cross-burnings and inflammatory racial language.
>
> While the themes in these two plays are structured not to be inflammatory in and of themselves, the mere presentation of these ideas and not including African Americans may be indefensible.[149]

This production brings up a question of whether it is possible for an audience to accept the presentation of an actor performing the role of a member of another race, even when the role is played straight and with sensitivity. This is an issue even in the professional theatre. The choice of a white, British actor to play one of the lead Asian roles in *Miss Saigon* when qualified Asian actors were available raised a furor at the time (the producers did have several arguments disputing the qualifications of various actors, including name recognition). In general, his portrayal was accepted by most audiences, and his performance was not meant to be a mockery of an individual or a race. In fairness, if it is possible to accept men playing women with no insult implied, then the same can be true across racial lines. That is not to say that there has always been this deference in performances at the club. In the early years at The Players, there were minstrel acts at Afterglows (white performers in blackface singing and doing comic routines), but while we would consider the material in minstrel shows racial stereotyping, they were typical of popular theatre in the United States in the first third of the twentieth century. For the most part, these performances dropped off the stage at The Players not long after they dropped off the popular public stage. Now, when Players want to produce a show because they think it is a good script, they play whatever the role requires, whether that requires makeup or heels. With America's social problems, general audiences are most likely not ready for this and will view the performance as insensitive, no matter the positive intent.[150]

One of the significant actions taken during the 1990s to combat the decline in membership was the decision to allow guests to attend in business suits. In 1996, the board of governors voted to allow guests to attend frolics in dark, conservative business suits. The board had been debating lifting the tuxedo rule for a while, but it had not been suspended since World War II. Not everyone was happy, including Chuck Steltenkamp, who was a member of the board at the time and an admitted traditionalist. He said that several older members of the board whose opinions he greatly valued explained that with the rising cost of tuxedo rental, a guest could be outlaying seventy dollars for "something that they really didn't know what they were getting into. The club is hard to describe ... the whole Players experience is hard to describe."[151] The board passed the measure, nonetheless, and the club has seen larger audiences on frolic nights, often thanks to a significant number of guests. This is good for the membership, as the men enjoy playing to larger houses, and the club gets to use its greatest recruitment tool: the Playhouse on a frolic night. The revitalization of Detroit and the resulting new construction near the Playhouse has also made it easier to recruit new members. Another addition during the 1990s was Bill Rohloff's "rookie show." Near the beginning of the season, one of the pieces at the frolic would be composed of as many of the new members as Rohloff could get. The sooner a new member got involved, the more likely he would be to stay. Now that Rohloff has passed on, it is unclear who will take on the responsibility of the rookie show.

The club staged its five hundredth frolic in April 1996. The board wanted to celebrate the event, but with it being so close to the May Show, some governors wanted to delay the celebration until the following season to "avoid back-to-back special events, thus avoiding an enthusiasm drop-off by both actors and theatre-goers in May."[152] Board members argued about what they could call the April frolic so that they could still have the five hundredth frolic celebration in the fall. They considered calling it "Frolic 499 1/2," but one governor insisted that every frolic afterward would have to be 500 1/2, 501 1/2, and so on. They considered numbering them out of order (501 would come before 500), but another governor said that would be dishonest and historically inaccurate. They finally decided on April remaining the 500th, but in "code." The number was replaced by the Roman numeral "D," and the frolic officially became known as the "Dth Frolic."[153]

The 501st frolic in the fall was a big Player musical, *The Players Take Manhattan*. Bud Pearse put together one of his famous revue shows for the November Invitational. The review described the show as a

> delightful variety romp over the entertainment index taxied at warp speed by the legends and milestones of show biz. Amazingly, we were treated in one rollicking mega gulp to dream girls, Burns and Allen, Harry Lauder, Carol Channing, Maurice Chevalier, Abbott and Costello and Marilyn Monroe.
> 
> Enough? Nope, plenty more. Add the tumbling, stumbling, bumbling magic of the Ed Sullivan Show, the entire "chorus line" of "Guys and Dolls," "Craig Whites" follies and the remarkable Players' remake of "West Side Story."
> 
> And yet none of the numbers in any of the eighteen scenes were parodies or simple imitation. Each segment was flavored and embellished by that special Players' twist that breathes new life into old adored plaster.[154]

The reviewer insisted that "if No. 501, 'The Players Take Manhattan,' portends the level of energy, glitz and craftsmanship of future shows, it will be impossible to listen to selflessness, singlemindedness and total spirit of ole 'Nunquam Renig' evidenced by this show, someone will be echoing similar sentiments at the No. 1001 Frolic ('The Players Take the World')."[155]

There was a sad note to this frolic. When the audition notice was sent out to the membership, they got the following reply from Bob Greene, which he allowed to be printed in *The Player*:

> It certainly sounds like one of "Bud's Best," and I wish you a huge success on the historic occasion of Players' 500th Frolic.
> 
> Five hundred? Incredible! As a longtime Life Member I was fortunate to attend and participate in several hundred of them, and they spawned cherished memories. I still have all my copies of *The Player* from those years, and their reviews and sketches provide much pleasant reminiscing.
> 
> ... As for me, the final countdown has begun. The doctors at Ford Hospital tell me they can no longer administer chemotherapy and radiation because of my age (90 in November), so it is time to move on. The

brass nameplate from my chair will take its place on the lobby wall, alongside so many other good friends of my generation.

Players take their final curtain call, but *The Players* will go on. It will survive and prosper for many years to come, with the warm support of all of us standing unseen in the wings.

Sincerely,
Bob Greene[156]

The Players lost both Bob Greene and Bud Pearse in 1997. A tree was planted in front of the Playhouse and a new set of curtains donated in honor of Pearse.[157] In 2003, a Japanese maple was planted for Player Frank Judge, joining Pearse's tree. Player Tom Brandel, a close friend of Judge's, spearheaded the movement to create an award in his honor. Prior to his death, Judge wanted to donate a statuette of Shakespeare to the club. According to Player Peter Dawson, the first recipient of the award, "It was Tom Brandel's idea, based on his admiration for Mr. Judge, to turn the statuette into an award at Players to recognize the 'spirit of Nunquam Renig.' The Frank Judge *Nunquam Renig* Award was to be given to a Player who had gone above and beyond the call."[158] Dawson knew about the award and was very surprised when he became its first recipient:

> I was Treasurer for two years and discovered we had been paying real estate taxes and other taxes that as a nonprofit theatre we should not have been paying, and I was able to get us officially exempt from them. ... While I was Treasurer, our office manager quit and I basically took over some of the functions of the office for several months. ... I also totally revamped the accounting system and got it all computerized there. When the office manager quit, I also started doing *The Player* from cradle to grave and the Directory since they might have gone left undone, so to speak.[159]

This may not be as glamorous as being under the lights, but it is an example of what perpetuates the club and is a good illustration of the attitude and improved outlook at the club since the end of the 1990s.

This new tradition has been welcomed. One last informal tradition deserves mention. For the twenty-third time at the December 2004 Afterglow, Player Jim Turnbull delivered his personal story of "An Altar Boy's Christmas in Scotland." This particular event was described in an article "ghostwritten" in *The Player* (Sam Slade is listed as the author):

> A Player's Christmas tradition is this re-telling of young Master Turnbull and his Christmas billiards match with Father McNulty, the pastor of the local Catholic Church in Selkirk. ... Much may be said of the story, but the message it presents and Father McNulty's disguised gift of something more valuable than a tangible or pecuniary present speaks to the true meaning of the season, that it is more blessed to give than to receive, that sometimes a gift of sacrifice or love or the act of giving alone, by itself, is more meaningful than a pence or a shilling or a dollar.[160]

The story is that Father McNulty, an accomplished billiards player, played five billiard games with the eleven-year-old after Midnight Mass. Turnbull, much to his surprise, won three out of the five. At the conclusion of the match, McNulty threw a fit and told him, "If I ever, ever, hear a word about this game tonight, it'll be the saddest day in your life." Years later, when discussing the priest with an old friend and fellow altar server, the friend asked him if he had ever played billiards with him. Turnbull was surprised to hear his exact experience related. It turns out that McNulty was too poor to give him a gift, so he gave him a billiard game instead. Turnbull insists that he has yet to get a finer Christmas present.[161]

Although Afterglows do not traditionally have caricatures made of them, Chris Monley has witnessed all twenty-three repetitions of the story and thought that it was time it made it to the walls of the Playhouse. After Turnbull completed the story to rousing applause, he was called back onto the stage, and Monley presented him with a caricature of himself telling the Father McNulty story.

Players have often stepped up to the plate to ensure that the club is there for future generations of Players. The club has established a Web page, stepped up their efforts to build the endowment, increased their community outreach efforts (including presenting a scholarship to a Wayne State University theatre student), and recruited significantly younger members. It now tapes its frolics for posterity, so Players can replay their favorite frolic moments. On 9 December 2000, the club celebrated its ninetieth birthday with a production (of course) of *Re-Doing Stratford* and a champagne toast at midnight. Now, with ninety-five years of history behind them, the Players are not looking back at what they have accomplished and survived, but are looking forward to their one hundredth anniversary in 2010.

Jim Turnbull's "A Selkirk Christmas": A long-standing Christmas tradition at The Players is for Turnbull to relate the story of the best Christmas present he ever received—a billiards game he played as an altar server in Scotland with Father McNulty.

# 6

# The Players Today

In 2005, the Players numbered 174. Almost all of the membership is more than forty years of age, and at least half is more than sixty. There is a far better balance of social brackets than in years past, and members come from all walks of life. Some are professional artists, others are doctors, lawyers, and educators. Despite a broad range of professions, "all are equal," in the words of Player Glenn Michael Corey. "It doesn't matter what occupation one has outside the club, once inside the doors of the Grand Lady we are all brothers."[1] All of them are firmly dedicated to their club. They speak of the Players Playhouse fondly as "The Great Lady," "The Grand Lady," or "The Beautiful Lady," and most of them can point with pride to a caricature of themselves in a show that hangs on the walls of the Playhouse. They still speak of Sam Slade as if they knew him, although he has been dead for more than sixty years. They can point out their favorite Legge sketch, and they know all of the words to "When the Day Is Done" (or can fake it pretty well).

The organization is leaner, to be sure, but the members have the gleam of zealotry in their eyes. They are genuinely proud of their productions and their Playhouse. As a group, they are friendly, welcoming, and relaxed. They all enjoy speaking of their experiences of the club and only need a willing ear to relate a story, or five, about their time at The Players. The members see their club as a unique organization, but most do not view their ranks as elitist. They welcome everyone. Even though I am a woman, they were excited to have someone interested in their club and its history. Although it was true that my gender prevented me from attending the monthly frolics, every other accommodation was made to allow me to document their history. I have attended invitationals and board meetings, and I have sat in on an audition (the only one I have ever attended where beer was served—this is, after all, The Players). I was never treated as an outsider. Anyone who shares their love of The Players is welcome.

## Theatre Arts Club, the Fine Arts Society, and The Players

The Theatre Arts Club and the Fine Arts Society still hold their productions in the Playhouse and receive a reduced rate. These organizations, like The Players, have survived the lean years. They have also cut down their number of performances, but they still are going strong. The Theatre Arts Club grants a scholarship every year to an outstanding woman in the Theatre Department at Wayne State University (the Eva Woodbridge Victor Scholarship). The clubs have revived the Tri-Effort, the last of which was Neil Simon's *Plaza Suite*, performed in August 1998. With this three-act play, the groups have returned to older versions of the Tri-Effort in which each group produces a separate act. They also participate in some social activities together, such as a joint Halloween party held in 2003. The three groups are facing possible changes. The Theatre Arts Club has held its performances in the afternoons for years. This time is no longer conducive to the schedules of the professional women who are members, and the group now holds weekend performances to encourage more participation from the membership.[2] They produce three shows a year, host an annual Christmas party, and hold their annual meeting in June. The middle production of the year is directed by the winner of the scholarship, and proceeds from that evening help fund the award. Their numbers are small, and the club struggles, but they have not given up.[3]

The Fine Arts Society celebrated their one hundredth anniversary during the 2005–6 season with a large party boasting music, food, dramatic sketches, and a slide show at the Playhouse, to which members of The Players and the Theatre Arts Club were invited. They commissioned a special logo and a song from their membership to celebrate their centennial. The Fine Arts Society continues to produce four shows a year (three plays and a musical). Originally, the club did not produce plays, and the 2004–5 president, John Denler, dates the production of plays to the building of the Players Playhouse. Prior to that, meetings with various art lovers were held in members' homes. At each contemporary performance, they invite a guest visual artist to show his or her work to the membership.[4]

## Player Frolics and Invitationals

The Players hold a Fall Invitational in October, frolics in November and December, a Millionaires' Party in January, then three more frolics in February, March, and April, followed by the May Show. The Script and Casting Committee still chooses the plays for each season. It considers upward of seventy scripts a year. Each member reads between thirty and forty scripts, and at least three members of the committee read each script. These three will recommend to the whole group whether the script should be produced. Like any other theatre company, the difficulty of the script, its appropriateness for the intended audience, and the complexity of production values (i.e., the kind of set needed, complicated lighting arrangements, difficult effects, etc.) are the major considerations used to determine which scripts will be chosen.

Instead of the random combination of most monthly frolics in the past, the Script and Casting Committee attempts to tie the scripts together with a theme to give the evening more unity when possible.[5] It probably makes for a more coherent bill, but it robs the frolics of some of the fun engendered by mixing up O'Neill families and Hitler stories.

Once a season's productions are chosen, a "Dream Sheet" is sent to all resident members. They can check off whatever position or role they may want, and the Script and Casting Committee compiles this information. If a show still lacks a director once all members have submitted their preferences, a member of the committee, a board member, or a dependable Player may be recruited to fill the gap. The director will ask potential actors if they are available. If there are roles that are still left open after all the membership has been approached, the frolic's producer or director may take the role. For a Fall Invitational, auditions may be held to encourage a broader range of Players to get involved. According to 1999–2000 president Glenn Scoles, begging is an effective way to fill the empty positions, and most directors become quite adept at convincing potential candidates to tread the boards in this manner.[6] It is still hard to get everyone together for rehearsals, but shows still manage to pull together for the frolic.[7] Recent editions of *The Player* do mention that memorization can be an issue, particularly if the show has had a limited rehearsal period.

Occasionally, shows come to the Script and Casting Committee fully formed. A group of friends at The Players will decide that they want to work on a particular play together. The committee still has to approve the script, and the group often has to wait a year until it can be produced so that it will not interfere with the shows that have already been chosen for a season.[8] In addition, The Players still enjoy revivals of past favorites. The 1999–2000 season opened with *My Three Angels*, a hit from the 1950s. In keeping with tradition, some members from the original cast reappear when possible, though not necessarily in the same roles.

One change from past years is that dress rehearsals are now open to invited guests. According to J. J. Jorgensen, "families, including women and children, and friends of cast members often come to the dress rehearsals. The evening is a long one, but the cast members really appreciate having an opportunity to strut their stuff before a live audience. Shameless prima donnas!"[9]

Player Playwrights still contribute topical one acts. One recent production spoofs the prison stay of the maven of household and entertaining ideas, Martha Stewart. Players Chris Nesi and Bob Zych's darkly humorous *Martha & Me* presents Martha at her "best," even in prison. Martha seems as concerned with providing just the right atmosphere, as always, but the audience is quickly cued into the fact that all is not "perfect" at the prison. Her guard is terrified of her, with some justification—she stabbed him in the thigh with knitting needles she made out of "egg whites and dried spaghetti."[10] Diane, a brand new inmate, is put in with Martha. Diane is anxious to get along with her new cellmate and not wind up in the infirmary with nervous exhaustion like Martha's three previous cellmates, who could not keep up with the Martha Stewart lifestyle. Martha quickly impresses her into domestic service to help her decorate for Halloween. Another inmate, Bertha, wants to make Diane her girlfriend, and Diane is desperate to avoid her. Conveniently, in her keepsake box made out of license plates, Martha has a shiv (knife) she made out of "an old toothbrush and a few pieces of fine Italian glass. I find it to be the perfect balance of subtle refinement and 'fuck you, bitch.'"[11] Martha gives Diane the shiv, and Bertha lunges for Diane, trips, and impales herself on the blade. Diane is hysterical, assuming that she will spend the rest of her life in prison for murder, but Martha is truly prepared for *every* occasion. Bertha becomes part of the Halloween decorations—and the refreshments—and the day is saved. *Martha & Me* easily made the May Show.

Chorus "girls" Robert G. Frear, Oren W. Blenkle Jr., and Robert L. Garrison

The Players' orchestra and chorus have been reinstated, though they are somewhat smaller than in years past:

> Yes there is an "orchestra" ... and I use that term *very* loosely. Again, it's a group of guys who play a variety of strange instruments, and get together to hack their way through some crappy songs ... and the crowd loves it, just as much as they love the crappy shows. It's fun. And anyone who has the nerve to get up and play before a Players audience deserves applause and recognition. We've always said that if it wasn't for the pianist (who is usually pretty good), we wouldn't have a clue as to what in the world the orchestra was playing.
>
> There's also a Players vocal group. It's unofficial at best, and yes they get together as required, or as the whim strikes them. The good news is that there are actually a few good voices in there, so it's not quite as painful an experience as listening to the orchestra.[12]

If past methods used to choose a May Show confused members, more recent methods are even more obscure. A statistician headed up the committee that chooses the May Show several years ago, and he tried out a system that weighted both what was voted on and who voted. If the person attended fewer frolics, then his vote was given less weight. To this was added the concerns of production, availability, and feasibility of reproducing some of these shows. This method was quickly abandoned, and most members still believe that in some cases the names of the shows are put in a hat and drawn at random.

## Tuxedos

Formal dress is still a critical part of participation in the frolics, and frequent reminders (and debates) show up in *The Player* about the exact definition of tuxedo or black tie. "Dr. Fashion" (with some help from Emily Post) provides advice to help Players uncertain about dress requirements. Former Player president Denne Osgood published a recent reminder to the membership on this subject:

> Players is our club. When this club was founded, it decided to set itself apart from other clubs. One of the distinctions is our preference for "black tie." It is a tradition that we wish to continue. Our traditions must be observed by our members as well as their guests.
>
> To introduce our beautiful "lady" to outsiders, we usually relax our tradition of black tie for guests....

It is the responsibility of every member to make sure that his guest know and follow our dress code.

The tuxedo is the essential evening dress of gentlemen. And is the PROPER dress for members to EVERY Frolic and Invitational.

The definition of "Black Tie" is: Tuxedo—black ... white shirt with wing collar or wide spread collar, if winged collar, the tie goes under. If you know how to tie a bow tie, tie your own, it has that slight irregularity that is the mark of great style.

A recent innovation, is bow tie and cummerbund in various colors and patterns or a black button at the neck. Shoes should always be black; pumps with a satin bow are the most traditional. Oh yes, and black socks!

Preferably no watch—Black tie is a party outfit so who cares what time it is.

In our Tuxedos we are an oasis of genteel charm in a barren desert of casual Fridays.[13]

The club does keep a bank of tuxedos for both guests and members that might not have their own, but guests can attend in conservative suits if they prefer. If a member wants to introduce a guest at a less formal event, he invites him to The Players' Traffic Hour.

## Traffic Hours

The whole point of the Traffic Hour is to allow "members and would-be members to mix in an informal atmosphere," according to 2005–6 president J. J. Jorgensen.[14] It also has the added benefit of finishing off the beer from the previous weekend's frolic. He explains that the frantic pace of the frolics is not always conducive to getting to know other members. Plus, the Traffic Hour is critical to recruiting for the club, as it gives potential members not just a chance "to mix and mingle with members, but to see these guys with their 'stuffed shirts' removed. There's nothing like meeting a past president in his plumber's work togs fresh from fixing a boiler somewhere in the Detroit Metro Area."[15]

There are several members who were first introduced to the club this way. Player John L. Daly recounted his first Traffic Hour: "I asked one of my co-workers if he was going to work late that evening and he said that no, he was going to have a drink at a club that a friend of his belonged to [and] asked if I would like to come. I fell in love with 'The Beautiful Lady' instantly and his friend, Chris Hawksley[,] became one of my sponsors."[16]

### Other Player Activities

Like the Traffic Hour, the Millionaires' Party, and the Christmas party, there are plenty of events that do not necessarily involve theatre and frolics (most still involve beer, though). Some of these are limited to members only, and others include Player family and friends. A number of these are "unofficial events" arranged by a member, such as participating in the Dragon Boat races on the Detroit River in the summer (Players won its division in 2004) or taking a trip to London. Some events have become traditions in their own right. Several years ago, four Players decided to put together a golf outing as a "lark." Player Geno Pirrami enjoyed the experience so much that he just "kind of picked it up and ran with it," and it turned into an annual event whose attendance can rival that of the annual meeting. It serves as another way to socialize for Players who might not get to work with each other on stage.[17]

Another traditional event is the summer work party. Jorgensen describes these events as "select scheduled Saturdays during the summer when members convene at the Playhouse to paint, clean, rig, skin flats, do landscape work, toss out our annual over-abundance of nasty furniture and props, etc." He sees these work parties as an opportunity to really get involved in the life of the club: "Eight years ago, I joined The Players late in the season. I had a role in the February rookie play and reprised it in three May Invitational evenings. Following that regular Frolic season, I participated in at least three Saturday work parties. This, rather than participating in those plays, really solidified my membership in The Players."[18]

### Membership in The Players

Membership still requires two sponsors and can be rejected if current members lodge objections against the candidate. Rejection is unlikely in such a close-knit organization in need of members, but it is still possible. It is no longer a "gentlemen's club" in the social elite sense of the word, and some of the older members lament the changes to the makeup of the club. In all honesty, one must expect that changing demographics would affect the nature of the club on some level. Even those men that remember the club as it was recognize that times have changed and that the club must change on some level to remain viable. As the club and society have changed, so has the exact definition of "gentlemen." In the 1987 version of "This Is Players," the club defines the term for both themselves and potential members:

> The Players has always been a gentlemen's club, in the best sense of that word. For we are not necessarily gentlemen by birth, business success or social position, although these are not necessarily hindrances. Rather, we are gentlemen by a spirit that crosses and bridges a wide variety of backgrounds and foregrounds.
> It is how we behave toward each other, and toward the traditions of our club, that furnish all the credentials a Player needs.[19]

Most members still think that The Players are the "greatest group of guys on earth." Longtime member Bill Rohloff admitted that he arranged his schedule around Player events, which were the focus of his social activities. He described the Players as an extended family, a community that was a significant part of his life.[20] This community has changed and diversified over time and is still in the process of changing. In a 2001 *Detroit News* article, the club acknowledges that "to help the club survive well into the 21st century, members … want to recruit more African-American members and more 30-something people to bolster the ranks."[21]

## The Players and History

In 1998, the board started preparations for the seventy-fifth anniversary of the Players Playhouse for the December 2000 celebration. As part of this, Player Thomas Brunk set about preserving the architectural drawings of the Playhouse and writing a history of the structure itself. *Re-doing Stratford* was revived for the seventy-fifth anniversary, and although it is now impossible to get any of the original cast, many members of the audience will remember one of its revivals on other Player anniversaries.

The club has made itself part of the larger historical picture in Detroit. As part of the celebration of Detroit's tricentennial in 2001 (Detroit 300), the Players Playhouse hosted *Detroit Je T'Aime*: "[A]n original musical recounting the earliest days of Detroit and its founding fathers, particularly Messr. Cadillac. There were three evening gala performances and in at least one of them then-Mayor of Detroit, the Hon. Dennis Archer, appeared in a small role costumed as a French colonial official."[22] Hosting this performance in their historic structure tied the club to the celebration of events that have shaped Detroit.[23]

## Player Ghosts

Like any self-respecting theatre, the Playhouse has a resident ghost. According to Player John Butterfield, it appears most often in the flies, the area above the stage for hanging scenery (or at least it has in his experience). He and Player Barry Trombley (a sergeant with the Michigan State Police) were by the pinrail, hanging scenery. "Barry had a glass and a bottle in his hands. He dropped both when he saw the shadow flick across the upstage catwalk. The figure could be anyone of thousands of guys who have been Players. I prefer to think it is Dick Forsyth. He ran Players for forty or more years. A good friend."[24]

Player Bill Rohloff (the man with his name on the shower door) had his own run-in with a ghost up in the flies. Rohloff was working late one night, alone in the theatre. He was up on the paint rail, which is basically a catwalk set high above the stage so that scenery can be pulled past it to be painted, thus allowing a person to be able to paint any part of a large piece of flat scenery while standing in one place. Though effective, it is also a little dangerous, and Rohloff claims that he turned to find Sam Slade standing not far away from him. He said that Sam appeared to be warning him to be careful. Far from being a frightening encounter, this merely made Bill feel like past Players were watching out for him.[25]

Player Chuck Steltenkamp has an interesting view of ghost stories. Although he admits that he does not know any ghost stories in relation to the Playhouse, he claims to feel a different kind of ghostly presence in the form of the words of members who have passed on. Steltenkamp relayed a story that Player Frank Judge (of the *Nunquam Renig* Award) recounted to him about the fiftieth anniversary of the club. At that time, Judge, then president, was very interested in The Players' getting involved in the community. Player Harvey Campbell, who had been a member for almost all of the club's fifty years, met this discussion with several "I remembers." He told the board that he remembered when they were gambling in the dressing rooms, and he reminded them that the bumps worn down the back stairs were from kegs being brought in during Prohibition.

Steltenkamp did not understand what this had to do with community service, so Judge explained that Campbell was questioning why The Players needed to present a reputable face. He was basically reminding Players not to take themselves too seriously, and these words serve to remind current members that the club is meant for fun.[26]

With a tradition as rich as that of The Players, there is room for more than one Player ghost. Campbell and Slade can take their place with the others. All of these men were used to working together. With Al Weeks's flamboyant personality and dedication to Players, it is difficult to believe that he is not wandering around the theatre in one of the dressing rooms and that both Hirschfields are not quietly looking over Players' shoulders as they put on their makeup for an evening's performance.

## The Doors

The following is a brief recap of those who have been memorialized by the club by having their names placed on doors.

Slade (1942): Sam Slade was the first Player ever honored with his name on a door. A stalwart of the Player stage, Sam appeared in a multitude of roles, but he probably was best known for his portrayal of Lincoln at the February frolics.

Elliott (1958): Another committed Player, William (Bill) Elliott was a fixture on the stage at Players. In addition to directing occasionally, he served on the board of governors, was a vice-president, was president in 1934–35, and spent decades on the Script Committee. He also appeared in Player classics such as Albert D. Conkey's *On High* (the satire about great historical figures in heaven; he played George III) and Noble and Jacobs's *Men Working* (the musical about the WPA).

Forsyth (1961): There are several anecdotes about Dick Forsyth, particularly in relation to actors flubbing lines in one of the shows he directed. Player Ned Schneider remembers Player Bob Garrison having trouble with lines in the production of *The Women*. Forsyth came through the French doors onstage in the middle of the performance, prompted, and returned backstage. He got such a workout in that performance that he took a bow during the curtain call. Bill Rohloff remembered him walking onstage during another performance, tearing the page out of the script, and handing it to the actor. Al Shelden Jr. remembers another time when someone forgot their lines during one of Forsyth's shows. There was a window upstage, Forsyth pushed up the sash, stuck his head onstage with the script, and delivered the line.[27]

Rohloff (1981): Bill's contributions to The Players are discussed elsewhere in this chapter, but Bill's door has the most interesting story behind it. Players Thom and Jefferies gave him the door as a gag, which backfired on them when he took it seriously. Rohloff was so well liked that no one was going to disillusion him. When he discovered that he had been given the door to the shower that had not worked in forty years, he good-naturedly hunted down parts and made the shower work again.[28] The board immediately considered putting his name on other items that needed repair.

Carroll (1981): The first woman to be honored with a door at the club was Leona Carroll. Lee Carroll spent forty-seven years as the executive secretary/office manager for The Players. Her meticulous records form part of the material used in the research for this book. Before it became Script and Casting responsibility to cast shows, Carroll used to pull out her list of cards of active members and start making phone calls, offering the parts to various Players.[29] Beloved by Players, a special frolic was thrown in her honor when she retired in 1991. The Lee Carroll Frolic followed all the standard rules for a typical frolic, with one exception—Lee was invited, thus making her the only woman to attend a noninvitational frolic.

Hirschfield (1982): The club named this door after Frances Hirschfield, but she would undoubtedly be glad to share the honor with her husband, Jake. Frances helped her husband prior to his death and took over his duties afterward. She costumed Players for more than fifty years, helping members with every aspect of costuming—including the subtleties of wearing panty hose.

### *Nunquam Renig*

Every member has a story about a Player going the extra mile (*Nunquam Renig*). William Colburn Standish Jr. joined in 1937, following in his father's footsteps. From 1954 to 1998, Standish produced dress rehearsal dinners. Previous to this self-imposed task, "the actors would go out to supper and not return to set up the stage until ????. I was a member of the Properties Committee and the Board of

Directors at the time and sometimes I would not get home until 1 or 2 o'clock a.m. So that is the reason I started to cook for Players."[30] A minimal fee was charged, which everyone assumed was to cover the cost of food. Years later, they found out they were wrong: Bill actually paid for the dinners out of his pocket and saved the money collected, which he donated to the Players endowment fund in 1998.[31]

J. J. Jorgensen replied to a call for *Nunquam Renig* stories with this one: "Nunquam Renig is the phrase I always use at the end of my e-mail notes when I'm really, really desperate." He was "nunquammed" to perform at an Afterglow once by Bill Rohloff: "It wasn't too bad, but I haven't been on stage since. Nunquam Renig can be dangerous to your well being."[32] This may be why the Frank Judge *Nunquam Renig* Award was established, to reward those unsung heroes who have stepped into the breach.

The Players is a working club, a point of pride for the members. According to Player Greg R. Thorn:

> This really is one of the few clubs in the area that a member can pay dues for the privilege of working really hard. ... But that's the whole story behind this club. It was started by a group of men who loved theatre ... all aspects of theatre, including set design, set building, lights, sound, costumes, make-up, etc., etc., etc.... not just acting and directing. Players allows members to try their hand at almost anything they've ever dreamed about doing in the theatre. Never pulled a curtain before? No problem. Never worked a light board before? Here's your chance. We really have never had a tough time getting people to work on the various committees because there's always someone who's always wanted to do that sort of thing....
>
> I must say that there were always a couple of committees from which members steered clear. Costumes was one of those areas that nobody really wanted to jump into. The good news is that there were always "a few good men" that loved that committee, and would sign up for it every year. We let them. The other committee that nobody wanted to work was Props. Again, several years ago, there was a group of guys that loved to rummage around in the prop room, drink beer, and smoke their cigars. They had their own little "club within a club."[33]

Periodic reminders to the membership to help out do appear in *The Player*, but most members who participate feel that they get more out of the experience than they put in:

> No matter how experienced we may be with the theatre, or life at The Players (not necessarily the same thing!), we too often take for granted the hours and sometimes days of behind-the-scenes toil that goes into

> our monthly Frolics. Such things as designing, building and painting the sets (no fellas, no one gets paid to do that and it takes a lot of time and effort, especially when it falls to one or two Players); costuming—yes, especially the female roles; working on the stage crew (to get us from one play to another—not only on Frolic night, but hopefully, at dress rehearsals as well) and make-up (showing up early for the Frolic, then often missing one or more of the shows, buried in the basement attending to the late-arriving actors). Okay, it's inglorious, tedious and mostly under-appreciated work. But someone's got to do all this, or we don't have a Frolic! For the most part, these support functions do not require extensive training or special skills—just a willingness to learn and contribute.
>
> One of the charms of The Players is the unpretentiousness of the group of Players, young and old, experienced or novice, striving for the common goal—to put together an evening of entertainment for our members and guests, and to sustain the traditions and the values that attracted us all to The Players, in the first place....
>
> ... You know, Players used to have a lot of regulars, who pitched in for a Frolic or two each season. And, if we have enough regulars involved, those few backstage stalwarts that have gotten us this far, won't burn out and leave us with no one to turn to. Getting involved in this way not only helps strengthen the Club, it offers you the opportunity to meet other Players and develop more camaraderie.[34]

The epitome of the spirit of *Nunquam Renig* was exemplified by Bill Rohloff. He was known affectionately as "Mr. Player." When asked how he earned this nickname, he replied, "Well, I have held every office. I've been on the board three times, served on every committee, chaired most of them, and done a lot of directing and acting."[35] But there was more to it than that. Rohloff may not have known this, but he was actually held up as an example to the younger members of the club. If any of them asked what it meant to be a gentleman or what it meant to be a Player, they were answered with, "It means you're Bill Rohloff." Chuck Steltenkamp eagerly admitted that he admired Rohloff: "He carries himself with such dignity and grace.... When I grow up, I want to be Bill Rohloff."[36]

Rohloff was the current generation's Sam Slade, and as a surprise, the club planned the October 2005 frolic as a celebration of his ninetieth birthday (actually August 5). Dubbed "Project R," the event was the brainchild of Player Larry Smith, who was inspired by conversations he had with Rohloff about the frolic that was held for Lee Carroll. Smith described his plan several months ahead of the actual event, with the festivities beginning at the Twenty Year Club dinner before the frolic:

> The southwest corner wall will have a painting, covered with a drape. At the end of the dinner, just before the start of the frolic, the full membership and guests will enter the founders room and announce that this frolic is dedicated to Bill Rohloff, that this frolic is now called "The Rohloff." The first event is to be the unveiling of an oil portrait of Bill, hanging in the founder's room (painted by Player Glen "Fuzz" Corey). We then will proceed to the auditorium were Bill will be seated in a special made throne where his usual table is.
>
> The programs are to be special keepsake booklets with a color insert, full of pictures and caricatures of Bill's past at Players (produced by Player Todd Rader). The cover logo and also the logo for the frolic is to be a stylized caricature of Bill (like that famous Hitchcock silhouette) designed by Player Chris Monley.[37]

The members managed to keep the secret, and Rohloff was stunned when confronted with his portrait and learned that the frolic was in his honor. The first show for the frolic was *Summer Comes to Diamond O*, by Betty Smith and Robert Finch. This was the first show in which Rohloff had appeared on the Players' stage. The audience loved this sentimental, Depression-era cowboy story, so much so that they even joined in the performance: "Veteran Player Henry Nelson as Stub provided the surprise of the evening. He tuned his Sears Roebuck guitar for a little bunkhouse singsong, when suddenly the entire audience joined in the chorus. Another Players' moment."[38] This was followed by a musical "salute" composed of music from different periods of Bill's life. Again, the audience joined in, followed by a roast (of Bill, not the frolic supper), a tribute from past Player presidents, the actual supper, a birthday cake, and a special caricature for the occasion by Player Chris Monley.[39]

There was no better way to honor Rohloff. In Player James Turnbull's review of the event, he closes, "The Players is never about one man, but once, every century or so, we come remarkably close to selecting such a patriarchal figure. We will never be closer than we were on the evening of October 1, 2005. God bless you, Bill Rohloff."[40] Rohloff died later that season.

One of the best *Nunquam Renig* stories comes from a 1979 edition of *The Player*:

# CHAPTER 6

Bill Rohloff caricature requested by the
Gourmet Group in honor of his ninetieth birthday

Allan Dick never believed in miracles. He had always been told they existed, but he was still skeptical.

"Show me some proof," he would cry, "and maybe then I'll believe."

On the twelfth day of Christmas, Allan got his proof.

Allan was the Producer of the 396th Frolic, and after taking on this tedious task, he was barraged with a series of problems. On December 14, he had no shows, no scripts, no directors, and no casts.

But little did Allan know that he was being watched over by the Guardian of Players Past, Present, and Future, St. Nunquam Renig.

And the following afternoon, the mysterious voice of St. Nunquam spoke to him. "We have two shows, two directors, and two casts."

"What?" the startled Allan replied. "Who's that?"

"Don't ask silly questions," the voice shot back, "just get out there and hold a production meeting. We need a stage crew, prop men, make-up men, set designers, set painters ... so don't stand there all day. Get rolling."

"You bet I will," screamed the jubilant producer. "Glory be to St. Nunquam Renig." ...

But the big grin didn't last long. He was asked to sing the Players' Song, and yet when he got to the Playhouse that night, he found there was no orchestra. "How can I sing without an orchestra?" Allan asked. He thought no one was listening, but the Guardian Angel was. "If there was only someone who could play the piano and sight-read music."

Just then, there was a flash of light and a puff of smoke. Allan coughed and covered his eyes with one hand as he fanned away the smoke with the other.

When the smoke cleared, Allan opened his eyes to see Player Bill Sinischo standing in front of him holding some sheet music. "C'mon, Allan. We're late ... sing the Players' Song."

And so the evening began.[41]

Even families get involved in the spirit of *Nunquam Renig*. Player Roy Jendrzejewski was making his debut in *An Evening for Merlin Finch*, but his pregnant wife went into labor that day. Once his daughter was born, his wife sent him back down to the Playhouse to perform.[42] Apparently everyone takes the idea of "None Shall Refuse" seriously.

### "When the Day Is Done"

The current Players are well aware of the uniqueness of their organization. Player Kensinger Jones has the best description of what makes The Players so special: "The sheer tenacity of an organization that is obviously obsolete, defies popular culture, maintains quaint traditions, and brings joy to the hearts of those who believe 'for men only' is a reasonable statement."[43] Player William S. Turner Jr. summed it up in the following sentence: "Nothing ever changes!"[44]

The board is currently evaluating ways to help the club perpetuate itself in the years to come. Recent goals set by the board include the following:

- A net increase of 20 new, actively involved members;
- Creation and implementation of a five-year strategic business

plan;
- Active solicitation to double our Endowment Fund;
- Completion and submission of application materials for grants to offset the cost of maintaining our "beautiful lady";
- Enhancing our long-term relationships with Fine Arts and Theatre Arts;
- Re-establishing strong community involvement.[45]

There are small and large fund-raisers for supplies, ranging from materials for the prop room to equipment for the theatre. Two recent ones were for a new beer cooler and a defibrillator for the Playhouse. There are more elaborate benefits. For five years, the Playhouse has hosted the Balduck Mountain Ramblers to raise money for the endowment fund. A more recent event is Wassailfest, "two evenings of Renaissance merriment, entertainment and food."[46] Providing entertainment at the Wassailfest is the Detroit Renaissance Dance Company with whom The Players splits the profits. The 2004 event doubled the previous year's profit.[47]

The board is trying to plan for the future, actively recruiting renters for the Playhouse (40 percent of the annual operating revenue of the club comes from rentals) and constantly reevaluating member needs so as to better serve their constituency.[48] When possible, newspapers and television stations are contacted to see if they want to do a human interest or historical piece on The Players. May Shows are packed at almost every performance, and members of the media attend the event. Every other year, this garners a mention or an article in the press. As a way to recruit new members, the board awards a scholarship to a local college student to increase awareness and membership. The board of governors welcomed the recipient for the 2004–5 season, Joseph Porter of Wayne State University, as a guest at the frolics, and he directed *The (Fifteen Minute) Dogg's Troupe Hamlet* by Tom Stoppard for the club in February 2005. The experience appears to have been successful, but it will take time to see if this raises the profile of the club or nets new members. At the very least, it is exposing a new generation to shows at The Players. The board has ambitious plans. If they succeed, the club may be on a stable footing for the next hundred years.

What is most amazing about The Players today is how little has really changed from the early years of the club. Sam Slade or C.

Membership gathered for a frolic

Hayward Murphy could come back and assume the same roles they played decades ago. Some of the logistics and technology of producing frolics have changed, as have the plays and faces, but little else. The gentlemen's theatrical club that Guy Brewster Cady envisioned is still pretty much as he left it. Although the membership base is more diverse, a group of men with a passion for theatre still meet in tuxedos October through May, one Saturday a month, to see a show, drink a beer, and spend time with the "greatest group of guys on earth."

# Conclusion

When I describe The Players to people, it always takes a moment before they realize that I am not talking about something that existed in the past, but something that is alive and active in the present. They are always surprised that the club is still in existence and that it still continues in pretty much the same way that it has since its founding. The only major change is the expansion of its definition of "gentlemen" to a far more inclusive one that is based on how a person acts rather than his status in society.

It would actually be less surprising if the club had *not* survived, as many clubs have withered over the last thirty years. Robert D. Putnam has examined this phenomenon in his book *Bowling Alone: The Collapse and Revival of American Community*, both confirming that the trend exists and determining what has caused it. His research has determined that, in the last thirty years, community groups of all kinds (volunteer organizations, social clubs, cultural groups) have been declining in number. Plus, for those that still exist, attendance and involvement are down.[1] This is not limited to formal organizations; the number of social visits and family dinners has declined also. Participation in sports has decreased, particularly among young people (this has contributed to the American obesity epidemic). In fact, across the board in any kind of participatory event, observing is up and participating is down.[2] Putnam blames four major factors in this process: (1) the decreasing amount of free time and money combined with the two-career family; (2) suburbanization, commuting, and urban sprawl; (3) electronic entertainment (particularly television); and (4) generational change (generations go through cycles of involvement, and the most involved generation is currently also the oldest one).[3] Mary Ann Clawson, who studies fraternal groups, blames the changes primarily on "changes in social relations between men and women, and the development of mass media entertainment."[4] What is most terrifying about the trend

Putnam tracks is that at the current rate of decline, he believes that clubs and organizations will disappear in twenty years.[5]

Another element that has contributed to this trend is the nature of contemporary society and the distance that it creates between people. Sociologist James A. Vela-McConnell describes the United States as a "society of strangers" that has been developing over time, as technology has made us less dependent on other people or on the larger community to survive.[6] The American "culture of individualism" has only intensified this impression that people need to take care of themselves and that the individual should always be valued more than the group.[7] The societal changes that have occurred over the course of the twentieth century have destroyed the old rules of how society should function, and the new rules have not yet been settled. This can be liberating, but it can also be frightening and confusing as members of society try to determine which rules and obligations should be kept and which ones discarded.[8]

So why has The Players survived these changes? What is the club providing that is important enough for the members to keep it alive? When we examine the club from the sociological perspective of community, certain key elements emerge. There are many definitions for community, but sociologist Anthony P. Cohen provides the most pertinent one to this case. Community is defined by a shared "system of values, norms, and moral codes which provide a sense of identity within a bounded whole to its members."[9] There are a few other tenets that also apply. The most basic is that human beings are essentially communal.[10] We want to be part of a group because we need to belong, to form bonds with other people, and to feel valued.[11] We also want a sense of continuity, particularly if we feel the world around us is unsettled.[12] Contemporary communities are more likely to be formed by what people know, rather than who they are (i.e., ethnic group, social class).[13] The importance of friendships has grown "as mobility, divorce, and smaller families have reduced the relative importance of kinship ties."[14] When a community provides these elements for its members, it is more likely to survive and thrive.

These elements are what people need, but the real question is *how* to provide them. Ritual crops up frequently in discussion of community. Cohen insists that ritual "is an important means through which people experience community."[15] The largest community experience at The Players is the frolic. It has a special night, a specific time and a uniform (the tux). It has a standard format that starts when all the members rise to sing The Players' Song, progressing through a shared meal and ending with a celebration (the Afterglow). When these men come together as a group, it reaffirms their sense of who they are as members of this community. The "collective experience" of the frolic emphasizes their relationship to each other and to other Players of years past who have participated in the same experience. Thus they have a sense of continuity, solidarity, and group identity necessary for a successful community.[16] According to sociologist Patricia Anne Masters, "Rituals create the bonds that transform individuals into members of a community."[17] When new members join the club, the president brings them to the stage during their first frolic, introduces them and gives them a beer mug with the Players' crest. They have thus been initiated and given a symbol that makes them a Player.

Both rituals and symbols can be used to keep members of community in line.[18] For example, the tuxedo that Players wear is a symbol that they are gentlemen, but it is also a reminder that they must *act* like gentlemen. Everyone wears it. Even when working backstage as a member of the crew, the tuxedo is part of the uniform. Furthermore, symbols are adaptable, and their meaning can change over time. Even though the meaning changes, however, the persistence of the symbol provides the *"appearance* of continuity."[19] Thus, although the tuxedo might have once been a mark of social status at Players, it has become a symbol of how these men want to be perceived and how they will act—as gentlemen. It also provides another sense of continuity, as members have been wearing them for more than ninety years.[20]

A sense of shared history strengthens community, particularly when it creates a sense of connection with the past life of the community.[21] Members of The Players have a strong sense of this history, and it crops up in conversations and in articles in *The Player*. Player Michael Jeffries related his experience of this:

> When I look back to that time, I think of the years Fran [Van Deusen] has been a member, and all the shows, both good and bad, that he has witnessed, I start to realize how much Players has changed for him over the years. Most of the faces are new, the plays are generally more modern and the beer is legal. However, the most important part of Players has stayed the same. The traditions go on as they did when Fran was first introduced to the Players.

> It's comforting to know that somewhere in this world there is someone sitting in wet diapers and that someday he too will be president of Players. I suggest you don't try to guess who he is because he's not a member right now; but when he becomes president the faces at Players will have changed a great deal for me, as they have done for Fran, but the traditions will still be the same.[22]

The sense of a shared history, a constant awareness of that history, and how the individual member fits into it is necessary to maintain a community.[23]

The location of a community also has an effect on its ability to survive. Definitions of community often include the fact that members are physically located near each other. This proximity is no longer considered necessary with the mobility of contemporary society. Communities can now consist of individuals who are nowhere near each other physically.[24] Despite this, a physical space related to the community can be critical. According to sociologist John G. Bruhn, "Places create emotion and feeling in us because they reflect the values and beliefs we learned and experienced in that setting."[25] Thus the Players Playhouse is critical to the club's community It is the place where the members have the clearest sense of belonging in their community, and it is the place most of the members have had the majority of their experiences as part of that community This is the place where they see shows together, tell stories, perform on the stage, or crew a show. It is the home for the Players' family. They can move away, but no matter how far away they may live, this is the home to which they can always return, and it will be familiar, no matter how many years have passed.

Another element that provides a sense of belonging to the group is gender. Communities define themselves as much by who they are as who they are not.[26] Thus, one of the uniting factors at The Players is that the membership is all male. One office manager described the Playhouse as their "treehouse."[27] It is also worth noting that members do not choose to define themselves merely as men but more specifically as "gentlemen." The Players is for fun, but members have a sense of decorum, even with the beer and pretzels. They value someone who distinguishes himself by his actions.

Membership in a community provides not only those necessities mentioned earlier (close bonds with other people, a sense of belonging, a sense of continuity) but also a sense of worth.[28] Everyone serves a necessary function on a frolic night, whether they are part of the show, part of the audience, serving the dinner, or pouring the beer. Each and every one is necessary to the experience, and the group is small enough that a member will be missed if he is not present. There is also a sense of friendship that would not necessarily be present at a larger club, or a club that is only a social club. Working on a show together, helping with a project around the Playhouse or helping cook a meal for a frolic allows the men to form more than simply casual ties. A statement I have heard from several Players is "of the four or five people I would call in the middle of the night if I needed to be bailed out of jail, at least three are members of Players." Although said somewhat jokingly (members hardly engage in frequent criminal activities, although directors might insist forgetting lines is a crime), they are quite serious about their close ties. They really would feel comfortable calling a member in the middle of the night if they needed help, and they are certain that they would receive it. In our disconnected society, being part of a group outside of our immediate families that would provide that kind of support is necessary to our well-being. Putnam lists several other immediate benefits of being part of a close-knit society: it encourages good character traits, including tolerance (just ask the directors), and it can provide useful information. If a member knows that another member needs something, be it a job or a babysitter, he will try to provide any helpful information he can. Last, being part of a strong community is actually a coping mechanism for individuals that makes them better able to handle stress, illness, and crises because they feel like they are not alone.[29] Several sociologists note that people who are part of strong communities that look out for their members are healthier both physically and mentally.[30]

In Patricia Anne Masters's sociological study, she discusses how "play" (in the sense of having fun) creates community. To do this, she examines how the volunteer groups and clubs that produce the Philadelphia Mummers' Parade function. Because performance, and the preparation for that performance, is their main activity, there are several parallels between what she found with the Mummers and what is present at The Players. She determined that playing together does "create a tightly knit community" by providing its members with personal satisfaction (play is satisfying in and of itself), by making the individuals feel like they are part of a larger group (for the Mummers, this was the city of Philadelphia; for The Players, it is the connection they feel with performers past and present), by creating a link with the past, and by "creat[ing] personal linkages that participants rely on when they face family problems that are beyond their capacity to solve."[31] She expands on this: "The Mummers are a family, and the sense of belonging that membership in the groups provides is one of the attractions that draws individuals into working hard to play. Belonging creates obligations, to be at the clubhouse in the final crunch ... and to help one another."[32]

The two elements that appear to be the most important in Masters's discussion are the effects of playing or performing together and creating a family. Simply, "playing together" converts separate individuals into a family in a way that simply spending time with a group of people would not.[33] In addition, the act of performing with other people and for a specific group with which one feels a connection intensifies the whole process. Plus, there is a sense of the ritual in any performance, which makes the experience of it (whether behind the stage, on it, or watching it) extraordinary.[34] That is not to say that this sense of the extraordinary is constant, but even fleeting moments are enough to make the experience satisfying for all involved. The sense of family created by working and playing so closely together is also significant. At The Players, members know that they have obligations to help one another if possible, but also that the community is obligated to help them in turn. The club motto, *Nunquam Renig*, reinforces this. The club constantly reminds members that if they are asked, they should not say no. Masters noted that when people did not have strong "kinship ties" (i.e., no close blood relations), the clubs could function as a primary family group providing support when needed.[35] Several members of The Players have told me that they believe certain of the older members are alive only because of the support they experience as part of the club. Younger members look out for them, provide rides to frolic nights, and even help with everyday needs when required.

Thus all of the elements that make The Players unique, and even those that make it an anachronism, have provided its members with a sense of community. Tuxedos and beer mugs are symbols, frolics are rituals, the Playhouse a home and a connection to the past, and caricatures on the walls a sense of continuity and history, particularly when a member first has one of his hung on the wall. Other members provide support and camaraderie and reaffirm an individual's worth. Members have a strong belief that anyone brave enough to get onstage at the Playhouse deserves to be praised, whatever the quality of the performance. All members are encouraged to participate and try new things, whether they have the experience or not. In a large urban environment, the club provides an awareness of stability and history, plus the safety of familiarity and a sense of welcome. When viewed in these terms it is clear why the club has survived when larger ones have not. Because the production of theatre is central to its activities, The Players has provided not only a supportive environment for creative activity but also a close-knit community. This, then, is why it has survived and, hopefully, will continue to survive in the years to come.

# Appendix A: Players Timeline

**1910**
*10 December* Founding of The Players: Guy Brewster Cady meets four friends at Richter's Café.

**1911**
*11 January* Articles of Association signed by Kirkland B. Alexander, Walter C. Boynton, Guy Brewster Cady, Leonard R. Carley, Alexander K. Gage, H. J. Maxwell Grylls, Charles P. Larned, Frederick S. Stearns, William W. Talman, and Ernest S. Witbeck.
*26 October* First official performance.

**1912**
Club is inactive.

**1913**
*January* Several members throw a party to revive The Players.
*April Hairlooms* first performed.
*November* Walter C. Boynton elected president and Guy Brewster Cady vice-president, putting The Players back on track.

**1915**
*January* Sam Slade elected to membership.
*March* Board decides that the May Show will showcase the best works of the season.
*October* The first Player goes off to war.

**1916**
During the 1915–16 season, theatrical design legend Norman Bel Geddes designs the second design of his long career: a set for an Afterglow for The Players.
*November* The Players moves to the Arts and Crafts Little Theatre.

*December* First edition of *The Player*, the club's newsletter.

**1917**

*February* Position of Glowworm (originally Toastmaster) established to plan the Afterglows.

*March* First discussion of building a permanent home.

*May* Annual meeting held in May for the first time so that the new board of governors will have the summer to plan for the upcoming season.

*October* First honorary member elected, Sam Hume, the president of the Detroit Society of Arts and Crafts.

**1918**

End of World War I. Fifty-four Players served; Player Harry W. Ford only war-related death.

**1919**

Player C. Hayward Murphy first appears as official stage manager.

**1920**

Russell H. Legge elected to membership.

Al Weeks's play *Her Family Tree* is on Broadway.

*5 April* Legge's caricatures first appear in *The Player*.

**1921**

Club is so popular that a waiting list must be established for membership.

*May* The May Show consists completely of Player-composed works.

**1923**

*February* Playhouse General Committee established to build a home for the Players, Player Joseph Meadon, Chair.

**1924**

Players Holding Company formed to finance and build the Playhouse.

## 1925
*10 December* The Playhouse opens with *Doing Stratford*, a musical with lyrics by Al Weeks and music by Bill Holliday. One of the songs from this show, "When the Day is Done," would later become The Players' Song.

## 1926
*2 November* Player Bill Holliday dies.

## 1928
*16 January* The Theatre Arts Club presents The Players with electric chimes for the theatre.
*The Players Book of One Act Plays* published by Walter V. McKee, Inc.
Marion Weeks draws caricature of the November frolic.

## 1929
Michael Todd takes over caricatures for the January and February frolics.

## 1930
The Depression hits home at The Players, and resignations start trickling in.

## 1932
Ownership of the Playhouse transferred from The Players Holding Company to the club.

## 1933
*May* Life membership instituted. Sam Slade is first inductee.

## 1934
*23 September* Founder Walter C. Boynton dies.

## 1936
*February* Offenbach's *The Rose of Auvergne* presented, may be the American premiere of the piece.
*March* Board of governors actively recruiting ex-Players.
*May* The tide of the Depression has been stemmed and membership is again increasing.

### 1937

"Meyerson" (no first name) draws the caricature of the March frolic.

*December* Players is able to hold the children's Christmas party for the first time since 1933.

### 1938

*Life* magazine publishes an article on The Players' 150th frolic.

### 1939

*December* National Bank of Detroit buys the mortgage on the Playhouse from Guardian Depositors Corporation, allowing The Players ten more years to pay it off.

### 1940

*3 April* Player Henry T. Ewald presents The Players with a portrait of Sam Slade painted by Player John S. Coppin. Ewald was also one of the men who donated the Honoré murals.

### 1941

Russ Legge dies.

*February* A movie is made of Sam Slade as Lincoln in *Nor Long Remember*.

*13 April* C. Hayward Murphy dies.

*May* Players' vote widened to include associates. Players' numbers are dropping. Associates are encouraged to take part in club activities.

*November* Board exempts from payment of dues all members of the service who are not in Detroit.

### 1942

*May* Player numbers are still dropping. The board lowers the initiation fee to encourage recruiting.

*21 June* Founder H. J. Maxwell Grylls dies.

*October* Temporary membership established for the duration of the war, allowing those in military and government service temporarily in Detroit to join The Players.

*December* Barrymore dressing room renamed "Slade."

## 1943
*January* Players allowed to come to frolics in business suits instead of tuxes.

## 1944
The Players start a mortgage fund to pay off the mortgage.
Lee Carroll becomes The Players' business secretary.

## 1945
*18 March* Founder Alexander K. Gage dies.
*May* The Players pay off the mortgage to the Playhouse. The copy of the mortgage is burned onstage, and the ashes are placed in the stage right Winningham vase.

## 1946
*October* Verne Minge takes over as caricaturist of the frolics.
*November* Minge's sketches first appear in *The Player*. First time a full-length play is used to open the season and is then repeated as an invitational.

## 1951
*June* Twenty Year Club established to encourage older members to attend the frolics.

## 1952
*January* Tradition of singing "When the Day Is Done" to open the frolic established.
*10 January* Founder Charles P. Larned dies.
*February* Memorial plaque installed for those Players that have died. Their chair plaques are removed and placed on the board that bears the inscription "Our Play Is Done."
*April* The board decides that women cannot attend dress rehearsals, but "little stags" (Players' sons) were welcome.

## 1954
*21 February* Founder Guy Brewster Cady dies.
*April* Vice-President Richard Nixon attends April frolic.

**1955**

*March* Historical Committee formed to collect and write a Players' history.

**1956**

First Drama Festival held: a joint venture between The Players, Theatre Arts, and Fine Arts, later called the Tri-Effort.

**1957**

*December* Minge stops drawing caricatures for *The Player*. Edward G. Robinson appears at the December Afterglow.

**1958**

Bill Elliott dies, a dressing room door is dedicated to him.
*May 20* Players Foundation incorporated to see to the perpetuation of the club.

**1959**

Bob Schafer takes over caricatures in *The Player*.

**1960**

*December* Fiftieth anniversary of The Players.
Articles appear in the *Detroit Historical Society Bulletin* and the *New York Times*.

**1961**

Dick Forsyth door dedicated.
James Strasburg dies.
Players get mugs emblazoned with their name and the club seal.
*March* W. Colburn Standish Jr. donates an act drop to the club on behalf of his family, quickly becomes known as the "Olie."
*September* First serious attempt by The Players to compile their history.
Playroom renamed Founders Room to attract renters.

**1962**

Jake Hirschfield and W. Colburn "Olie" Standish die.

**1963**

Al Weeks and Loren T. Robinson die.

**1965**
First Mid-Winter Party held in place of the January frolic.
Minge was again doing caricatures during the mid-1960s and early 1970s, but several editions of *The Player* have been lost, so it is unclear when this happened.

**1967**
*July* Race riots change the face of Detroit.

**1971**
Dick Forsyth dies.

**1972**
First edition of "This Is Players" published, describes to nonmembers the club and its traditions.
Fall Invitational becomes a permanent part of the Players' season (first Fall Invitational was in 1946).
The Players stop holding Christmas parties for orphans. The Christmas party was later reinstated for Players and their guests. Toys were collected for underprivileged children instead.

**1973**
Willie Awards established to spoof the year at the annual meeting.

**1974**
Bloody Run historical marker, originally cast by the Michigan Stove Works, stolen.
*November* Traffic Hour established as an opportunity for Players to socialize after work.

**1975**
The Players hosted an event for the International Organization of Little Theatre Groups.
A Coppin nude once again hangs in the Playhouse.
*May* Bob Greene takes over caricatures of frolics.
*9 December* The Players celebrate the sixty-fifth anniversary of the club and the fiftieth anniversary of the Playhouse.

### 1976
*Summer* Break-in at the Playhouse, Coppin nude and Sam Slade paintings are stolen. Both are later returned.

### 1977
Club membership has dropped almost in half since the riots of 1967.
Ray Jacobs dies.

### 1980
Player Marshal Bruce, known for singing The Players' Song at the beginning of every frolic, dies.

### 1981
Bill Rohloff receives a door with his name on it—from the decrepit shower, which he promptly fixes.
The office door in the Playhouse is dedicated to Lee Carroll.
Gourmet Group founded. The group of twelve Players serves dinner at Fine Arts functions and uses the money to refurbish the Playhouse.

### 1982
Glenn Scoles takes over caricatures for The Players.
*February* Walter Hodges, noted Shakespearean scholar, visits the Playhouse. Hodges was trying to gain interest in rebuilding Shakespeare's Globe Theatre.
*April* Frances Hirschfield has a dressing room door named after her.

### 1983
Chris Monley takes over caricatures for the club.

### 1985
Playhouse becomes a Michigan historic site.
*December* Seventy-fifth anniversary of The Players.

### 1987
Playhouse listed as a national historic site.
Second edition of "This Is Players" published.

**1991**
Lee Carroll becomes the only woman to be invited to a frolic when she retires after forty-seven years of working for The Players.

**1993**
Bud Pearse's silver heels donated to Players' historical exhibit.

**1996**
Board allows guests to come in business suits.

**1997**
*15 May* Bob Greene dies.
*7 June* Bud Pearse dies.

**1999**
Nonprofit status reaffirmed.

**2000**
*December* Seventy-fifth anniversary of the Playhouse and ninetieth anniversary of The Players.

**2003**
Frank Judge *Nunquam Renig* Award established. Player Peter Dawson is the first recipient.

**2005**
Rohloff Frolic.

# Appendix B: Membership List

Aaron, William H. 1986
Aaron, William H., Jr. 1962
Abbey, Dan R. 1964
Abbott, Chester G. 1931
Adams, Beard. 1939
Adams, Charles D. 1938
Adams, H. W. 1918
Ainsworth, Charles H. 1926
Ainsworth, Ralph. 1922
Aird, Paul D. 1949
Ajlouny, Joseph S. 2004
Albachten, E. Walter. 1949
Albee, William N. 1919
Aldrich, Henry. 1969
Aldrich, Ralph L. 1927
Alexander, Donald. 1925
Alexander, Frederick. 1916
Alexander, Kirkland B. 1910 (founder)
Alexander, Willard L. 1948
Alford, A. B. 1946
Alfs, William A. 1943
Alger, Frederick Moulton. 1913
Allan, Richard W. 1950
Allan, Robert W. 1928
Allen, Eugene D. 1959
Allen, Lee Harrison. 1953
Allen, Richard W. 1947
Alling, Robert B. 1923
Allison, Douglas F. 1957
Allison, Richard H. 1976
Allmand, John. 1942
Alvord, William Roy. 1928
Amos, Frank B. 1927
Anderson, Arthur B. 1953
Anderson, Carl D. 1987
Anderson, D. R. 1937
Anderson, E. J. 1935
Anderson, John Wendell. 1913
Anderson, Lee. 1918
Anderson, Wayne A. 1962
Anderson, Wendell W. 1930
Anderson-Smith, B. C. 1950
Andrews, Frank R. 1973
Andrews, Fred W. 1920
Andrews, Roger M. 1931
Angell, John H. 1945
Anger, Roy W. 1918
Angove, R. L. 1949
Anklam, W. F. 1924
Ankney, Ralph A. 1968
Anthony, Walter Melville. 1916
Arlund, William T. 1930
Armstrong, A. Gordon. 1943
Armstrong, Edwin E. 1913
Arnold, Gerald A., Jr. 1969
Aronson, Orvil R. 1948
Ash, Roy R. 1968
Asselin, Dean R. 1955
Athay, R. M. 1942
Atkinson, Percy L. 1940
Austin, Chris. 1996

Austin, Ronald H. 1981
Averbach, J. E. 1928
Avery, W. A., Jr. 1915
Axsom, Russell H. 1945
Babcock, Harry N. 1923
Bachman, Paul M. 1967
Backus, Standish. 1915
Bagamery, Frank J., Jr. 1970
Bahl, George L. 1920
Bailey, Walter A., Jr. 1974
Baillargeon, William A. 1986
Baits, Stuart G. 1929
Baker, Edwin W. 1925
Baker, George S. 1926
Baker, L. H. D. 1923
Baks, Richard P. 1990
Baldwin, Michael J. 1987
Ballantine, Andrew J. 2003
Ballantyne, Ford. 1925
Ballantyne, Howard P. 1925
Ballard, Harold L. 1944
Ballard, James Alfred. 1923
Bangs, John K., Jr. 1925
Bannister, H. T. (Tim). 1994
Barbour, William T. 1926
Barnes, Russell. 1921
Barrett, E. Daniel. 1974
Barrett, Robert Dick. 1959
Barry, James B. 1922
Barry, Jeffery W. 1968
Barry, Patrick A. 1978
Barter, Percy Leverett. 1916
Bartley, Edward A. 1977
Bartley, Lloyd V. 1936
Bartram, John G. 1980
Bashara, George N., Jr. 1966
Baskerville, Gerald M. 1964
Bass, Edred B., Jr. 1961
Bassett, Arthur F., Jr. 1974
Bassham, Kelly M. 2005

Batchelor, Edward Armistead. 1920
Batchelor, Edward A., III. 1996
Bateman, Ralph W. 1944
Baubie, James A. 1953
Bauchat, James L. 1950
Bawol, Aaron W. 2003
Bawol, Brian W. 2001
Baxter, Aldrich. 1917
Baxter, Charles Ernest. 1911
Beach, George W. 1945
Beal, Leland W. 1961
Beall, James E. 1957
Beattie, Daniel C. 1944
Beattie, Harold T. 1962
Beauchamp, Cleve J. 1969
Beaumont, Arthur C., Jr. 1957
Beauvais, Albert L. 1949
Beer, Joseph F. 1956
Begg, George O. 1918
Begole, Ari M. 1943
Belanger, Richard J. (R. J.). 1999
Bell, J. Bertram. 1947
Bellanca, Peter J. 1981
Beltaire, Mark A., III. 1943
Beltaire, Mark A., IV. 1983
Bement, Austin F. 1926
Benfield, John D. 1954
Bennett, Charles D. 1917
Bennett, Clark. 1933
Bennett, John W. 1948
Benson, Halge G. 1962
Berke, Joseph J. 2001 (honorary)
Bernard, William R. 1948
Berridge, George I. 1918
Berry, J. Leslie. 1942
Berry, Jay. 1952

Berry, Raymond H. 1933
Berry, Sterling P. 1968
Berteel, Albert M. 1956
Berthet, T. D. 1967
Bigelow, Horace W. 1924
Bingay, Malcolm W. 1917
Bird, Charles S. 1949
Black, Edwin. 1938
Black, Fred L. 1928
Blackburn, C. Versal, Jr. 1958
Blackburn, James B., Jr. 1966
Blackwell, Harry E. 1925
Blair, Frank W. 1928
Blanchett, William Ellis. 1974
Bleakley, Donald E. 1933
Blenkle, David Oren. 1977
Blenkle, Oren W., Jr. 1950
Blessed, Clarence D. 1928
Blood, Howard E. 1932
Blunck, Herbert C. 1943
Bodde, John R. 1926
Bodman, Henry Edward. 1913
Boehmer, Paul. 1987
Bogan, Chester S. 1957
Bogle, Henry C. 1933
Bohn, Z. Stephen. 1954
Bolton, Frederick R. 1955
Bommarito, Salvatore. 1972
Bonbright, Howard. 1928
Bond, William B. 1956
Bondy, Duane. 2004
Boomer, Lynes D. 1940
Boomer, Roy E. 1943
Boone, John T. 1976
Booth, John Lord. 1942
Booth, Ralph W. H. 1920
Borgman, Harold H. 1941
Borre, Herbert. 1945
Borsodi, Robert J. 1977
Bosquette, Thomas J. 1913

Boudreau, Samuel B. 1950
Bourke, Richard M. 1926
Boutell, C. M. 1948
Bowen, Charles C. 1920
Bowen, Daniel W., Jr. 1952
Bowen, Edgar W. 1911
Bowen, Julian. 1920
Bowen, Lem W. 1913
Bowen, Paul M. 1920
Bowen, William T. 1953
Bower, Edwin H. 1944
Bowman, Robert H. 1978
Boydell, John F. 1943
Boyer, Joseph. 1913
Boynton, Frank D. 1948
Boynton, Walter Channing. 1910 (founder)
Brackett, Clare L. 1928
Brackett, Jerry W. 1976
Brand, C. Richard. 1923
Brand, R. C. 1918
Brandel, Thomas J. 1982
Brandon, Walter C. 1926
Braniecki, William G. 1975
Brauns, Curt K. 1926
Bray, Charles A. 1915
Breck, Samuel L. 1919
Brennen, John V. 1920
Bretelle, Horace T., Jr. 1958
Brethen, Richard H. 1955
Briggs, Walter O. 1917
Briggs, Walter (Spike) O., Jr. 1939
Brinkman, William J. 1946
Brisco, Frank. 1915
Britt, L. V. 1923
Broderick, Kevin P. 1972
Brodman, David G. 1984
Brogan, E. B. 1960
Brooks, Mark. 1977

Brosch, George. 1943
Brossy, Francis E. 1918
Brossy, Francis E., III. 1954
Brother, D. P. 1940
Brotherton, Norton T. 1919
Brow, Norman N. 1973
Browder, George R. 1953
Brown, Cecil H. 1942
Brown, Guy C. 1925
Brown, Ira A., Jr. 1956
Brown, James D. 1986
Brown, Kendrick B. 1946
Brown, Lewis F. 1934
Brown, Patrick J., Jr. 1947
Brown, Peter T. 1963
Brown, Sedley. 1927
Brown, Spencer D. 1951
Brown, William H. 1920
Brown, William Rolston. 1931
Browne, C. G. 1949
Browne, Harry C. 1927
Brownfield, Keith W. 1980
Browning, W. McPherson. 1915
Bruce, A. J. 1945
Bruce, Charles. 1969
Bruce, John M., Jr. 1969
Bruce, Marshall. 1950
Bruce, Michael R. 1968
Brucker, Wilber M. 1934
Bruegel, David R. 1983
Brunk, Clifford F. 1938
Brunk, Thomas Walter. 1982
Brunsink, Bruce A. 1989
Bruske, Paul W. 1948
Buchanan, Roger S. 1962
Buchinger, William G. 1959
Buell, Daniel H. 1955
Buell, Don J. 1937
Buell, J. Lawrence. 1915

Buermele, James. 1987
Buffmyer, Edward G. 1969
Buhl, Arthur Hiram. 1915
Buhl, Theodore D. 1929
Buhler, Herbert. 1934
Buhler, Herbert, Jr. 1947
Bulkley, John M. 1937
Bunker, Frank. 1996
Burchenal, Seldon D. 1917
Burdon, Harold W. 1928
Burke, Charles G. 1943
Burke, John C. 2002
Burke, John D. 1937
Burke, Martin R. 1969
Burleigh, Manfred. 1941
Burns, Thomas F. 1952
Burris, Robert L. 1968
Burritt, H. W. 1933
Burroughs, Clyde H. 1921
Burt, Lou. 1924
Busby, Edward B. 1931
Bush, Charles T. 1929
Bushman, J. W. 1954
Bushnell, George E., Jr. 1956
Butterfield, John M. 1958
Buttrick, T. R. 1921
Bye, Mortimer. 1925
Bylica, Alexander A. 1964
Cadieux, Eugene R. 1964
Cady, David D. 1911
Cady, Guy Brewster. 1910 (founder)
Callaway, Lew L., Jr. 1948
Calvert, Michael R. 1991
Calvert, Richard E. 1966
Campau, A. Macomb. 1926
Campau, H. C. (Pat). 1989
Campbell, Endres M. 1948
Campbell, Harvey J. 1914
Campbell, Richard S. 1972

Campbell, Robert B. 1961
Candler, George V., Jr. 1931
Candler, Henry (Harry) E. 1914
Candler, J. Boyer. 1927
Canever, Victor W. 1956
Canis, Otto R. 1975
Canon, John S. 1991
Canty, Alan. 1949
Capler, Gregory M. 1989
Carey, E. H., Jr. 1949
Carey, Matthew. 1944
Carey, Philip D. 1958
Carey, Reginald G. 1955
Carey, Rolph D. 1979
Carleton, Daniel W. 1995
Carley, Leonard Rainford. 1910 (founder)
Carlson, Robert W. 1997
Carlson, Stephen F. A. 1979
Carlson, William. 1944
Carmichael, Curtis C. 1955
Carpenter, Marshall M., Jr. 1961
Carpenter, Scott. 1947
Carreiro, Jaime V. 1970
Carrico, John F. 1953
Carrier, Edward R., Jr. 1949
Carrow, Herbert P. 1918
Carruthers, George B. 1961
Carter, George W. 1926
Case, Louis H. 1918
Case, Storrs J. 1939
Casey, Matthew J. 1920
Casgrain, Wilfred V. 1937
Cashin, Leo J. 1961
Cassidy, George L. 1944
Castelli, Albert L. 1949
Castorri, Ronald A. 1969
Cataldo, John B. 1964

Caulkins, Horace J., Jr. 1925
Cedargreen, Irving H. 1943
Chabot, Albert E. 1975
Chaffee, Neal. 1961
Chaffin, Edward J. 1939
Chalmers, Hugh. 1915
Chamberlain, Carl B. 1926
Chamberlain, R. E. 1920
Champion, William J., III. 1996
Chaney, Austin B., Jr. 1966
Chapin, Dallas J. 1942
Chapin, Roy D. 1913
Chappellie, Stephen G. 1982
Charette, Paul. 1994
Charles, Martin. 1980
Cheever, Markham S. 1948
Chesterfield, A. P. 1918
Chirite, J. Douglas. 1947
Chittenden, William J. 1913
Chodkowski, Robert J. 1991
Christian, Eric. 1999
Chronowski, Alois J. 1953
Church, Aloysius S. 1956
Cicotte, Alan. 1994
Cipriano, Salvatore. 1975
Ciure, Robert J. 1982
Clark, Albert A. 1937
Clark, Emory W. 1913
Clark, Frank Scott. 1920
Clark, Frank Scott, III. 1943
Clark, George R. 1914
Clark, Robert M. 1984
Clarke, Carl F. 1921
Clarke, Howard A., Jr. 1950
Clarke, Howard A., Sr. 1926
Clayton, Thomas S. 1934
Clayton, Wallace E. 1959
Cleland, James, Jr. 1916
Clement, Leonard H. 1921

Clements, Frank Milton, Jr. 1957
Clover, G. R. 1930
Coche, Woodfin E. 1971
Cochran, John P. 1954
Cody, Frank. 1920
Cody, Fred. 1952
Coe, John William. 1951
Coffin, Dean. 1937
Coffin, Howard Aldridge. 1922
Colburn, William R. 1914
Colby, Howard H. 1933
Cole, Bernard V. 1943
Cole, Fred H. 1933
Cole, Walter C. 1920
Coleman, S. S. 1921
Colett, Anthony William. 1954
Collins, Alpheus. 1916
Collins, Ray J. 1957
Collins, Russell S. 1927
Comlossy, Frederic B. 1965
Compton, Fred A. 1950
Comstock, William A. 1923
Conkey, Albert D. 1935
Conklin, James M. 1984
Conley, Joseph J. 1998
Conley, Thomas F. 1998
Conley, Timothy. 2003
Connor, C. L. 1925
Conway, George W. 1972
Conway, Michael A. 1966
Cook, G. Robert. 1963
Cook, Grant L. 1932
Coolidge, David A. 1948
Coolidge, Frank, Jr. 1942
Coon, Patrick A. 2004
Cooper, Frank R. 1965
Cooper, James D. 1956
Cooper, James H. 1932
Cooper, Robert H. 1948
Coppin, John S. 1939
Corbett, Sidney B. 1958
Corbin, Arthur E. 1915
Cordes, Tim. 1997
Cordner, Frank N. 1943
Corey, Glenn (Fuzz) M. 1994
Corlis, William B. 1972
Corning, Donald C. 1997
Corrigan, A. M. 1929
Costello, Russell T. 1941
Cotner, Jacob, Jr. 1915
Cotter, John L. 1929
Cotter, Thomas H. 1932
Cottrell, S. V. 1939
Couger, Warren D. 1962
Coulter, John E. 1919
Couzens, James. 1913
Covington, Harry S. 1928
Cowall, Frank A. 1970
Cowhey, James C. 1956
Coyle, William J. 1973
Crandall, Allison G. 1929
Crandall, David R. 1959
Crary, Douglas D. 1938
Craven, Norman E. 1920
Craves, Edwin. 1930
Crawford, Robert W. 1943
Cray, Cloud L. 1926
Creedon, Gaylord M. 1981
Crittenden, F. A. 1917
Crittenden, Ronald L. 1974
Crittendon, George A. 1924
Crocker, George J. 1955
Crombie, Charles. 1924
Cronenweth, John D. 1941
Crooker, Robert H., Jr. 1958
Crooks, Lee. 1951
Cross, Cameron T. 1981

Cross, Charles W. 1917
Cross, John K. 1953
Croteau, Kenneth C. 1963
Crotser, Joseph M. 1928
Crouse, Charles B. 1920
Crow, Allen B. 1950
Crowl, H. B. 1916
Crowley, A. H. 1953
Crowley, Joseph J. 1920
Crowley, William C. 1917
Crum, Frank. 1952
Cruz, Cosme. 1976
Cumming, Robert E. 1937
Curran, Robert W. 1955
Currie, Gilbert S. 1926
Currie, Thomas E. 1931
Currier, Gerald A. 1960
Curtin, Kevin B. 2001
Curtis, Roswell G., Jr. 1945
Curtis, William G. 1918
Cusack, Thomas O. 1924
Cushing, George W. 1917
Cushman, Bennet T. 1920
Cutler, Dwight. 1913
Cutting, Albert J. 1959
DaDeppo, George J. 1977
Dahlhofer, Brad. 2003
Dailey, Glenn C. 1955
Daisley, Edwin T. 1957
Daly, John L. 1978
Danaher, John E. 1961
Danahy, John J. 1970
Daniels, J. Eric. 1955
Danielson, J. C. 1964
Darwin, Charles A. 1917
Davidson, Peter S. 1973
Davies, Horace A. 1929
Davies, Karl R., Jr. 1946
Davies, Lewis. 1964
Davies, Ted. 1953

Davies, Thomas D. 1987
Davis, Charles S. 1943
Davis, Charles S., Jr. 1974
Davis, Ernest G. 1928
Davis, James Vernor. 1952
Davis, Jeffrey. 2003
Davis, Ralph N. 1947
Davis, Robert K. 1918
Davis, William L. 1925
Dawson, Peter W. 1995
Dawson, William A. E. 2005
Day, Clarence E., Jr. 1956
Day, Ray. 1933
Dayton, John R. 1964
Dean, Hugh. 1939
Dear, William (Bill). 2005
Dearth, Robert A. 1951
Decker, John R. 1926
Dell, Gary J. 1978
DeMass, Orrin Alden. 1927
Demchak, Michael J. 1977
Dempsey, Bruce J. 1962
Den Uyl, Simon D. 1935
Denby, Edwin. 1913
Denby, Garvin. 1913
Deneen, William F. 1950
Dennes, William J. 1952
Dennis, Frederic W. 1924
Derrick, Robert C. 1929
Dettlinger, Frederick W., Jr. 1961
Devers, John J., Jr. 1971
DeView, Harden W. 1966
DeVisser, John H. 1920
DeVlieg, Howard R. 1950
Devoe, James E. 1918
Dewart, Timothy R. 1979
Dewey, Fred G. 1937
Dewey, Joseph A. 1955
Dewey, Victor F. 1926

DeWitt, M. C. 1918
D'Haene, Nobyn H. 1949
DiChiera, David. 1970
Dick, Allan G. 1975
Dickinson, Don M., Jr. 1926
Dickinson, Frederick. 1920
Dickinson, Selden S. 1917
Diedrich, Arthur V. 1944
Diedrich, Arthur V., Jr. 1949
Diefendorf, Harry Goodrich. 1915
Dietrich, Paul A. 1962
Diffendal, Thomas D. 1991
Dillon, William M. 1931
Dixon, E. B. 1930
Dodge, Joseph M. 1927
Doering, Harry H. 1932
Dole, Harry. 1931
Doll, James B. 1961
Dols, Harold D. 1965
Dolsen, Fred R. 1933
Donohue, John. 1942
Donovan, Edward J. 1957
Donovan, Frank J. 1964
Doody, Daniel J. 1938
Doran, Felix, Jr. 1935
Doran, Kenneth W. 1943
Dostie, Gordon P. 1972
Doughty, Edward Crosby. 1913
Doughty, Robert T. 1950
Douglas, Morgan D. 1930
Downey, Thomas J. 1982
Downey, William D. 1943
Doyle, James C. 1953
Dozier, D. Preston. 1930
Drake, Kenneth S. 1953
Dresbach, James. 1927
Dretzka, Leo. 1924
Driscoll, Jerome F. 1970

Drumpelmann, W. J. 1923
Dubey, George. 1996
DuCharme, Fred T. 1913
Dudeck, Paul H. 1951
Duff, E. Hoover. 1952
Duffield, Bethune. 1913
Duffy, R. Patrick. 1963
Dumser, John M. 1954
Duncan, Noel F. 1970
Dunham, George W. 1916
Dunham, Walter C. 1920
Dunleavy, Lawrence C. 1932
Dusenbury, George A. 1938
Dyer, James L. 1986
Dykhouse, David J. 2000
Dyle, David L. 1979
Eagan, Emmett. 1948
Eagan, P. John. 1960
Ecker, Elmo. 1932
Eckert, Edwin. 1918
Eddy, Ezra B. 1916
Eddy, Frank Woodman. 1913
Edgett, Richard J. 1969
Edlund, Herbert E. 1969
Edwards, Robert S. 1948
Edwards, V. Lee. 1966
Eklund, Coy G. 1956
Eldred, Andrew J. 1930
Eldredge, Gordon C. 1916
Eliason, Paul G. 1972
Eliason, Stephen G. 1979
Elliot, William (Bill) H. 1918
Elliott, Edwin A. 1915
Elliott, John D. 1941
Elliott, John D., Jr. 1967
Ellis, Griffith Ogden. 1916
Ellis, Guy W. 1917
Ellis, Robert. 1918
Ely, Herbert. 1914
Emerson, Philip. 1913

Emmert, John H. 1927
Emmons, Harold H., Jr. 1958
Emmons, Walter T. 1946
Endicott, Charles M. 1957
Eoff, Richard G. 1971
Esper, Fred C. 1943
Esselstyn, Horace H. 1918
Essington, George E. 1944
Esterling, Charles J. 1916
Eubanks, Henry H. 1974
Evans, E. S. 1925
Evans, James M. 1928
Evans, R. B. 1939
Ewald, Henry T. 1916
Ewing, Alonzo P. 1916
Ewing, Harold W. 1972
Ewing, Richard D. 1922
Failing, John N. 1953
Fair, Earl D. 1947
Falsone, A. James. 1979
Falzon, Lawrence C. 1997
Farley, I. Joseph. 1935
Farmer, Robert E. 1975
Farquhar, William James. 1953
Farrell, Robert P. 2003
Farrell, W. B. 1937
Faulk, Raymond B. 1948
Favorite, W. P. 1935
Fead, Maxwell E. 1935
Fedele, William J. 1981
Feikens, John. 1949
Fell, Robert T. 1960
Fellows, Waldo E. 1916
Fenkell, Richard. 2002
Ferguson, Robert R. 1946
Ferrara, Richard. 1990
Ferry, Robert R. 1937
Field, Charles B. 1937
Field, Joseph E. 1926

Field, Robert E. 1949
Fielder, John. 1996
Filiatrault, Robert M. 1974
Fink, George R. 1927
Finn, William J. 1943
Finney, Frank H. 1956
Finnie, Haldeman. 1939
Fisher, John W. M. 1933
Fisher, Lawrence Peter. 1928
Fisk, Robert S. 1965
Fitzgerald, Edward T. 1918
Fitzgerald, J. W. 1917
Fitzgerald, Richard. 1932
Fitzpatrick, John P. 1961
Fitzpatrick, Leo. 1929
Fitzpatrick, William J. 1994
Fitzsimmons, P. W. A. 1916
Flanders, Phillip R. 1943
Fleck, Robert M. K. 1980
Flint, L. J. 1931
Flintermann, Carl H. L. 1922
Flintermann, Edgar D. 1943
Flintermann, Rudolph F. 1926
Flom, Fred J. 1972
Flum, Steven. 1995
Foersterling, E. H. 1932
Foley, Paul. 1948
Follmer, Gordon R. 1986
Foran, James T. 2004
Foraker, Burch. 1927
Ford, Edgar Kay. 1913
Ford, Edsel Bryant. 1924
Ford, Emory Leyden. 1913
Ford, Harry W. 1916
Forrester, Edward J. 1976
Forrester, Kurt. 1978
Forrester, Timothy W. 1976
Forsyth, Richard A. 1926
Forsyth, Richard A., Jr. 1955
Foster, Daniel P. 1934

Fowler, Richard C. 1916
Fox, Edward W. 1943
Frabutt, Donald R. 1998
Franco, Anthony M. 1962
Frank, Michael. 1998
Frankman, Donald A. 1953
Franz, Norman G. 1963
Fraser, Stuart A. 1920
Frawley, J. E. 1939
Frayne, Richard J. 1984
Frazell, Gary L. 1973
Frazho, James M. 1964
Frear, Robert G. 1949
Freda, Donald A. 1968
Frederick, E. R. 1933
Freeman, F. J. 1927
French, Dainforth B. 1963
Freydl, Arnold D. 1944
Friedrich, Ronald N. 1965
Fritz, Richard V. 2002
Frost, Albert C., Jr. 1926
Frost, Harry W. 1913
Frost, Jack A. 1943
Frost, Leon W. 1936
Frost, Richard Burton. 1953
Fruehauf, Harry. 1941
Fruehauf, Harvey C. 1941
Frutig, Edward C. 1956
Fry, John A. 1924
Frye, George R. 1966
Frye, George R., Jr. 1947
Frye, James H. 1968
Gage, Alexander K. 1910 (founder)
Gage, R. David. 1961
Gage, Raymond D. 1955
Gage, William H. 1912
Galinis, N. Michael. 1992
Gall, Richard A. 1954
Gammicchia, Steve. 2003

Garlinghouse, John G. 1933
Garner, Richard W. 1960
Garrison, Charles H. 1917
Garrison, Robert L. 1948
Gartley, Perry C. 1929
Garvey, C. Warren. 1960
Gaston, George T. 1957
Gatward, W. A. 1948
Gaughen, Frank X. 1937
Gaughen, John B. 1930
Gebauer, Gerald J. 1961
Genter, Ralph R. 1949
Gentile, James R. 1959
George, Edwin O. 1947
George, Ralph W. 1913
Georgi, Carl, Jr. 1945
Getler, Charles. 1945
Getsinger, Ralph C. 1928
Getz, John G., Jr. 1940
Gibbs, Francis C. 1950
Gibbs, Richard. 1964
Giffen, John F. 1956
Gilbert, Glenn W. 1967
Gilbreath, W. S. 1917
Giles, J. P. 1960
Gillary, Jack E. 1964
Gillis, Gaylord W., Jr. 1947
Gillis, Philip A. 1963
Gilpin, A. W. L. 1934
Gingras, B. E. de M. 1915
Girardot, E. D. 1936
Gladding, George M. 1931
Glass, John S. 1970
Glaza, Vincent J. 1948
Glaza, William C. 1948
Gleeson, Jack W. 1955
Glover, Fred. 1920
Goebel, Fritz. 1913
Gohle, Arthur W. 1963
Goidich, Gregory A. 1966

Goodell, Michael. 1990
Goodenough, Luman Webster. 1913
Goodson, George Frederick. 1935
Gorgas, Allen W. 1999
Gorham, Marvine. 1913
Gorman, John J. 1943
Gorman, John J., Jr. 1954
Gorman, Richard C. 1933
Gotschall, Neil D. 1943
Gotshall, William W. 1952
Goudie, James Q. 1917
Gould, J. Kingsley. 1916
Grace, E. R. 1921
Graham, James M. 1972
Graham, Walker. 1947
Graham, Walter L. 1944
Graham, William H. 1925
Graham, William L. 1944
Granse, William H. 1930
Grant, Michael. 2004
Granzow, Wellington. 1939
Grawn, Carl B. 1927
Gray, Cliff F., Jr. 1955
Gray, David M. 1913
Gray, Hugh M. 1937
Gray John B. 1957
Gray, Paul R. 1913
Green, Carl M. 1915
Green, Clarence C. 1947
Green, George F. 1959
Green, Joseph H. 1957
Greenberg, Jeffry. 1987
Greene, Guy. 1921
Greene, Robert L. 1948
Greenhoe, Joe Arthur. 1949
Gregory, Francis R. 1963
Gregory, Robert F. 1979
Gregory, William Bruce. 1937

Greiner, D. James. 2000
Greko, Peter M. 1985
Grier, John C., Jr. 1935
Grierson, Elmer P. 1923
Griffiths, Albert A. 1918
Griffiths, Orville. 1924
Grigg, Stuart W. 1982
Grinnell, Lloyd G. 1928
Grix, Henry M. 1982
Gruenberg, Axel A. 1935
Grumbache, Edward S. 1940
Grunau, E. G. 1943
Gruschow, Hugo F. 1917
Grylls, H. J. Maxwell. 1910 (founder)
Grylls, John K. 1960
Grylls, John R. J. 1926
Guenther, Henry J. 1962
Guest, Edgar A. 1913
Guest, Edgar A., III. 1962
Guest, Harry. 1947
Guiney, Benjamin H. 1961
Gump, John G. 1961
Gunderson, John C. 1945
Gurry, Edmund A. 1932
Gushee, Edward T., Jr. 1956
Guske, Carl W. 1918
Gutowski, Thad A. 1983
Haass, E. W. 1918
Habel, Mark W. 1978
Haberkorn, C. Henry, Jr. 1924
Hadden, George C. 1992
Hadley, S. C. 1936
Haeussler, Hubert R. 1938
Hagman, Harlan L. 1970
Hahn, J. Thomas. 1967
Halbeisen, John F. 1957
Hale, Merle C. 1934
Hall, Robert. 1946
Hamer, Alvin C. 1935

Hamilton, L. Grant. 1926
Hamilton, N. Frank. 1920
Hamlin, A. Norman. 1993
Hammond, James. 1933
Hammond, John. 1940
Hanford, William B., Jr. 1956
Hanley, Robert J. 1972
Hanley, Stewart. 1929
Hanna, Jay Eaton. 1930
Hanna, Phil S. 1931
Hanselman, Leon H. 1956
Hanson, Lee C. 1961
Hapman, Henry W. 1949
Harfst, Richard. 1919
Harfst, Richard D. 1943
Harger, R. N. 1923
Harkins, Daniel J. 1937
Harlan, M. S. 1937
Harland, James S. 1956
Harnden, Robert M. D. 1948
Harris, Del E. 1962
Harris, George G. 1915
Harris, Graham. 1919
Harris, John J. 1915
Harris, Newton J. 1929
Hart, Albert J. 1970
Hart, John O. 1950
Hart, Leon J., Jr. 1993
Hart, Linton. 1941
Hartigan, J. J. 1932
Hartigan, John T. 1956
Hartigan, Joseph J., Jr. 1954
Hartke, J. Ward. 1944
Harty, Fillmore. 1931
Hartz, J. Fred. 1918
Harvey, John G. 1923
Harwood, Laurance J., Jr. 1954
Hassberger, J. B. 1928
Hasse, Richard D. 1950

Hastings, Harold M. 1940
Hastings, Murray. 1913
Hatcher, Thomas. 1950
Haun, Ray H. 1935
Hawkins, George F. 1981
Hawkins, Norval A. 1915
Hawksley, Christopher R. 1975
Hawley, George E. 1920
Hawley, Kenneth J. 2003
Hay, Eric V. 1943
Hayes, Joseph J. 1915
Hayes, Robert C., Jr. 1978
Hayes, Walter J. 1918
Haynes, Charles E. 1960
Haynes, Richard H. 1953
Hayward, Richard Folson. 1950
Healy, Carleton. 1962
Heaslet, James G. 1916
Heaton, E. H. 1945
Hebb, G. Kenyon. 1935
Hebb, George K. 1925
Heckel, Edward G. 1922
Hecker, C. H. 1915
Hedgcock, M. A. 1943
Hedge, Frank S. 1948
Heffernan, Robert J. 1999
Heftler, Victor R. 1934
Helfenstein, Robert R. 1961
Helmer, Harold. 1918
Henderson, Arthur D. 1955
Henderson, H. J. C. 1928
Henderson, Norman M. 1951
Henderson, Thomas W. 1911
Hendley, Robert Rex. 1953
Hendricks, William J. 1947
Hendrickson, Jack R. 1961
Hendrie, William. 1925
Hendrikson, Carl. 1987

Henritze, Richard N. 1971
Henritzy, Charles L. 1979
Henry, Thomas R. 1923
Hentkowski, Stanley L. 1978
Herbert, William H. 1914
Herbertson, Alex. 1988
Herman, Raphael. 1913
Hewat, David A. 1966
Hibbard, J. M. 1920
Hicks, Charles C. 1932
Hicks, Clarence J. 1972
Hicks, Nelson E. 1924
Higbie, Carlton M. 1927
Hill, Harold Carl. 1941
Hill, Ted. 1938
Hill, Willard S. 1911
Hilton, Charles E. 1913
Hiltz, Richard B. 1957
Hinchman, T. H., Jr. 1913
Hinkley, Arthur M. 1959
Hinks, David M. 1957
Hirschfield, Jake R. 1955
Hitchcock, Floyd G. 1929
Hitchcock, Hugh W. 1929
Hittinger, Danny N. 1973
Hoag, Donald H. 1987
Hobart, Lynn M. 1915
Hobbs, C. H. 1918
Hobill, W. E. 1918
Hodges, Theodore R. 1920
Hodges, Wetmore. 1913
Hoeft, Rudolph H. 1943
Hoensheid, Ralph J. 1944
Hoffman, Arthur R. 1943
Hoffman, Luther H. 1918
Hoffman, Martin H. 1933
Holden, James S. 1913
Holland, James G. 1926
Holley, Earl. 1919
Holliday, Joseph R. 1931

Holliday, William (Bill) F. 1917
Hollinshead, M. A. 1935
Hollinshead, Melvin A. 1951
Holmes, Harold W. 1917
Holt, Frederick Holford. 1913
Holt, William R. 1928
Holvick, Olaf, II. 1970
Holzbaugh, Earl. 1949
Hood, Roy M. 1937
Hookey, John A. 1933
Hooper, George P. 1945
Hoover, Edwin K. 1938
Hopkins, James Frederic. 1938
Horton, Donald H. 1943
Hoskins, Neal L. 1930
Hoskins, William R. 1943
Hosmer, Harry L. 1927
Hossack, Robert. 1950
Hotchkiss, Andrew D. 1926
Hougland, Allen W. 1955
Houston, Alfred J. 1961
Houston, Henry A., III. 1953
Howard, Earl C. 1918
Howard, Kenneth. 1963
Howard, Stuart A. 1917
Howard, Walter S. 1962
Howe, Howard A. 1929
Howland, William. 1918
Howse, Harry R., Jr. 1966
Howson, Charles H. 1958
Hoyt, Douglas B. 1955
Huck, Louis C. 1932
Hudson, Earl J. 1946
Hudson, Matthew J. 1950
Huegli, Wilfred A. 1957
Huff, Daniel A. 1955
Huff, James R. 1974
Huffaker, Melvin S. 1947
Hughes, Charles A. 1925

Hughes, James Bennett. 1954
Hughes, Robert T. 1955
Hughes, S. Harvey. 1926
Hull, Charles B., Jr. 1913
Hull, George M. 1960
Hume, Sam. 1917
Humpage, F. R. 1919
Hund, Henry B. 1925
Hunt, George H. 1929
Hunt, Ormond E. 1919
Hunter, Covert R. 1950
Hurttienne, Brian V. 1993
Hutchinson, B. E. 1930
Hutchinson, Donald J. 1941
Hutchinson, O. C. 1920
Hyde, Austin W. 1926
Hyde, Owen G. 1937
Ide, O. Z. 1948
Ingersoll, William M. 1971
Inglis, James. 1913
Irwin, William H. 1975
Isaacs, W. H. 1918
Ives, Charles F. 1944
Jablonski, Jerome L. 1970
Jackman, Dan. 1975
Jackman, Leon E. 1945
Jackson, James B. 1960
Jacobs, Raymond (Ray) A. 1927
Jacobs, Raymond H. 1942
Jacobs, Rex C. 1937
Jacobson, Charles L. 1941
Jacques, Thomas A. 1957
Jaglois, Joseph. 1973
James, Edward W. 1956
James, William A. 1923
Jamieson, A. Douglass. 1939
Jamieson, Charles H. 1943
Janover, Robert H. 1980
Jaques, Arden D. 1952

Jarnagin, Marvin D. 1953
Jarrett, George J. 1941
Jarvis, Alfred H. 1975
Jaynes, Richard V. 1955
Jefferies, Michael L. 1972
Jendrzejewski, Roy A. 1978
Jenkins, Donal. 1957
Jenkins, Warner Haddon. 1913
Jenkins, Warner Haddon, Jr. 1926
Jenks, Nathan. 1913
Jennings, George A. 1935
Jennings, John J. 1916
Jennings, Joseph J. 1926
Jennings, Joseph N. 1949
Jenzen, Howard E. 1970
Jesser, John H. 1961
Jewell, Frank S. 1933
Jewell, W. Ralph. 1963
Jewell, Wayne D. 1937
Jewett, A. B. 1928
Johnson, Allan R. 1953
Johnson, Charles B. 1920
Johnson, Clark C. 1976
Johnson, Courtney. 1929
Johnson, David M. 1987
Johnson, Edward W. 1943
Johnson, Homer S. 1919
Johnston, F. Earl. 1936
Johnston, George. 1935
Johnstone, William D. 1959
Jolly, Raymond P. 1970
Jones, Daniel L., Jr. 1979
Jones, Ernest A. 1943
Jones, Ezra H. 1917
Jones, Jeffrey K. 1966
Jones, Joseph M. 1943
Jones, Kensinger. 1960
Jordan, R. Gerald. 1962

Jordan, Ralph E. 1937
Jordan, Robert J. 1975
Jordan, Walter C. 1930
Jorgensen, James J. (J. J.). 1997
Joslyn, Lee E., Jr. 1930
Joswick, Edwin F. 1952
Joy, Henry Bourne. 1915
Joy, Henry B., III. 1964
Joy, Leslie W. 1957
Joy, Richard P. 1926
Joy, William E. 1917
Judge, Frank. 1952
Judge, Frank T., Jr. 1952
Judkins, Roger B. 1960
Judson, Frank H. 1947
Kackley, James E. 1974
Kaess, Fred W. 1953
Kahler, Michael. 1987
Kahn, Mitchell J. 1980
Kaiser, Webster L., Jr. 1968
Kales, Robert G. 1939
Kandt, Frederick (Frank) J. 1914
Kane, Frank G. 1918
Kanter, Charles A. 1931
Kanzler, Ernest C. 1924
Kapp, William (Bill) E. 1923
Karcher, Roy A. 1962
Katulic, Joseph. 1987
Katzenmeyer, William H. 1956
Kay, Ward R. 1988
Keane, J. E. 1920
Keen, Albert S. 1917
Keena, Kemp. 1927
Kefgen, Bruce C. 1971
Kegler, John W. 1994
Kelch, James W. 1932
Keller, John H. 1950

Keller, Leonard A. 1938
Keller, Ralph E., Jr. 1949
Keller, Sam T. 1942
Kelley, Bethel B. 1968
Kelley, Paul J. 1955
Kellogg, Mark. 1921
Kelly, Frank A. 1917
Kelly, John E. 1961
Kelly, Lawrence B. 1971
Kelly, Peter J. 1978
Kemp, Arthur J. 1944
Kemp, Edward G. 1922
Kendrick, Charles L. 1949
Kenealy, John E. 1967
Kennedy, Frank I. 1936
Kennedy, William (Bill) F. 1962
Kent, Jack. 1950
Keplinger, John C., Jr. 1941
Kernkamp, Ralph. 1943
Kerr, Harry W. 1927
Kerr, William A. 1926
Kerwin, Thomas C. 1971
Ketchum, Berrien C. 1965
Keys, John F. 1921
Khuen, Ralph F. 1931
Kilbourn, Orrin P. 1932
Killins, Charles G. 1958
Kilpatrick, Arthur W. 1926
King, Edward D. 1923
King, George C. 1913
King, John L. 1957
King, Lawrence S. 1937
King, Ralph B. 1923
King, William Grafing. 1916
Kinsey, John W. 1943
Kinsey, V. Everett. 1955
Kirby, Alfred K. 1955
Kirby, Sigmund. 1957
Kirlin, John A. 1970

Kirsch, A. John. 1972
Kiskadden, Donald S. 1925
Kitchen, Robert. 1990
Kizer, Thomas J. 1944
Klare, H. William. 1924
Klemann, Robert B. 1947
Kliebert, Devin N. 1999
Kline, Harry D. 1925
Klingler, Harry J. 1940
Kludt, W. David. 1959
Kluender, H. F. 1934
Knapp, Joseph L. 1968
Knight, Douglas H. 2005
Knight, Edward D. 1973
Knight, Frank J. 1943
Knowles, James W. 1961
Knowlson, A. T. 1917
Knudsen, S. E. 1941
Knudsen, William S. 1938
Knudson, Eric J. 1983
Kocaj, William. 1978
Koch, Henry J. 1924
Koebel, Robert F. 1956
Koether, Bernard G. 1916
Kohl, Frank. 1940
Kokowicz, Paul R. 1976
Kolle, J. L. 1930
Kreller, Edward A. 1937
Kroll, Harvey V. 1971
Krysinski, Paul E. 1995
Kubasiak, Brett T. 1986
Kuhn, Donald W. 1973
Kumler, Alden D. 1960
Kummerow, Arnold. 1983
Kunz, Armand D. 1964
Kurtz, Jeffrey S. 1975
Kurtz, Kenneth W. 1970
Lacy, Arthur J. 1935
LaDuke, John C. 1955
Lagomarsino, Chess, Jr. 1953

Lahodny, George L. 1956
Laine, Virgil M. 1963
LaKomy, David A. 1993
Lalley, W. H. 1915
Lamb, Ernest. 1920
Lamb, Frederic H. 1961
Lamb, Kenneth. 1914
Lamb, Robert E. 1945
Lamb, Woodrow L. 1960
Lamberson, Frank A. 1944
Lamparter, Carl A. 1962
Landis, Cullen. 1932
Lane, Ralph S. 1918
Lane, Thomas Edison. 1943
Lang, Neal. 1953
Langford, David W. 1977
Langworthy, Michael. 1977
LaPointe, Alexander E. 1955
Larkin, Scott J. 1983
Larned, Abner E. 1913
Larned, Charles Pierpont.
 1910 (founder)
Larsen, Everett C. 1970
Lathrop, Charles G. 1916
Laub, Kenneth D. 1916
Laudani, David A. 1969
Laughlin, C. F. 1932
Laurie, William D. 1926
Lauver, H. J. 1937
Lawless, E. T. 1932
Lawrence, A. N. 1916
Lawrence, Richard H. 1925
Lawton, J. Fred. 1918
Leak, Clarence E., Jr. 1953
Leazenby, Arthur. 1953
Leckie, George C. 1932
Ledyard, Harry. 1925
Lee, James L. 1911
Lee, John R. 1927
Leemon, Roy N. 1943

Leffler, Carey. 1965
Legge, Russell H. 1920
Leggette, R. E. 1931
LeGro, Albert L. 1919
Lehman, Ira A. 1943
Lehman, Robert C. 1936
Leib, Lawrence J. 2002
Leininger, William H. 1943
Leisinger, Lewis M. 1952
Leonard, H. Bayard, Jr. 1968
Lepper, Louis J. 1940
Lerchen, A. T. 1916
Lerchen, William Godfrey. 1911
Leslie, R.Y., Sr. 1951
Lewis, Eugene W. 1914
Lewis, Tom. 1942
Lewton, W. Neil. 1957
L'Hommedieu, C. H. 1917
Liebold, Ernest J. 1940*
Liebold, Robert H. 1950
Lilly, Paul A. 1943
Lindegren, Carl. 1925
Lindzay, Burt L. 1948
Linen, James A. 1936
Ling, Louis C. 1911
Lingeman, Carl F. 1957
Lippincott, Hall. 1945
Little, Henry G. 1953
Littlejohn, Edward. 1957
Littler, Mark D. 1954
Livingston, Ralph L. 1960
Livingstone, T. W. P. 1926
Livingstone, William A. 1916
Lodge, John Christian. 1917
Lomas, Darrell. 1999

Lombard, Cameron. 1965
Long, George W. 1956
Longley, Clifford B. 1930
Lonius, Ralph L. 1941
Loomis, Allan. 1915
Loranger, Clifford B. P. 1935
Lord, Charles B. 1945
Lord, Charles N. 1964
Lorimer, George D. 1925
Loud, Brewster. 1916
Loud, Edward E. 1926
Loud, William C. 1953
Louisell, Joseph W. 1952
Love, Harold O. 1937
Love, Robert E. 1960
Lovgren, Kenneth C. 1948
Lowe, W. B. 1920
Lowe, Walter C. 1966
Lowery, P. C. 1929
Lowrie, Frederick L. 1924
Lucas, John D. 1934
Luce, Barnard C. 1917
Luchtman, Louis J. 1956
Ludlam, T. R. 1917
Ludwig, William R. 1975
Lukas, Stephen. 1971
Lundell, Arvid. 1952
Lundell, Carl Philip. 1960
Lundgren, Clifford L. 1954
Lungershausen, Arnold W. 1955
Lunghamer, Joseph E. 1966
Lupiloff, Steven. 1987
Luther, W. G. 1937
Lyons, Raymond M. 1948
Lytle, George D. 1956

---

* Liebold is listed in the club records simply as "E. G. Liebold," but the address matches an Ernest J. Liebold in the City Directory.

Macauley, Alvan. 1911
MacDonald, Glenn. 1944
MacDonough, William A. 1939
MacEdward, Gordon K. 1928
MacFarland, Edward W. 1941
MacFarlane, H. M. 1922
MacGlashan, L. C. 1953
MacGlashan, William. 1917
MacInnes, Peter A. 1970
Mack, Douglas. 1997
Mack, Harry. 1925
Mack, Joseph. 1916
MacKenzie, John. 1948
Macklin, Charles. 1920
MacLachlan, William. 1918
MacMahon, Charles H. 1923
MacManus, Theodore F. 1913
MacPherson, G. B. 1948
MacRae, Charles B. 1964
Madej, Joseph S. 1982
Madge, A. L. 1960
Maenza, Steven L. 1956
Magnuson, Arnold N., Jr. 1966
Malcomson, George W. 1928
Malott, Andrew Lorne. 1935
Malow, A. F. 1943
Manning, John C. 1920
Manos, James A. 1973
Manson, Roy C. 1920
Manton, W. P. 1917
Manton, Walter. 1920
Mapletoft, Kenneth E. 1960
Mara, W. A. 1923
Marco, Larry. 1966
Marco, Phillip. 1953
Mardney, Patrick A. 1981
Maree, Andrew M., Jr. 1928
Marentette, Lloyd R. 1944

Marks, Oliver D. 1944
Marschner, F. W. 1940
Marsden, Thomas J. 1926
Marsh, Howard R. 1919
Marshall, Douglas W. 1984
Marshall, Norton C. 1951
Marshall, Richard B. 1937
Martin, Douglas B. 1948
Martin, Frank V. 1918
Martin, Hugh. 1930
Martinek, C. Edward. 1937
Mason, George. 1931
Mason, Harry B. 1917
Mason, Richard. 1999
Matheson, Charles W. 1926
Mathews, Mark. 1939
Mattimore, W. J. 1924
Maunders, James Thomas. 1953
Maurer, Michael T. 1971
Mauser, Ferdinand F. 1968
May, Arthur A. 1933
May, Charles R. 1962
Maynard, Horace S. 1932
Mayo, William Benson. 1930
McAllister, Frank D. 1946
McAlpine, Archibald Duncan. 1926
McBrearty, William J. 1935
McCabe, Gordon E. 1953
McCabe, John C. 1968
McCann, Matthew A. 1959
McCauley, William Thomas, Jr. 1971
McClelland, Carl C. 1930
McClennan, George W. 1961
McClintock, James I. 1933
McCord, Darris P. 1975
McCulloch, Marc L. 1983
McCullough, Howard. 1952

McCullough, William D. 1918
McDonald, Allan Dunning. 1928
McDonald, Allan W. 1918
McDonald, Donald Fraser. 1936
McDonald, Harry A. 1926
McDuffee, Gregory R. 1973
McEvoy, James. 1932
McFawn, Joseph J. 1929
McFawn, William T. 1926
McFeely, Charles A., Jr. 1955
McFellin, Atlee C. 1946
McGaughey, William H. 1941
McGill, C. C. 1929
McGinn, Neil D. 1929
McGuire, Matthew. 1995
McHattie, William A. 1948
McHenry, Frank R. 1932
McHenry, John C. Thomas. 1975
McIntosh, Julian G. 1949
McIntyre, Donald G. 1969
McIntyre, Francis J., Jr. 1955
McIver, Stephens. 1917
McKay, Arch. 1937
McKay, Timothy. 1985
McKee, J. L. 1943
McKee, Ronald T. 1952
McKee, Walter V. 1923
McKenna, Robert A. 1966
McKinney, Herbert R. 1929
McKinney, L. LeRoy. 1952
McLean, Cameron. 1925
McLellan, R. Malcolm. 1948
McLeod, N. H. F. 1932
McLeod, W. C. Gordon. 1930
McMahon, George P. 1917
McMahon, Maurice H. 1918
McMaster, E. E. 1916

McMechan, Jervis B. 1966
McMillan, James. 1943
McNair, Russell A. 1933
McNamara, Emmett J. 1947
McNamara, John F. 1950
McPherson, Mark F. 1982
McRae, Milton A. 1911
McShane, J. Michael. 1978
Meadon, Joseph. 1916
Means, Cyril C. 1949
Meldrum, Bernard. 1950
Mellish, Charles F. 1924
Mello, Robert M. 1963
Mengden, Joseph M. J. 1962
Mercier, Lawrence C. 1958
Mercier, Michael L. 1981
Mercier, Peter J. 1961
Mercier, Thomas H. 1955
Meredith, Newland. 1916
Merker, Harvey M. 1923
Merker, Henry M. 1947
Merlo, Michael C. 1973
Merriam, DeWitt H. 1920
Merriam, Seward L. 1920
Merrill, William W. 1941
Metzger, Hoyt. 1935
Meyer, Frederick J. 1977
Mezey, Clifford W. 1956
Mijatovic, Milan (Moose). 2005
Mike, Gerald J. 1976
Milbrand, Otto. 1951
Miles, Leon E. 1958
Miller, Bruce E. 1956
Miller, Edwin L. 1924
Miller, George D. 1934
Miller, Gerald E. 1937
Miller, Gordon H. 1945
Miller, John. 1931
Miller, Norman L. 1962

Miller, Ray. 1944
Miller, Richard R. 1968
Miller, Robert F. 1937
Miller, Sidney T. 1913
Miller, Sidney T., Jr. 1924
Miller, Thomas C. 1971
Miller, W. A. C. 1911
Miller, W. A. C., Sr. 1920
Miller, W. Leslie. 1934
Miller, William A. C., III. 1935
Milligan, R. E. 1944
Mills, Joseph B. 1920
Mills, Russell H. 1928
Milroy, George S. 1963
Miners, Michael (Mickey) Case. 1994
Minge, LaVerne (Verne) W. 1946
Miotke, Ronald. 2003
Mitchell, C. Piquette. 1913
Mitchell, D. R. 1931
Mitchell, Harry T. 1936
Mitchell, Kyle W. 1974
Mitchell, Louis. 1975
Mitchell, W. Ledyard. 1920
Mockler, Stanton G. 1967
Moehlman, Arthur B. 1919
Moffett, William A. 1949
Mog, H. J. 1943
Mohrhoff, William H. 1943
Moler, Harry A. 1943
Molyneux, Richard F. 1949
Monaghan, George F. 1915
Monahan, E. C. 1934
Mongan, J. Michael. 1983
Monihan, John Guy. 1918
Monley, Christopher G. 1983
Monley, Richard P. 1960
Montgomery, Jeffrey M. 1975
Montgomery, John. 1966

Montgomery, John C. 1934
Montgomery, John O. 1966
Moock, Harry G., Jr. 1948
Moody, George Taylor. 1913
Moon, M. B. 1913
Moons, D. C. 1992
Moore, Arnold D. 1926
Moore, Jerry. 1951
Moore, Kenneth A., Jr. 1961
Moran, J. Bell. 1926
Moran, John. 2004
Morand, Louis J. 1934
Morang, Elmer N. 1943
Morang, Michael D. 1975
Morgana, Charles. 1927
Morley, Warren A. 1925
Morris, Harold L. 1931
Morrison, Frank A. 1944
Morse, Anthony J. 1958
Morton, Henry J. 1942
Moseman, Edward N. 1931
Moss, William E. 1926
Motley, Arthur H. 1934
Motley, Ralph Earl. 1951
Mountz, Myron B. 1968
Moyer, Arthur W. 1915
Mueller, Douglas H. 1962
Muer, Joseph W., Jr. 1958
Muir, W. Howie. 1913
Mulford, Ora J. 1916
Mullen, Frank J. 1938
Mumford, Samuel C. 1920
Munce, Hugh V. 1974
Munz, C. E. 1940
Murawski, Craig A. 1979
Murdock, Robert M. 1955
Murphy, Charles Hayward. 1911
Murphy, Henry T. 1925
Murphy, J. Harold. 1927

Murphy, John E. 1917
Murphy, L. F. 1920
Murphy, Michael Joseph. 1926
Murphy, Ralph E. 1943
Murphy, Robert J. 1961
Murphy, Thomas F. 1918
Murphy, William H. 1923
Murray, William J. 1978
Muzzy, H. Gray. 1930
Myers, Charles L. 1967
Myers, Clarence. 1943
Myers, L. C. 1938
Nagle, Donald R. 1966
Nagle, Paul. 1949
Naumann, Gerard O. 1955
Navin, Charles F. 1927
Nawrocki, Henry E. 1974
Neebe, Joseph H. 1920
Nelson, Dwight M. 1954
Nelson, Frederick B. 1947
Nelson, Henry M. 1986
Nelson, John W. 1955
Nesi, Christopher. 2002
Newberry, Phelps. 1923
Newberry, Truman Handy. 1926
Newkirk, Dallas E. 1956
Newkirk, Robert C. 1955
Newman, Henry L. 1942
Nicholay Paul. 1925
Nichols, John A., Jr. 1924
Nicholson, Donald F. 1960
Nicholson, Walter G. 1916
Nielson, Aage E. 1955
Nigro, Don J. 1954
Nigro, Ray. 1956
Niles, George S. 1975
Nimmo, Harry M. 1913
Nixon, Geoffrey G. 1986
Noble, Sheldon R. 1926

Nolan, Fred A. 1931
Noonan, Dermott. 1955
Norton, Chauncey C. 1959
Nutten, Clyde V. 1944
Nyland, Neal. 1934
Nyman, Lloyd C. 1944
Oakman, Carl Shepherd. 1911
O'Brien, Terrence A. 1974
O'Connor, Arthur C., Jr. 1938
O'Connor, R. D. 1961
O'Daniel, Patrick. 1972
O'Dea, J. M. 1917
Odenweller, Charles J. 1960
Oderman, H. S. 1934
O'Heron, Russell C. 1951
Ohliger, Willard. 1915
O'Keefe, Howard G. 1956
O'Leary, J. Robert (Bob), III. 1996
Olmsted, John G. 1976
Olsen, A. E. 1934
O'Neal, Albert E. 1963
Oostdyk, Charles A. 1944
Opie, Robert J. 1960
Orr, William R. 1913
Ortved, Niels C. 1931
Osborn, Wayne R. 1955
Osgood, Bradley T., II. 1978
Osgood, Denne. 1975
Osgood, Milton, III. 2000
Osgood, Milton B., Jr. 1995
Osgood, Richard E. 1956
O'Shea, Arthur W. 1978
Osius, Richard J. 1966
Osius, Theodore S. 1942
Osten, Frederic C. 1958
Osterhous, George C. 1916
Otter, Clarence E. 1920
Ottevaere, Donald G. 1973
Ottevaere, James A. 1978

Otto, C. Carroll. 1944
Otto, Walter E. 1936
Overesch, F. W. 1929
Owen, Ernest W. 1943
Owen, John L. 1958
Owen, Percy. 1916
Owen, Ramon L. 1963
Oxtoby James Veech. 1923
Oxtoby, Walter Ewing. 1916
Pabst, Norman A. 1914
Packer, John H. 1956
Packer, W. M. 1943
Palazzolo, Thomas. 1990
Palazzolo, William. 1997
Palmer, Bruce. 1937
Palmer, C. Williams. 1942
Palmer, George B. 1936
Palmer, Louis G. 1928
Palms, Charles Louis. 1911
Parcells, Charles A. 1920
Parcells, Charles A., Jr. 1954
Park, A. Colton. 1945
Park, John E. 1950
Parker, Charles M. 1911
Parker, Frank D. 1957
Parker, George E., Jr. 1943
Parker, Walter E. 1925
Parks, William N. 1964
Parmeter, Rolland C. 1916
Parnell, Emory. 1931
Passmore, John J. 1961
Patch, Charles O. 1915
Paterson, Edmund T. 1946
Paterson, Hamilton H. 1932
Patterson, Robert R. 1942
Patterson, W. Calvin. 1936
Peabody, Horace Baxter. 1911
Peabody, Witter J. 1913
Peacock, Henry W., Jr. 1968
Pearce, Harry. 1987

Pearce, Russell G. 1916
Pearse, Bernard (Bud) P. 1950
Pearse, Christopher W. 1972
Pearse, Paul T. 1965
Pearson, Alan H. 1920
Pearson, Ray C. 1981
Pease, Marshall. 1915
Peckham, Judson. 1940
Peed, L. G. 1930
Pehrson, Ralph S. 1956
Peirce, Thomas H. 1957
Pelletier, E. LeRoy. 1918
Peloso, Thomas. 1989
Peltier, Ray D. 1956
Peltier, Raymond D. 1976
Pelton, Chauncey R. 1923
Penrose, Clement A., Jr. 1937
Perakes, Dan. 1988
Pericin, John A. 1958
Perkin, Frank S. 1937
Perkins, Ralph A. 1925
Perring, Raymond T. 1944
Perron, Francis J. 1951
Perry, T. Stanley. 1923
Peters, Earl J. 1952
Peters, James H. 1956
Peters, John O. 1947
Peters, Thomas R. 1965
Petersen, Donald J. 1998
Peterson, Douglas Alden. 1980
Peterson, Edwin R. 1966
Pettey, Robert. 1987
Pew, Frederic C. 1936
Pfeffer. C. A. 1916
Phelps, George Harrison. 1921
Phillips, Robert J. 1972
Phillips, T. Glenn. 1916
Pierce, Harold M. 1943

Pierce, Howard O. 1921
Pierce, T. H. 1957
Pierrot, George F. 1933
Pike, Charles Sumner. 1920
Pillon, James A. 1963
Pinckard, Karl G. 1935
Pingree, Everett W. 1920
Pingree, Roy Edward. 1913
Pinney, N. Earl. 1943
Piper, Walter C. 1926
Pirrami, Geno. 1984
Pitkin, Maxwell I. 1923
Plaggemeyer, H. W. 1922
Plath, John J. 1917
Platt, Richard. 1977
Platten, Arthur J. 1937
Platts, Charles L. 1945
Plaun, Karl Eric. 1976
Poehle, Herbert F. 1954
Poinier, Arthur B. 1943
Pollard, William. 1943
Popham, Edmond W. 1951
Popowitz, Theodore. 1960
Porath, Edward W. 1943
Porter, Christopher. 2006
Pott, Christopher. 1993
Potter, Louis B. 1962
Potter, Ray L. 1950
Potter, Robert B. 1911
Potter, Walter N. 1944
Potthoff, Douglas J. 1974
Potts, Charles H., Jr. 1956
Power, William S. 1923
Powers, Joseph A. 1958
Powers, Robert Bruna. 1935
Prendergast, John J. 1935
Prescott, Joel H. 1929
Pressman, Warner. 1974
Price, Frank E. 1917
Price, Gordon A. 2003

Priebe, Edward J. 1999
Priehs, George W. 1956
Priest, R. Walter. 1943
Primost, Stephen C. 1973
Pringle, Andrew C. 1945
Provenzano, Nunzio. 1987
Pulcher, Martin L. 1917
Purdy, C. H. 1916
Purdy, Remington J. 1945
Purdy, Remington J., Jr. 1980
Puthuff, Edgar R. 1968
Putnam, Jack S. 1957
Putnam, Leslie C. 1941
Quakenbush, Howard M. 1943
Quirk, Daniel L. 1918
Quirk, Daniel L., Jr. 1929
Rader, Todd A. 2003
Radlick, Alan R. 1972
Radtke, Leonard O. 1966
Rahm, Phillip L. 1960
Rampp, Louis Edward. 1953
Ramsey, John J. 1929
Ramsey, Louis J. 1965
Ramstrum, Eric P. 1948
Ramstrum, Gunnar G. 1945
Ranger, Edward M. 1968
Raseman, Richard P. 1939
Rasmussen, Douglas J. 1970
Rast, James L. 1956
Rathbun, Robert R. 1961
Rea, V. Benton. 1942
Reading, Richard W. 1939
Reaume, Leonard P. 1926
Reck, Franklin M. 1937
Reddick, Joseph R. 2001
Redding, Peter J. 1991
Redebaugh, G. Arthur. 1957
Reed, J. Theodore. 1911
Reed, Paul F. 1968

Reeme, Clyde H. 1950
Reihmer, Richard A. 1987
Remick, Jerome H. 1913
Remillet, John J., Jr. 1953
Remus, Stanley R. 1983
Renaud, Laverne B. 1960
Renick, John B. 1971
Rexford, Walton K. 1931
Reynick, Henry F. 1921
Reynolds, Harry N. 1916
Reynolds, R. P. 1940
Rhoades, Thomas P. 1950
Rhoades, Thomas P., Jr. 1980
Ricard, Roland J. 1972
Rice, Nelson E. 1949
Rich, Herbert M. 1921
Richardson, Fred W. 1936
Richardson, G. F. 1934
Rickel, John M. 1966
Rickenbacker, Capt. Eddie V. 1923
Riddell, Wilfred A. 1968
Ridenour, George W. 1922
Riley, Wilfred J. 1950
Rinehart, T. Mel. 1935
Rinsche, Frank C. 1925
Rives, Kent K., Jr. 1960
Robb, David. 1972
Robb, W. C. 1931
Roberts, Aubrey C. 1955
Roberts, Charles E. 1987
Roberts, Preston. 1929
Robertson, B. Frank. 1915
Robertson, James M. 1955
Robertson, Willard. 1961
Robertson, Woody. 1984
Robinson, Frederick (Fred) R. 1916
Robinson, L. J. 1915
Robinson, Lewis S. 1930
Robinson, Loren T., Jr. 1951
Robinson, Loren T., Sr. 1917
Robinson, T. E. 1929
Robinson, William C. 1960
Robinson, William L. 1952
Robinson, William L., Jr. 1979
Rochm, Charles M. 1924
Rodger, Robert M. 1957
Rogala, David M. 1977
Roger, Michael K. 1991
Rogers, Edward F. 1969
Rogers, Roger M. 1944
Rogind, Hans. 1961
Rohloff, Douglas F. 1969
Rohloff, Willard (Bill) A. 1952
Rohrbach, Richard G. 1959
Rolinson, Fairbank F. 1947
Rolinson, Sam S. 1948
Rollins, Fred H. 1946
Romaine, Arthur J. 1937
Romaine, William W. 1937
Roney, Edward C. 1940
Roney, Edward C. 1985
Roney, Richard B. 1959
Rose, Arthur L. 1918
Rose, Howard J. 1949
Ross, O. Richard. 1972
Rothang, Donald W. H. 1953
Rowland, R. M. 1933
Roy, Hubert F. 1934
Ruda, Charles R. 1986
Rueger, Carlisle F. 1954
Ruelle, Alexander, III. 1931
Ruffner, Frederick G., Jr. 1991
Ruffner, L. Chapin. 1916
Ruffner, Peter E. 1990
Rumbaugh, LeRoy 1954
Rumney, Mason P. 1922
Russel, George B. 1925
Russel, Henry. 1915

Russel, Philip S. 1927
Russel, Walter S. 1911
Russell, Donald M. 1943
Russell, John Ross. 1913
Russell, Sidney. 1923
Russell, William C. 1953
Russo, Anthony A. 1954
Ryan, Louis W. 1935
Sage, Thomas. 1950
Sajewski, Charles J., Jr. 1978
Sales, Murry W. 1926
Sample, Morris DeFrees. 1920
Samuel, Ronald G. 1970
Sanford, Frederic L. 1924
Sanford, James S. 1969
Sanford, Sterling S. 1966
Sanger, Harry H. 1924
Sapere, Arthur J. 1976
Saunders, Fred W. 1931
Saunders, Murray. 1934
Savage, George L. 1964
Savidge, Myron H. 1955
Sawitzky, Lawrence F. 1947
Sawyer, Donald E. 1985
Sawyer, W. Whitney, Jr. 1947
Schaefer, A. Leslie. 1967
Schafer, Jack. 1946
Schafer, Robert L. 1960
Schaltenbrand, Robert A. 1972
Schan, Robert. 2003
Schantz, Arnold Augustus. 1915
Scherer, John A. 1970
Schiffer, Robert E. 1959
Schindler, William S. 1963
Schlotman, Joseph B. 1916
Schmitt, W.J. 1929
Schneider, Edward (Ned) N. 1956
Schneider, Louis James. 1954
Schotanus, P. 1933
Schram, Ross. 1920
Schroat, Martin N. 1971
Schrom, Donald R. 1987
Schuller, Walter. 1957
Schulte, Leo J. 1960
Schultz, Jeremy C. 2004
Schwab, Richard O. 1979
Schwartz, Conrad P. 1987
Schwarzer, Harry D. 1975
Schweikart, William E. 1949
Scoles, Glenn R. 1975
Scott, E. Ray. 1967
Scripps, William E. 1932
Scripps, William John. 1937
Scully, Arthur J. 1925
Scully, David A. 1926
Seagrave, Fred. 1916
Sedlacek, Karel. 2000
Seegar, Lockwood B. 1956
Seeley, D. Jack. 1972
Seely, Arthur H. 1955
Seifeldine, Rageh. 1998
Seiffert, Karl. 1952
Seitz, Frederick W. 1955
Selby, H.G. 1933
Seldon, Harry M. 1929
Seltzer, Frederick W. 1979
Sevald, William T. 1963
Shaeffer, George B. 1933
Shafter, Royce R. 1935
Shanahan, C. Richard. 1950
Shannon, John L. 1944
Shannon, Richard. 1947
Shappelle, Richard A. 1920
Sharette, Roland J. 1967
Sharkey, Eugene. 1931
Sharrock, Norman W. 1938
Shaw, Charles P. 1917

Shaw, Danny W. 1979
Shearer, Charles E. 1946
Sheilds, C. John. 1920
Sheill, Donald A. 1979
Shelden, Alger (Al), Jr. 1950
Shelin, Kenneth. 1987
Sheridan, John J. 1957
Sherman, W. L. 1949
Sherwood, David, Jr. 1998
Sherwood, David G., III. 1999
Sherwood, L. C. 1918
Sherwood, Michael. 1997
Sherwood, Myron L. 1949
Shiel, Samuel Ashe. 1998
Sholty, Lester J. 1959
Shower, Charles J. 1943
Shuart, H. H. 1928
Shude, F. William. 1958
Shuell, Frank W. 1923
Shuler, Thomas H. 1955
Shumaker, Elliott. 1954
Shurley, Burt R. 1913
Sibley, Mark M. 1920
Sidor, Stanley J. 1970
Simms, Leonard. 1935
Simon, Cedric G. 1964
Simonds, Ralph W. 1973
Simpson, H. Lee. 1925
Simpson, Howard L. 1916
Sincere, Victor W. 1944
Sinclair, R. Sidney. 1963
Sinclair, Timothy R. 1968
Sinischo, William R. 1978
Sisson, Franklin G. 1966
Skaff, George. 1976
Skerrett, W. H. W. 1926
Skillman, Harry. 1915
Skillman, Harry, II. 1940
Skillman, Newton. 1924
Slade, Blount. 1942

Slade, Sam I. 1915
Slocum, George M. 1916
Slutz, Donald. 1937
Slyfield, Henry S. 1929
Small, Sidney R. 1913
Smart, Douglas L. 1946
Smith, A. Laurence. 1914
Smith, A. Mark. 1937
Smith, Brian J. 1983
Smith, Budd F. 1974
Smith, Charles O. 1922
Smith, Craig R. 1920
Smith, Creon D. 1995
Smith, David R. 1961
Smith, Don B. 1944
Smith, E. Merrill. 1918
Smith, Frank G. 1915
Smith, Fred Louis. 1911
Smith, George H. 1942
Smith, H. K. 1938
Smith, Hal C. 1918
Smith, Hal Horace. 1919
Smith, Harry C., Jr. 1960
Smith, Heber H. 1913
Smith, Hiram K., Jr. 1941
Smith, Howard F. 1928
Smith, J. Meredith. 1960
Smith, James Cosslett. 1913
Smith, Lawrence L. 1998
Smith, Lawrence P. 1914
Smith, Oscar W. 1923
Smith, Willard S. 1960
Smock, Adam. 1998
Smyly, John B. 1955
Sneckenbergter, Robert C. 1966
Snell, Lawrence W., Jr. 1926
Snook, Harold R. 1944
Snow, Neil W. 1913
Snowday, H. Terry, Jr. 1956

Snyder, James W., Jr. 1974
Snyder, W. Howard T. 1939
Sobson, Henry H. 1967
Southcott, John J., III. 1971
Southcott, John J., Jr. 1971
Sovereign, Otto E. 1931
Sowden, Richard M. 1945
Spadea, Joseph R. 1937
Spain, Charles C. 1923
Sparling, Ralph. 1923
Spaulding, Oliver. 1935
Spayde, S. H. 1939
Spears, Robert S. 1954
Speed, John J. 1948
Spence, H. Wibert. 1918
Spencer, Donald R. 1951
Spencer, Herbert, Jr. 1950
Spencer, R. S. 1920
Spink, Shepard. 1935
Spitzley, Joseph H. 1946
Spivak, Peter B. 1968
Sreenan, Charles M. 1931
St. Amour, Ronald J. 1986
St. Clair, John P. 1935
St. John, Raymond A. 1946
Stadler, William L. 1935
Staffeld, Stanley E. 1937
Staley, John W. 1915
Stalker, David D. 1958
Stalker, Peter, II. 1960
Standart, R. W., Jr. 1916
Standart, William Esty. 1916
Stander, Mel S. 1952
Stander, Richard B. 1970
Standish, James D., Jr. 1927
Standish, William Colburn, Jr. 1947
Standish, William Colburn (Olie), Sr. 1913
Stanek, John D. 1982

Stanten, John P. 1976
Stapleton, David W. 1949
Stark, George W. 1915
Starkman, Steven. 1992
Starling, William F. 1943
Starynchak, Thomas. 1988
Stearns, Frederick Kimball. 1913
Stearns, Frederick Sweet. 1910 (founder)
Steele, Charles M. 1914
Steffke, Glenn T. 1968
Steltenkamp, Charles J. 1990
Stephens, Sidney E. 1945
Stephenson, Bertram S. 1925
Stephenson, E. C. 1946
Stevens, Clark H. 1935
Stevens, Henry G. 1913
Stevens, Mark C. 1966
Stevens, William Carter. 1971
Stevens, William P. 1915
Stevenson, Morley S. 1974
Stewart, Carl. 1943
Stewart, Maitland N. 1968
Stewart, Oscar F. 1953
Stewart, R. P. 1941
Stewart, Robert D. 1945
Stieber, Donald A., Jr. 1983
Stiebling, James K. 1964
Stirling, Robert B. 1913
Stobbe, G. Dorr. 1962
Stockmeyer, Steven F. 1969
Stockwell, Robert G. 1962
Stoetzer, Gerald L. 1956
Stoetzer, James B. 1969
Stone, Ferris D. 1937
Stone, J. Blinn. 1921
Stouffer, R. A. 1936
Stoughton, Edwin R. 1911
Strasburg, James. 1911

Stretch, Harold A. 1931
Striker, Francis H. 1940
Stringer, Charles A. 1914
Stringham, Joseph S. 1911
Stroble, George C. 1917
Stroh, Bernard, Jr. 1913
Stroh, Edwin R. 1913
Stroh, Gari. 1918
Sturman, Robert H. 1981
Suhrheinrich, Richard F. 1971
Sukert, Lancelot. 1924
Sullivan, Edward F. 1953
Sullivan, John M. 1950
Sullivan, Michael J. 1974
Sullivan, Paul. 1943
Sullivan, Robert F. 1965
Sutherland, J. M. 1942
Sutherland, Paul M. 1943
Sutter, David M. 1946
Swain, Walter S. 1916
Swan, James R. 1915
Sweeney, Theodore J., Jr. 1982
Sweet, Thurlow L. 1963
Swenson, Charles E. 1957
Swift, N. Parker. 1943
Talman, William W. 1910 (founder)
Talman, William W., Jr. 1937
Tannahill, R. B. 1917
Tappan, Bruce N. 1942
Tarnow, Richard. 2004
Tatti, Michael R. 1998
Taylor, David H. 1963
Taylor, David S. 1972
Taylor, Douglas L. 1978
Taylor, Jack R. 1974
Taylor, Orla B. 1913
Teagan, J. Gerard. 1991
Tempest, R. W. 1928
Templeton, Marshal E. 1970

Tenerowicz, John F. 1970
Terns, John B. 1919
Terry, Charles W. 1917
Teske, Thomas E. 1975
Texter, E. Clinton. 1946
Texter, Elmer C. 1938
Theobald, Carl J. 1965
Thom, George H., Jr. 1955
Thorn, Greg R. 1972
Thomas, Burt R. 1922
Thomas, Fay M. 1943
Thomas, Frederick W. 1913
Thomas, Henry A. 1922
Thomas, L. Murray. 1964
Thomas, Luther. 1924
Thomas, Ralph. 1940
Thomas, Reginald. 1966
Thomas, Richard W. 1927
Thomas, Walter L. 1962
Thomas, Willis P. 1941
Thompson, Harold. 1950
Thompson, Hayward S. 1927
Thompson, Walter. 1926
Thomsen, Howard J., Jr. 1972
Thomson, J. Russell. 1917
Thorburn, Albert J. 1960
Thorburn, Donaldson B. 1955
Thornhill, John L. 1948
Thurston, Harrison E. 1927
Thweatt, Melvin M. 1952
Tiedemann, A. C., Jr. 1938
Tigchon, John H. 1926
Tintinalli, John. 1999
Tobin, Benjamin F., Jr. 1927
Todd, Guerin, Jr. 1952
Todd, John. 1944
Todd, Michael W. 1920
Todd, William M., Jr. 1951
Todhunter, John A. 1973
Toepel, Frederick A. 1948

Tomlinson, Edwin A. 1937
Toms, Robert (Bob) M. 1918
Toner, T. J. 1920
Toppin, Clare I. 1946
Torma, J. Arnold. 1970
Toro, Carlos E. 1956
Towers, Walter K. 1917
Tracy, William R. 1929
Traicoff, Michael G. 1970
Traverso, Peter V. 1954
Travis, DeHull N. 1927
Travis, Frederick I. 1975
Treder, Paul F. 2001
Trego, Carroll. 1925
Trendle, George W. 1919
Trendle, George W., Jr. 1968
Trent, David Michael. 1979
Trese, Earl. 1920
Trible, W. C. 1916
Trix, Herbert. 1923
Trombly, Barry A. 1985
Trout, Donald M. 1965
Trowbridge, Luther Stephen, Jr. 1913
Trube, Robert D. 1997
Truesdell, Alfred L. 1951
Truettner, Walter F. 1929
Trump, Hal G. 1920
Tuchow, Gerald. 1983
Tucker, Edward. 1936
Tucker, Vernon W. 1915
Tucker, William A. 1943
Tullar, Frank S. 1947
Tullock, Daniel M. 1974
Turnbull, James (Jim). 1979
Turner, Frederick C. 1980
Turner, William S., Jr. 1970
Turrell, Harry C. 1944
Tutag, Edward J. 1954
Tuttle, Carl B. 1926

Tuttle, James L. 1976
Tweedy, O. S. 1919
Tyler, Maurice L. 1973
Ulrich, Hugo. 1943
Ulrich, William J. 1943
Uridge, Owen F. 1942
Vail, Clair Fremont. 1943
Vallet, V. E. 1936
Valley, Don F. 1932
Van Allen, M. C. 1936
Van Auken, Howell. 1935
Vanderkloot, James M. 1974
Vanderkloot, M. A. 1938
VanderKloot, Robert (Bob) C. 1938
VanderKloot, William R. 1957
VanDerPyl, Robert A. 1947
Van Deusen, Francois (Fran) B. 1936
Van Deventer, Frank G. 1979
Van Dusen, C. B. 1932
Van Dyke, Frank G. 1915
Van Husen, Edward C. 1926
Vann, James Allen, III. 1983
VanOsdal, N. K. 1943
Varney, Henry R. 1917
Vary, Calvin P. 1923
Vaughan, J. W. 1921
Vaughn, Clarence S. 1923
Veauvais, Albert. 1949
Verdier, Lawrence J. 1952
Vernor, James, Jr. 1942
Vieweg, Robert A. 1978
Villerot, George E. 1938
Vincent, George C. 1975
Vincent, Jesse Gurney. 1939
Vinci, Anthony J. 1967
Viotto, John E. 1980
Voelker, Charles M. 1924
Vogler, Raymond E. 1979

Volz, William H. 1990
Von Bernthal, Hans Eric. 1961
Von dem Bussche, C. F. 1927
Von Schmittou, Rudy M. 1979
Von Wormer, Chris. 2006
Vopni, Edward R. 1962
Vossler, Albert E. 1960
Wachner, Clarence. 1955
Wade, Daniel E. 1916
Wade, James W. 1971
Wade, Thomas G. 1931
Wadleigh, Ray E. 1949
Wadsworth, Harold L. 1925
Wahl, William G. 1953
Wakevainen, John M. 1977
Walbridge, George B. 1925
Waldo, C. G., Jr. 1916
Waldon, Sidney D. 1915
Wales, A.A. 1942
Wales, Philip H. 1974
Walker, Arthur C. 1960
Walker, Gordon L. 1955
Walker, Harrington E. 1913
Walker, Harry C. 1915
Walker, James Marshall. 1917
Walker, Mickey M. 1966
Walker, Richard Earl. 1972
Walker, Roger V. 1933
Walker, Thaddeus. 1925
Walker, William T. 1928
Wall, Vincent C. 1943
Wallace, Harry L. 1923
Walter, William E. 1947
Wandschneider, Robert D. 1979
Ward, Harry T., Jr. 1976
Ward, Robert S. 1943
Wardwell, Harold F. 1913
Warner, Daniel S. 1939
Warner, H. J. 1921

Warren, Gerald E. 1952
Warren, Glen W. 1940
Warren, Wadsworth. 1916
Warrick, Charles F. 1944
Washburn, Joseph H. 1948
Waterman, Cameron B. 1913
Waterman, Ira D. 1913
Waterman, Reuben M., Jr. 1974
Watkins, Edward B. 1935
Watkins, James K. 1925
Watkins, John R. 1928
Watling, John W. 1916
Watts, C. J. 1924
Watts, John B. 1937
Wayne, Arthur. 1937
Weaver, Henry G. 1933
Weaver, W. W. 1953
Webb, Jefferson (Jeff) B. 1918
Webb, Jervis B. 1927
Webb, Joseph F. 1937
Webber, Oscar. 1923
Webster, J. O. 1936
Webster, John W. 1959
Weeks, Albert (Al) Loren. 1915
Weighell, J. E. 1917
Weikel, Charles W. 1949
Weiss, Roy J. 1944
Weitzel, Anthony. 1946
Welch, Barret F. 1941
Welday, Donald F., Jr. 1957
Weldon, James Lee. 1947
Wells, C. Thompson, Jr. 1965
Wells, Carl S. 1937
Wells, David C. 1971
Wells, Everett H. 1937
Wells, Pearson. 1918
Wells, Sidney A. 1937
Wemhoff, B. F. 1943

Wendel, Charles F. 1923
Wendell, Murray R. 1913
Wendin, Richard H. 1963
Wendin, Sigurd R., Jr. 1962
Werfelmann, George A. 1960
Wernecken, Frank E. 1925
Werner, Eduard. 1924
Werthmann, Cletus A. 1957
Wesley, Walter P. 1957
West, Eugene L. 1958
Wetherbee, R. Noble. 1938
Wheeler, Kenneth M. 1971
Whildin, W. G. 1928
Whims, Timothy A. 2001
Whitcomb, James S. 1937
White, Craig. 1985
White, H. Kirk, Jr. 1915
White, Kirby B. 1918
White, Mark R. 1999
White, R. K. 1937
White, Wayne E. 1947
Whitehead, James T. 1922
Whitehurst, Russell B. 1957
Whiting, Henry. 1930
Whitley, Bernard. 1948
Whittaker, Alfred Heacock. 1933
Whittemore, James. 1913
Whittingham, Manfred G. 1968
Wichert, Hugh A. 1953
Widger, G. Russell, Jr. 1971
Widger, William F. 1962
Wilcox, Wayne J. 1941
Wilcox, Wayne J. 1962
Wild, Robert G. 1951
Wilding, N. E. 1933
Willard, Walter E. 1960
Wille, Rudolph Jon. 1956
Williams, Arthur. 1978

Williams, Henry P. 1917
Willis, Sidney. 1929
Wilsher, Donald J. 1941
Wilson, Alfred G. 1926
Wilson, Allan F. 1941
Wilson, Burton C. 1937
Wilson, Burton C., Jr. 1948
Wilson, C. Haines. 1918
Wilson, George D. 1925
Wilson, George E. 1976
Wilson, George V. 1959
Wilson, H. Dwight, Jr. 1954
Wilson, Hansel Dwight. 1952
Wilson, Harold. 1923
Wilson, John N. 1955
Wilson, Joseph O. 1953
Wilson, Paul R. 1951
Wilson, Ralph C. 1944
Wilson, Raymond H. 1955
Wilson, Walter A. 1966
Wilt, John R. 1955
Wilton, H. L. 1917
Winningham, C. C. 1918
Winslow, Palmer E. 1917
Winstanley, Ernie. 1949
Winter, Arthur W. 1919
Winter, Leonard L. 1955
Wise, Henry D., Jr. 1948
Wismer, Otto G. 1938
Wissman, M. C. 1938
Witbeck, Ernest S. 1910 (founder)
Wolfe, Earl W. 2000
Wolfenden, Richard J. 1958
Wolff, Howard B. 1951
Wolff, William F. 1965
Wood, Bert. 1930
Wood, James J. 1981
Wood, Warren A. 1936
Woodall, H. J. 1943

Woodbridge, C. K. 1927
Woodhouse, John T. 1913
Woodruff, Fremont. 1915
Woodruff, J. Fred. 1917
Worcester, Willard S. 1929
Worden, John R. 1920
Worley, Donald M. 1955
Wormer, C. C., Jr. 1915
Wright, James W. 1954
Wright, Nathaniel C. 1922
Wright, Wynn. 1932
Wurster, Harold J. 1997
Wurzer, F. Henry. 1929
Wyatt, Harry H. 1932
Wyckoff, Richard H. 1956
Yares, Robert. 1981
Yavruian, John V. 1991
Yerkes, George B. 1918
Yerkes, Robert G. 1926
Yonker, Ralph L. 1927
Yonkers, Edward R. 1950
Yost, George C. 1948
Yost, Robert J. 1975
Young, Ben E. 1933
Young, Donald E. 1974
Young, DuBois. 1928
Young, Murray. 1954
Zander, Richard M. 1963
Zaremba, Thomas E. 1979
Zeder, Fred M. 1936
Zeese, David S., Jr. 1966
Zeunen, Lee E. 1966
Ziegfeld, William K. 1927
Zimmer, Dennis R. 1973
Zimmerman, George H. 1942
Zuber, Eugene M. 1935
Zych, Robert. 2003

# Appendix C: Famous Players

ALGER, FREDERICK MOULTON. 1913: The Alger family was one of the four leading families in Detroit in the early 1900s (the Joys, McMillans, and Newberrys were the others).[1] Frederick was also one of the early major donors to the Detroit Symphony Orchestra.[2]

ANDERSON, JOHN WENDELL. 1913: A lawyer by trade, one of Anderson's clients was the A. Y. Malcomson Coal Company, which brought him into contact with Henry Ford. Alexander Malcomson was about to become one of the original—and major—investors in the Ford Motor Company (he had 250 shares to Ford's 255). Anderson saw an opportunity to get in on the ground floor of a major investment, as his boss was helping Ford set up the company and wrote a desperate letter to his father for money to invest in the company. His father agreed, and he became the proud owner of 50 of the total 1,000 shares of stock available at the time.[3]

ANDERSON, LEE. 1918: Anderson started out as a reporter and worked his way up to editor for the *Detroit News*. He then moved into advertising: first as advertising manager for Chalmers Motor Company, then as vice-president for Hupp Motor Car Corporation, and finally as vice-president of MacManus, Inc., National Advertising Agents.[4] At one time he also had his own firm, Lee Anderson Advertising Company.

BACKUS, STANDISH. 1915: Backus was the son-in-law of Joseph Boyer, a lawyer who became president of Burroughs Adding Machine Company in 1920.[5]

BATCHELOR, EDWARD ARMISTEAD. 1920: Batchelor was a reporter for the *Detroit News* and the *Detroit Free Press*, editor for the *Free Press*, the *DAC News*, and *Detroit Saturday Night*. He later worked in advertising at Advertisers, Inc., and at Lee Anderson Advertising Company.[6]

BEATTIE, DANIEL C. 1944: Beattie worked as a scriptwriter for the WXYZ radio station, particularly on *The Lone Ranger* program. There are several connections with other Players. Dick Forsyth's son, Sandy, used to work on the shows as a child.[7] John Todd played Tonto, and George Washington Trendle was both co-owner of the station and the person who originally conceived the idea. Fran Striker developed the story for Trendle. The program began in 1933 and moved to television in 1949.[8] Beattie also worked on several other classic radio programs, including *The Green Hornet* and *Sgt. Preston of the Yukon*. The Popular Culture and American Culture associations honored him for his work when they held their convention in Detroit in April 1980.[9]

BENNETT, CHARLES D. 1917: Bennett was president of Bennett Insurance Agency.[10]

BINGAY, MALCOLM W. 1917: Bingay was a reporter for, then editor of, the *Detroit News*, and he was in charge of the London Bureau for the paper. He changed papers and became the editorial director for the *Detroit Free Press* and public relations counsel for Theodore F. MacManus, Inc. Bingay authored *Detroit Is My Own Home Town* and several journalism textbooks.[11]

BODDE, JOHN R. 1926: Bodde was a banker with People's Savings Bank and its successors.[12]

BODMAN, HENRY EDWARD. 1913: Bodman was a Detroit attorney, vice-president of Packard Motor Car Company, and a founder of the Guardian Detroit Bank, one of the banks that collapsed during the 1933 Detroit bank crisis.[13]

BOWEN, CHARLES C. 1920: Bowen was president of the Standard of Detroit Group of Insurance Companies.[14]

BOWEN, LEM W. 1913: Bowen was president of the D. M. Ferry seed company and an original investor in the Henry Ford Company (not to be confused with the Ford Motor Company), a forerunner to Cadillac Motor Car Company (the investors changed the name when Ford resigned from the company, much to the relief of the investors who could not control him).[15]

BOYER, JOSEPH. 1913: Boyer became president of Burroughs Adding Machine in 1902 and was an original investor in the Packard Motor Car Company.[16]

BOYNTON, WALTER CHANNING. 1910: Boynton worked in publishing and newspapers before becoming an advertising copywriter for Campbell-Ewald and later joined the C. C. Winningham agency as its vice-president before returning to Campbell-Ewald. The French Academy inducted him as a member for his work translating French plays and literature into English.[17]

BRENNEN, JOHN V. 1920: Brennan was a judge in the Detroit Recorder's Court during Prohibition.[18]

BRIGGS, WALTER O. 1917: Briggs was president and general manager of Briggs Manufacturing Company, which made auto bodies (they supplied Ford).[19] Briggs was also a founder of the Guardian Detroit Bank, one of the banks that collapsed during the 1933 Detroit bank crisis.[20] In 1938, Briggs became the second owner of the Detroit Tigers baseball team after he purchased it from Frank Navin. He renamed the stadium "Briggs Stadium," and it later became known as Tiger Stadium, which was last used by the team in 1999 before moving to Comerica Park.[21] For a time, he was president of the Detroit Zoological Commission.[22]

BRIGGS, WALTER (SPIKE) O., JR. 1939: In 1952, Spike resigned from the vice-presidency of Briggs Manufacturing and became president of the Tigers after his father's death. He shared ownership of the team with his mother and four sisters until the family was forced to sell four years later.[23]

BRUCKER, WILBER M. 1934: Brucker was the Republican governor of Michigan during the Depression years of 1931–32. As a young man, he served with the Michigan National Guard in the campaign against Pancho Villa and received a silver star for his accomplishments as an infantry officer in the 186th Infantry, 42nd (Rainbow) Division, during World War I.[24] After his term as governor, Brucker returned to practicing law. He was the U.S. Senate candidate that defeated Couzens in the primary in 1936, but lost the final election. In 1955, President Dwight D. Eisenhower appointed him to general counsel of the Defense Department, and later he became secretary of the army.[25]

BRUNK, CLIFFORD F. 1938: Brunk was a physician on the staffs of Children's, Harper, and Deaconness hospitals. He was also a director of the Detroit Civic Opera.[26]

BRUNK, THOMAS WALTER. 1982: Brunk is an art and architectural historian with several books to his credit: *Pewabic Pottery: Marks and Labels* (1978), *Leonard B. Willeke: Excellence in Architecture and Design* (1986), *Grosse Pointe Artists Association: Over Half a Century of Artistic Excellence in the Community* (1992). He also co-authored *Arts and Crafts Movement in Michigan, 1886–1906* (1986) with James E. Conway and Thomas K. Maher and edited by Mary Jane Hock. He is currently working on an architectural history of the homes in Indian Village in Detroit.

BUHL, ARTHUR HIRAM. 1915: Buhl was the son of Theodore De Long Buhl. He was president and manager of Buhl Sons Co. (wholesale hardware), vice-president of Parke, Davis and Co. and of the Buhl Aircraft Company, and a director of Burroughs Adding Machine Co. Later he became president of Buhl Malleable. Along with his brother, mother, and a niece, he financed construction of the Buhl Building.[27]

BUHL, THEODORE D. 1929: Theodore Buhl was the secretary of the family-owned Buhl Stamping, a metal-fabricating company, and was a major investor in the Paige-Detroit Motor Car Company.[28]

BURROUGHS, CLYDE H. 1921: Burroughs began working for the Detroit Institute of Arts when it was still the Museum of Art when he was nineteen and worked his way up to secretary and curator. He founded the Michigan Artists Exhibition at the museum, which he ran for thirty-six years until his retirement.[29] He was also president of the Association of Art Museum Directors and a founder of the Scarab Club.[30]

CADY, GUY BREWSTER. 1910: Principal founder of The Players, he ran his own advertising display business, Guy Brewster Cady and Staff, and was a partner in Cady and Wentz, direct-mail advertisers.[31]

CAMPAU, A. MACOMB. 1926: Campau was the secretary and treasurer of the family real estate and insurance company, A. M. Campau Realty Company. He was also a naval veteran from the Spanish American War onboard the *U.S.S. Yosemite*, along with fellow Players Edwin Denby, Henry B. Joy, and Truman Newberry, and he served as a naval officer during World War I.[32]

CARLSON, ROBERT W. 1997: Bob Carlson was first introduced to the Players stage by his grandfather, William, who was a member. The early theatre influence carried on into his later life. After moving to San Antonio to pursue a career in banking (he is currently a senior vice-president of Broadway Bank), Carlson became involved in the Arneson River Theatre, an open air theatre with seating on one side of the river and the stage on the other. He raised almost $ 1 million to repair it and another $1 million to set up an endowment fund. Not one to rest on his laurels, he is now trying to help the Sunken Garden Theatre, an outdoor theatre located in an old quarry.[33]

CARLSON, WILLIAM. 1944: William Carlson was a former vaudeville actor.[34]

CHALMERS, HUGH. 1915: Chalmers was fired from his position as vice-president of the National Cash Register Company in 1907, but soon he was approached by another future Player, Roy D. Chapin of Thomas-Detroit Motor Car Company. He refused the company's original offer, but the partners in Thomas-Detroit offered to change the name to Chalmers-Detroit Motor Car Company, and he was persuaded.[35] Chalmers was known for his sales technique, and it was his idea to give an "annual award to baseball's leading batter."[36] After a controversy in the first year regarding whether it should be awarded to Detroit's Ty Cobb or Cleveland's Napoleon "Larry" Lajoie (both received it),[37] Chalmers decided that the award should not be based on batting average but by a vote of the sportswriters. This developed into today's Most Valuable Player Award.[38] He also served as the first president of the reorganized Detroit Athletic Club in 1913.[39]

CHAPIN, ROY D. 1913: Chapin first made waves in the auto world when he was a mechanic/tester for Olds Motor Works. Ransom E. Olds had an idea for a publicity stunt to get people interested in travel by car. In 1902, Olds had Chapin drive a car from Detroit to New York in time for the automobile show. Part of the trip was made driving along the towpaths for the

Erie Canal, but he made New York in time. Ten years later, Chapin was president of Hudson Motor Car Company. While still at Olds in the position of sales manager, Chapin befriended Howard E. Coffin, an engineer who wanted to design a car of his own. Chapin took up the cause and set about finding interested investors. He managed to attract the interest of Erwin R. Thomas, a millionaire already involved in the auto business, and they named the car in part in his honor, Thomas-Detroit. To sell the car, he recruited Hugh Chalmers after he had left the National Cash Register Company. Not long after, Chapin and Coffin left to form Hudson Motor Car Company, where Chapin became chairman of the board. Hudson was a success, making them millionaires and allowing them to retire early. A supporter of the arts, he was also the vice-president of the Detroit Symphony Society.[40] In 1932, Herbert Hoover appointed Chapin secretary of commerce. This is somewhat ironic considering that he was a founder of the Guardian Detroit Bank, one of the banks that collapsed during the 1933 Detroit bank crisis.[41] For additional information, see J. C. Long, *Roy D. Chapin: The Man behind the Hudson Motor Car Company* (Detroit: Wayne State University Press, 2004).

CHITTENDEN, WILLIAM J. 1913: Chittenden was the manager of the Ponchartrain Hotel.[42]

CLARK, EMORY W. 1913: Clark was a banker, president of the First National Bank of Detroit, and a leader in the movement to repeal Prohibition.[43]

COFFIN, HOWARD ALDRIDGE. 1922: Coffin was the general manager of the White Star-Ohio division of the Socony-Vacuum Oil Company, Inc. (petroleum).[44]

COMSTOCK, WILLIAM A. 1923: Comstock was the governor of Michigan from 1933 to 1934. He "initiated a 3-percent sales tax to help the state out of debt."[45]

COUZENS, JAMES. 1913: Couzens was actively involved in the business of the Ford Motor Company from 1903 to 1915. In the early years, Couzens kept the company afloat, including personally selecting all of the Ford dealers.[46] In many ways, he was the real boss of the business. Norval A. Hawkins, a former sales manager of the company, gave him credit for 50 percent of the success of the company.⁴⁷ Ford was in charge of manufacturing, but Couzens had control over finance, purchasing, and sales.⁴⁸ Although both men would later take credit for the idea, it appears that Couzens was the driving force behind the Five-Dollar Day at Ford Motor. Couzens was worried about unemployed workers, particularly those who were laid off periodically during the year. Couzens talked Ford around, and the two of them convinced one of the other shareholders to support the idea (Horace Rackham), which was all the quorum needed to enact it. Not only did they determine that pay would be five dollars a day, but they also lowered the number of hours from nine to eight. This also moved the factory from two nine-hour shifts to three eight-hour shifts.⁴⁹

He left the company in 1915 when he disagreed with some of Ford's public statements about preparedness for World War I. Soon after, the mayor appointed him police commissioner, and he went on to become mayor of Detroit (1919–22). Later he was appointed to finish Player Truman Newberry's term as U.S. senator when Newberry resigned in 1922. In the following elections in 1924 and 1930, he was elected to the seat in his own right. He sought reelection and lost in 1936, but he died in office before his term expired. Couzens founded the Children's Fund of Michigan with a $10 million gift, the most impressive achievement in a long line of philanthropic acts that primarily benefited children. For more information, read his biography by Harry Barnard, *Independent Man: The Life of Senator James Couzens* (1958; repr., Detroit: Wayne State University Press, 2002).

DEMASS, ORRIN ALDEN. 1927: DeMass was a "merchant, sportsman, writer, lecturer" who did everything from mining in the Rockies to exploring in Canada to hunting in most of the states.⁵⁰

DENBY, EDWIN. 1913: Grandson of a U.S. senator and son of the first American ambassador to China, Edwin was one of the original investors in Hupp Motor Car (he provided $5,000 of the $8,500 originally invested in the company). He was also a naval veteran from the Spanish American War onboard the *U.S.S. Yosemite*, along with fellow Players A. Macomb Campau,

Henry B. Joy, and Truman Newberry,[51] He successfully ran for Congress in 1910 (against Truman Newberry), but he resigned his seat to enlist in the army during World War I. Denby is best known for his stint as secretary of the navy under Warren Harding, from 1921 to 1923, and under Calvin Coolidge, from 1923 to 1924, because of his involvement in the Teapot Dome Scandal in which Albert Fall sold naval oil reserves to his cronies.[52] Although Denby was cleared of any involvement, he was censured for not paying close enough attention to Fall's actions. Denby High School in Detroit is named for him.[53]

DENBY, GARVIN. 1913: Denby was president of Denby Truck.[54]

DICHIERA, DAVID. 1970: DiChiera is the founding general director of both the Michigan Opera Theatre in Detroit and Opera Pacific in Orange County, California. A pianist, a Fulbright Scholar, and an educator, he taught at both the University of California, Los Angeles, and Oakland University, where he was an assistant dean and then the music department chair. In 1971, he founded the Michigan Opera Theatre. In 1996, the Michigan Opera Theatre moved into the Detroit Opera House, a renovated 1922 movie palace, originally known as the Capitol, then as the Grand Circus Theatre (it is located just off of Grand Circus Park). The project began in 1988 and necessitated restoring the severely damaged interior and building the stage and support areas virtually from the ground up. The opera house is located near the theatre district and played a key part in its revival.[55] DiChiera is the son-in-law of another Player, Bob VanderKloot, who in turn was the son-in-law of Player William Knudsen.

DODGE, JOSEPH M. 1927: President of the Detroit Bank, Dodge was appointed to chair the War Department Price Adjustment Board and served as director of the Renegotiation Division for the Army Service Forces in 1943.[56] After World War II, Dodge was a financial advisor to the Supreme Allied Command and one of the architects for an economic program to rebuild Japan's economy.[57]

EDDY, FRANK WOODMAN. 1913: Eddy was vice-president of the Detroit Trust Company and the first president of the original Detroit Athletic Club.[58]

ELLIS, GRIFFITH OGDEN. 1916: Ellis was married to Ellen Winifred Scripps. He was the president of Sprague Publishing Company, which published *American Boy Magazine* (which he also edited), and was also president of William A. Scripps Company. In addition, Ellis was vice-president of the Bank of Detroit and then the Guardian-Detroit Bank. He was also Trustee for the Detroit Institute of Art.[59]

EWALD, HENRY T. 1916: An advertising pioneer, Ewald was one of the cofounders of Campbell-Ewald Company, an advertising firm that specialized in automotive advertising and grew into one of the largest advertising firms in America.[60] In addition to founding his own company, he was also one of the founders of the Adcraft Club and the National Outdoor Advertising Bureau.[61]

FINK, GEORGE R. 1927: Fink founded a securities company, with fellow Players Carlton M. Higbie and Ernest Kanzler, named Kanzler, Fink, and Higbie.[62] He was a founder of the Guardian Detroit Bank, one of the banks that collapsed during the 1933 Detroit bank crisis.[63]

FISHER, LAWRENCE PETER. 1928: Fisher began as a mechanic in his family's firm, Fisher Body. At the time General Motors bought it, he was vice-president. General Motors retained his services and eventually made him president of Cadillac Motor Car Company, and later, vice-president of General Motors.[64] In 1927, the seven Fisher brothers announced plans for the Fisher Building on Grand Boulevard, across from the General Motors Building, which later purchased Fisher Body. Designed by Albert Kahn, the building is one of Detroit's most impressive Art Deco skyscrapers. The elaborate building boasts 430 tons of bronze, including the 256 elevator doors, and forty different kinds of marble in its arcade.[65]

Fisher was also one of the first to build in the Grayhaven community, an island that was part of the Detroit shoreline on the Detroit River. This private development was designed so that every home would have a dry dock, and several would have direct access to the water. Fisher began his $1.5 million mansion in 1928 on one of the canals. Stairs led directly from the library down to the Pewabic-tiled boatwell. After being sold by Fisher's widow, eventually the Hari Krishnas purchased and renovated the building, reopening it as the Bhaktivedanta Cultural Center for the International Society for Krishna Consciousness.[66]

FITZGERALD, EDWARD T. 1918: Fitzgerald was secretary to Detroit mayors Oscar B. Marx and James Couzens.[67]

FORAKER, BURCH. 1927: Foraker was president of Michigan Bell Telephone.[68]

FORD, EDSEL BRYANT. 1924: Edsel Ford was the son of Henry Ford, president of Ford Motor Company, and a major philanthropist. Edsel grew up with Ford Motor Company, becoming president of the company in 1918 when he was only twenty-five. In addition to dealing with the expansion of the massive Rouge Complex and keeping the company's defense contracts on time during the two world wars, Edsel was actively involved in the company's experiments with aviation.[69] Before the Depression and his father interfered, Edsel's interest in aviation also extended to exploration. Admiral (then Commander) Richard E. Byrd approached Edsel seeking support for an expedition to the North Pole. Byrd wanted to be the first person to fly over the North Pole at a time when no one was even sure that planes could fly under the harsh conditions. Edsel was taken by the idea and became a contributor for both what may have been a successful flight over the North Pole in 1926 (scholars dispute whether he actually crossed the pole based on the records in his diary)[70] and one over the South Pole in 1929. While in Antarctica, Byrd named a mountain range he discovered after Edsel.[71]

Edsel's biggest area of philanthropy was not aviation but the arts. He studied painting, attended cultural events, and belonged to various arts societies. He was appointed by the mayor to the Arts Commission that oversaw the Detroit Institute of Arts (DIA) in 1925 and became its president in 1930 until his death in 1943. Edsel set up a fund at the museum in his name for the purchase of artwork, plus he and his wife, Eleanor, donated additional money for other purchases that led to the acquisition of works by a range of artists including Titian, Caravaggio, Donatello, and Raphael.[72] His generosity was not limited to purchases for the museum. During the Depression, the budget for the museum was slashed so severely that it would have been impossible to keep the doors open. Edsel donated enough money to ensure that it could, and he also provided for the publication of its monthly newsletter.

Edsel's most significant contribution of an individual piece of art was not his most expensive donation, but his most controversial. He contributed the funds for Diego Rivera to paint the murals collectively known as "Detroit Industry" on the walls of the Garden Court in the DIA. Many people were not pleased to have a Mexican communist being paid to paint the walls in a city-owned museum during the Depression, while others objected because of supposed blasphemy in one of the mural panels.[73] Edsel refused to be swayed by public opinion and insisted that the murals be left alone for future generations to decide their value.[74]

In addition, Edsel was a founder of the Guardian Detroit Bank, one of the banks that collapsed during the 1933 Detroit bank crisis.[75] Interstate 94 through Detroit is named after him. There are several good biographies of Edsel, particularly Henry Dominguez, *Edsel: The Story of Henry Ford's Forgotten Son* (Warrendale, PA: Society of Automotive Engineers, 2002) and Richard Bak, *Henry and Edsel: The Creation of the Ford Empire* (Hoboken, NJ: John Wiley and Sons, 2003).

FORD, EMORY LEYDEN. 1913: Emory Ford was vice-president and treasurer of Michigan Alkali Company.[76]

FORD, HARRY W. 1916: Ford was a sportswriter in Chicago, a member of the advertising department at National Cash Register Company, advertising manager for Chalmers-Detroit in 1908, general manager of Chalmers-Detroit by 1913 and, later that year, the president of Saxon Motor Car Company. Ford bought out the other original investors in Saxon in 1915. The company did not survive long after his death in World War I in 1918.[77]

FORSYTH, RICHARD A. 1926: Forsyth was a lawyer and the government attaché in Sweden.[78]

FOSTER, DANIEL P. 1934: Foster was a physician at Henry Ford Hospital and a director of the Detroit Civic Opera.[79]

FROST, HARRY W. 1913: Frost started out in newspaper and magazine publishing, but then moved into manufacturing of railway supplies (a significant industry in Detroit) with his own company, Frost Railway Supply.[80]

GAGE, ALEXANDER K. 1910: Gage was one of the club founders and was a lawyer who eventually became the assistant prosecuting attorney for Wayne County.[81]

GOEBEL, FRITZ. 1913: Goebel was the president of Banner Brewing Company.[82]

GRAY, DAVID M. 1913: Gray was sales manager, vice-president, and secretary of Frederick Stearns and Co. (pharmaceuticals). Both Frederick Stearnses (father and son) were also members. The junior Stearns was a founding member.[83]

GRINNELL, LLOYD G. 1928: Grinnell was married to the daughter of the president of Grinnell Brothers (a large Detroit music business). He was an assistant secretary of the company and was also director and vice-president of the International Music Festival.[84]

GRYLLS, H. J. MAXWELL. 1910: Grylls was born in England but came to the United States in 1881 when he was sixteen. He became a partner in the architectural firm of Smith, Hinchman, and Grylls in 1906.[85] A founding member of The Players, his firm designed and built the Players Playhouse and other Detroit landmarks, such as the Penobscot and Guardian buildings. This firm, now known as the SmithGroup, is still a significant architecture firm in Detroit and has several offices in large cities across the country.[86]

GUEST, EDGAR A. 1913: Guest started out at the *Detroit Free Press* as part of the bookkeeping staff and quickly moved into a reporting job working under the city editor (and Player), John C. Lodge. Newspapers once used snippets of poetry as filler. Guest tried his hand at some verses and slipped them under the Sunday editor's office door. They were printed on 11 December 1898.[87] Soon he had a weekly column, "Blue Monday Chat," and a daily column, "Breakfast Table Chat." By 1916, his poetry was nationally syndicated. His biographer described Guest's inspiration as "the common experiences, the universal emotions of the whole human race. The triumphs, the tragedies, the joys and sorrows, the moments of dignity and indignity which every man comes to know."[88] Several collections of Guest's poetry were published: *Home Rhymes*

(1909), *Just Glad Things* (1911), *Breakfast Table Chat* (1913), and *A Heap O' Livin'* (1916). In addition, he wrote plays, was a radio announcer, and briefly had a television show. He was beloved enough in Michigan to have the Michigan legislature unanimously pass a resolution designating him as Michigan's poet laureate.[89] In addition, mayors of Detroit proclaimed several "Eddie Guest Days."

HASTINGS, HAROLD M. 1940: Hastings was an advertising executive who worked for Hudson Motor Car Company; Power, Alexander, and Jenkins (an advertising agency); and the C. C. Winningham Advertising Agency. He was secretary and manager of the Adcraft Club.[90]

HAWKINS, NORVAL A. 1915: The first general sales manager for Ford Motor Company, Hawkins "was credited with being the genius who, under James Couzens, perfected the great Ford sales organization and made the Ford Motor Co. the wonder of the world."[91]

HEASLET, JAMES G. 1916: Heaslet designed a twenty-horsepower motor for E-M-F Motor Car.[92]

HIGBIE, CARLTON M. 1927: Higbie founded a securities company, with fellow Players George R. Fink and Ernest Kanzler, named Kanzler, Fink, and Higbie.[93] He also was a founder of the Guardian Detroit Bank, one of the banks that collapsed during the 1933 Detroit bank crisis.[94]

HOLLEY, EARL. 1919: Holley was president and the cofounder, with his brother George, of the Holley Carburetor Company.[95]

HOLLIDAY, WILLIAM (BILL) F. 1917: Holliday worked in advertising, but was best known for his work in radio. He was the first voice of WWJ-radio.[96]

HOPKINS, JAMES FREDERIC. 1938: Hopkins was the manager of the radio station WJBK.[97]

HUGHES, CHARLES A. 1925: Hughes was a charter member of the reorganized Detroit Athletic Club in 1913 and its secretary for many years. He was founder, editor, and owner of the *DAC News*.[98] He "was also instrumental in organizing the syndicate that created Detroit's first professional hockey team, the Cougars (they eventually became the Red Wings)."[99]

HUNT, ORMOND E. 1919: Hunt was the chief engineer for Chevrolet.[100]

HUTCHINSON, B. E. 1930: Hutchinson was treasurer (and later vice-president) of Chrysler Corporation when it bought out the Dodge brothers.[101]

IDE, O. Z. 1948: Ide was a lawyer by trade. Most friends called him "Ozie" or "Oz." He was a captain in the field artillery during World War I and served with the judge advocate general's staff in Europe and North Africa during World War II. He was on the legal staff at Ford Motor where he negotiated with the Brazilian government for the acquisition of 6 million acres of rubber plantation. He was appointed to a judgeship on the Recorder's Court and later was elected to that position.[102]

JACOBS, RAYMOND (RAY) A. 1927: Jacobs was vice-president of First National Bank in Detroit and mayor of Huntington Woods, 1931–33.[103]

JAMIESON, A. DOUGLASS. 1939: Jamieson was vice-president of the Union Guardian Trust Company.[104]

JENDRZEJEWSKI, ROY A. 1978: Although not "famous" in the traditional sense, Jendrzejewski's name has become something of a Player tradition due to the difficulty of spelling it properly. When speaking of him, he is occasionally referred to as "Roy Alphabet," and in various editions of *The Player* his name has appeared as "Ray *sic*] Alphabitzz," "Roy 'Wheel of Fortune' Jendrzejewski ... Because whenever somebody sees his name, they immediately want to buy a vowel," "Roy Jendralphabet" and my personal favorite, "Roy Jendrezewabcdefghijklmnopqrstuvwski."[105]

JOY, HENRY BOURNE. 1915: Scion of one of the four major Detroit families that built Detroit, Henry B. Joy was heir to millions. Along with other prominent Detroiters, he served in the navy on the *U.S.S. Yosemite* during the Spanish American War.[106] His interest in automobiles and engines led him to invest $25,000 in 1902 with the Ohio Automobile Company, which soon moved to Detroit and became the Packard Motor Car Company.[107] He also got his brother-in-law, Truman Handy Newberry, to invest in the company. He was president of Packard Motor from 1903 until 1916.[108] Joy's father, J. F. Joy, was a lawyer who "financed and coordinated the building of the Soo Locks," for which the state of Michigan rewarded him with 750,000 acres of land, thus firmly establishing the family as one of the major players in Detroit.[109] Joy also played a role in the repeal of the Eighteenth Amendment. Originally a supporter of Prohibition, when he saw the difficulty of enforcement firsthand (his shoreline property had frequent run-ins between smugglers and police), he became one of the leading figures in the Association for the Appeal of the Prohibition Amendment.[110] He was a director of the Chamber of Commerce of the United States and vice-president of the Detroit board.[111] Joy was also one of the early major donors to the Detroit Symphony Orchestra and a major sponsor of the coast-to-coast Lincoln Highway.[112]

JOY, RICHARD P. 1926: Richard Joy was brother to Henry and one of the original investors in Packard Motor Car Company.[113] Richard was the first president of the National Bank of Commerce (one of the banks that collapsed during the Detroit bank crisis in 1933).[114]

JUDGE, FRANK. 1952: Judge spent more than forty years at Ford Motor Company and was civic affairs director when he retired.[115]

KANZLER, ERNEST C. 1924: Kanzler was a close friend and brother-in-law to Edsel Ford, plus a vice-president of Ford Motor. He was at one time the head of the Universal Credit Corporation, which provided financing for Ford vehicles.[116] In 1926, he joined the list of many good men summarily fired by Henry Ford for supposedly wielding too much influence over Edsel. Henry also disliked him because he had pushed for the abandonment of the Model T.[117] Along with fellow Players George R. Fink and Carlton M. Higbie, he founded a securities company named Kanzler, Fink, and Higbie.[118] Kanzler was also a founder of the Guardian Detroit Bank, one of the banks that collapsed during the 1933 Detroit bank crisis. His banking practices contributed to that collapse.[119]

KAPP, WILLIAM (BILL) E. 1923: Kapp was an architect for Smith, Hinchman, and Grylls, the firm that built the Playhouse and the Detroit Historical and Dossin Great Lakes museums.

KEANE, J. E. 1920: Keane was an investment broker who was a founder of the Guardian Detroit Bank, one of the banks that collapsed during the 1933 Detroit bank crisis.[120]

KENNEDY, WILLIAM (BILL) F. 1962: Kennedy was a newscaster for WWJ-radio, contract actor with Warner Brothers, news anchor in Los Angeles, and finally a television movie host in Detroit.[121]

KNUDSEN, WILLIAM S. 1938: Knudsen was a Danish immigrant to the United States with an innate sense of how to organize manufacturing processes to make them more efficient. His abilities impacted the fortunes of Ford Motor Company, General Motors, and finally, the entire United States of America plus some of its allies during World War II. In a 1994 exhibit remembering Knudsen's and General Motors' contributions during World War II, Knudsen was remembered as the "father of the 'Arsenal of Democracy'" whose leadership in the national conversion to wartime production was "unmatched in history."[122]

Knudsen's expertise was vital in setting up the moving assembly line that would drive Ford production, and he was instrumental in the planning and construction at Ford's River Rouge complex beginning in 1915.[123] Henry Ford's typical level of interference with his top executives finally drove Knudsen away, but General Motors (GM) hired him within a year of his leaving Ford Motor Company. At GM he turned the Chevrolet division around and went on to become the president of GM. The improvements at GM knocked Ford out of its position as the number one automaker and forced Henry Ford to abandon his beloved Model T, shut down his plants, and retool for the Model A.[124]

During World War II, President Roosevelt appointed him lieutenant general of the army to deal with war production. He was the only civilian ever to receive that high a rank. For his work for the military, Knudsen received the Distinguished Service Medal in May 1944 and had an oak leaf cluster added to it in May 1945 (adding an oak leaf cluster to a medal is the equivalent of being awarded the medal again). More details can be found in Knudsen's biography: Norman Beasley, *Knudsen: A Biography* (New York: McGraw-Hill, 1947).

LACY, ARTHUR J. 1935: Lacy was a judge with the Detroit Court of Domestic Relations and a lawyer in John Anderson's firm, Anderson, Wilcox, Lacy, and Lawson.[125]

LARNED, ABNER E. 1913: Larned was the president of a clothing company that manufactured overalls and a chairman of the

Detroit Regional Labor Board.[126] Larned was also one of the early major donors to the Detroit Symphony Orchestra.[127]

LEGGE, RUSSELL H. 1920: Legge founded Russell H. Legge Studios, which specialized in commercial illustration.[128]

LERCHEN, WILLIAM GODFREY. 1911: Lerchen was an investment banker and partner in Watling, Lerchen, and Hayes.[129]

LIEBOLD, ERNEST J. 1940: Liebold was vice-president of the Detroit, Toledo, and Ironton Railroad.[130]

LING, LOUIS C. 1911: Ling was a drama critic for the *Detroit Journal*.[131]

LIVINGSTON, WILLIAM A. 1916: Livingstone was president of the Dime Savings Bank.[132]

LODGE, JOHN CHRISTIAN. 1917: Lodge was an editor for the *Detroit Free Press* before moving into politics. He was a longtime member of the Detroit Common Council and a beloved mayor of Detroit.

LONGLEY, CLIFFORD B. 1930: Longley was the Ford family attorney and a president of the Union Guardian Trust Company.[133]

MACAULEY, ALVAN. 1911: Macauley was general manager of Burroughs Adding Machine Company until Packard Motor Car Company lured him away in 1910 to assume the same position. He eventually became president and chairman of the company until 1948. During World War I, Packard was vital to the production of the Liberty motor. Not only did it design and build the first Liberty motor, it produced more of them by the end of the war than any other manufacturer.[134] Macauley was also a founder of the Guardian Detroit Bank, one of the banks that collapsed during the 1933 Detroit bank crisis.[135] During World War II, Macauley was president of the Automotive Council for War Production.[136]

MACMANUS, THEODORE F. 1913: MacManus was coauthor with Norman Beasley of *Men, Money, and Motors* (1929). MacManus spent years in advertising for "Ford, General Motors, Peerless, Hupmobile, Graham Brothers, Goodyear Tires, Fisher Bodies, Chrysler, Dodge Brothers, Packard," and other auto-related businesses.[137] His years of experience culminated in the founding of MacManus, Inc., a national advertising firm. At one point he also claimed Cadillac as a client.[138] When his son, Hugo, died in 1929, MacManus built St.

Hugo's Church in Bloomfield Hills as a memorial.

MALOTT, ANDREW LORNE. 1935: Malott was president of Andrew L. Malott, Inc., a real estate management company.[139]

MARTIN, HUGH. 1930: Martin was president of the Detroit Gray Iron Foundry Company.[140]

MAYO, WILLIAM BENSON. 1930: Mayo was an engineer for Ford Motor Company. He was in charge of "several large construction projects for Ford, including the Rouge Complex," in addition to playing a significant role in Ford's aviation business.[141]

MCALPINE, ARCHIBALD DUNCAN. 1926: McAlpine was a surgeon at Harper Hospital.[142]

MEADON, JOSEPH. 1916: Meadon was president and general manager of the Franklin Press and was founder and editor of the *Graphic Arts and Crafts Yearbook*.[143]

MILLER, SIDNEY T. 1913: Miller was an elite lawyer in Detroit and was a supporter of culture. He was on the Detroit Public Library Committee and a founder and director of the Detroit Symphony Society.[144] He was also on the board of directors of Reliance Motor Car Company and was one of its major stockholders.[145]

MINERS, MICHAEL (MICKEY) CASE. 1994: Miners was president of The Players from 1997 to 1998. Miners founded Youtheatre at the Detroit Institute of Arts, which exposed over 5.8 million metro Detroit children to the theatre.[146]

MINGE, LAVERNE (VERNE) W. 1946: Minge was a caricaturist for the *Detroit Free Press*.

MITCHELL, W. LEDYARD. 1920: Mitchell was a founder of the Guardian Detroit Bank, one of the banks that collapsed during the 1933 Detroit bank crisis.[147]

MULFORD, ORA J. 1916: Mulford was one of the organizers of the Gray Motor Car Company.[148]

MURPHY, CHARLES HAYWARD. 1911: Murphy was the secretary and treasurer in Simon J. Murphy Company and a vice-president of the Detroit Symphony Society.[149] Murphy was also president of the Detroit Fire Commission.

MURPHY, MICHAEL JOSEPH. 1926: Murphy was one of the founders of the Detroit Board of Commerce, secretary and vice president of the Globe Furniture and Manufacturing Company, and international vice-president of the Brotherhood of Railroad Trainmen.[150]

MURPHY, WILLIAM H. 1923: Murphy was the son of "millionaire lumber merchant" Simon Murphy. The family held significant real estate holdings in Detroit at the beginning of the twentieth century. William was an original investor in the Henry Ford Company, a forerunner to Cadillac (the name was changed when Ford resigned from the company, much to the relief of the investors, who could not control him).[151]

NEWBERRY, PHELPS. 1923: Phelps Newberry, the son of Truman Newberry, was involved with Newberry Estates, Inc., and vice-president of Union Guardian Trust Company.[152] Phelps served in the military during World War I and World War II. During World War II he was a lieutenant colonel in the U. S. Army Air Corps.[153]

NEWBERRY, TRUMAN HANDY. 1926: Newberry was a member of one of the four big old money families in Detroit; the Newberry family made its original money in lumber.[154] Newberry also made a significant amount of money as an original investor in Packard Motor Car Company (his brother-in-law, Henry B. Joy, had convinced him to invest).[155] He started out working in the railroad business, but quickly progressed to being an officer or director in several Detroit companies, such as Detroit Steel Castings, Union Trust Company, and Packard Motor Car. In 1895 he organized the Michigan Naval Brigade, and soon after enlisted in the navy, which led to his service onboard the *U.S.S. Yosemite*, which saw action near Puerto Rico during the Spanish American War. This experience, combined with his father's political contacts, led to Theodore Roosevelt's appointing him as assistant secretary of the navy in 1905 and secretary of the navy in 1908. Newberry returned to Detroit when his term ended and ran unsuccessfully for Congress in 1910 against Edwin Denby (another Player, who was appointed secretary of the navy by President Warren Harding).

In 1918, Newberry ran for the U.S. Senate against Henry Ford. Newberry won by a solid but relatively small margin. The campaign was so contentious that Ford brought a suit against Newberry charging him with violating the 1911 Federal

Corrupt Practices Act. The act set the limit for the primary and final election campaign spending at no more than the value of half of the elected position's salary. In this case, that meant that only $3,750 could be spent in pursuit of the Senate seat. Newberry spent $176,568 on the campaign, mostly on advertising, as he was out of state serving in the navy in New York. Newberry was convicted and sentenced to fines and jail time, but he fought the conviction all the way to the Supreme Court, which overturned the ruling and declared the law unconstitutional. Newberry finally took his seat in 1922, only to resign later that year from continued allegations of wrongdoing and threats to put him through another trial. For a detailed analysis, see Spencer Ervin, *Henry Ford vs. Truman H. Newberry: The Famous Senate Election Contest* (New York: R. R. Smith, 1935; repr., New York: Arno Press, 1974) or Donald Findlay Davis, *Conspicuous Production: Automobiles and Elites in Detroit, 1899–1933* (Philadelphia: Temple University Press, 1988).

NIMMO, HARRY M. 1913: Nimmo was founder and editor of the newspaper *Detroit Saturday Night*. He was an opponent of Prohibition and used his paper to point out the impossibility of controlling the flow of alcohol and the waste of tax dollars attempting to do it.[156]

NOBLE, SHELDON R. 1926: Noble was an investment broker and partner in the firm of H. W. Noble and Company.[157]

NOLAN, FRED A. 1931: Nolan was general manager of the Department of Street Railways.[158]

OVERESCH, F. W. 1929: Overesch was an advertising executive with Maxon, Inc., an advertising agency.[159]

OWEN, JOHN L. 1958: Owen had a distinguished career in law. After two years in private practice, he became the assistant prosecuting attorney for Wayne County. Over his career, he split his time between private practice and public service, holding the positions of deputy probate register, a trial attorney in the Office of Regional Counsel Wage Stabilization Board, the assistant U.S. attorney for the eastern district of Michigan, and a Detroit Recorders Court traffic court referee. In addition to his interest in the arts, he was highly involved in the Shriners charities.[160]

PALMS, CHARLES LOUIS. 1911: Palms was a "stove manufacturer, publisher, banker ... and one of the principal heirs of the Palms real estate fortune."[161]

PEABODY, HORACE BAXTER. 1911: Peabody was on the staff of the *Detroit Journal* for ten years and later was president of Detroit Garages, Inc.[162]

PELLETIER, E. LEROY. 1918: Pelletier was an advertising man for both Ford and E-M-F Motor Car companies. Norman Beasley called him "the first great publicist of the new industry."[163]

PIERROT, GEORGE F. 1933: Pierrot was the president of *American Boy* magazine, for which he traveled extensively.[164] Later he used this material to host a "travelogue" series during the 1960s.[165]

PINGREE, EVERETT W. 1920: Everett Pingree was a nephew of Hazen S. Pingree (a former mayor of Detroit, affectionately known as "potato patch Pingree" due to some creative ways he tried to deal with poverty in the city). In 1913, he formed the F. C. Pingree Sons Company (shoe manufacturers) with his brother Roy. After 1925, he was involved in real estate.[166]

PINGREE, ROY EDWARD. 1913: Roy Pingree, brother to Everett and nephew to Hazen, was a partner with Everett in the F. C. Pingree Sons Company.

PRENDERGAST, JOHN J. 1935: Prendergast was an instructor of obstetrics at Wayne State University and director of the Hospital Professional Service at Detroit Receiving Hospital.[167]

RECK, FRANKLIN M. 1937: Reck was assistant managing editor of *American Boy* magazine and a contributor to that magazine and to *St. Nicholas* magazine. He also authored twenty-five books, several of them for young adults. He literally died at his typewriter.[168]

RICKENBACKER, EDWARD V. 1923: Captain Rickenbacker was "America's greatest World War I flying ace."[169]

ROBINSON, LOREN T., SR. 1917: Robinson was vice-president of Campbell-Ewald Company, an advertising firm.[170]

ROBINSON, WILLIAM L. 1952: Robinson was a vice-president of Burton Abstract and Title Company.[171]

RUSSEL, HENRY. 1915: Henry Russel was an owner (along with his brother, George H. Russel) of Russel Wheel and Foundry (which manufactured logging cars). Henry was vice-president and chief counsel for the Michigan Central Railroad and had a hand in the establishment of the Michigan State Telephone Company.[172]

RUSSEL, WALTER S. 1911: Russel founded Russel Wheel and Foundry Company with his brothers.[173] He was also head of the Russel Steel Construction Company that provided the steelwork for such Detroit landmarks as the Masonic Temple and the Free Press Building.[174]

RUSSELL, JOHN ROSS. 1913: Russell was president of the Great Lakes Engineering Works of Detroit, "steel ship and engine builders."[175]

SANGER, HARRY H. 1924: Sanger was a vice-president of Manufacturers National Bank.[176]

SCHANTZ, ARNOLD AUGUSTUS. 1915: Schantz was president of the Detroit and Cleveland Navigation Company (passenger shipping line).[177]

SCHNEIDER, EDWARD (NED) N. 1956: Schneider was a war correspondent in Korea in 1952. When he returned, he became an Episcopalian minister and was chaplain at the National Cathedral School for Girls in Washington, D.C. He was the minister for St. James Episcopal Church until he retired.[178]

SCHNEIDER, LOUIS JAMES. 1954: Schneider was a lawyer and state legislator.[179]

SCRIPPS, WILLIAM E. 1932: Scripps was president of the *Detroit News* and founded WWJ-FM, WWJ-AM, and WWJ-TV. A colorful character, he bought an airplane in 1912 and taught himself how to fly. He also donated a miniature railway system to the Detroit Zoo on behalf of his paper.[180]

SCRIPPS, WILLIAM JOHN. 1937: Son of William E. Scripps, William served in the army in the Office of Strategic Command during World War II and was a general manager of the radio station WWJ and later a director of the *Detroit News*.[181] The station WWJ, the world's first commercial radio station, was founded by his father, who named the station using his son's initials.[182]

SHANNON, RICHARD. 1947: Shannon is famous—or rather infamous—only at The Players for an inflammatory incident at the Playhouse. Shannon was a percussionist in the orchestra at

The Players and could be spotted on frolic nights behind his drum set on the left side of the pit. Unfortunately, he was also a smoker, and he managed to drop a lit cigarette onto the head of the drum, setting it aflame rather quickly. Luckily, one of the Players in the front row calmly doused the fire with pitcher of beer ... and the show went on.[183]

SHURLEY, BURT R. 1913: Shurley was a laryngologist at Harper Hospital and the founder of the Detroit Medical College.[184]

SLADE, SAM I. 1915: Although he trained and then worked as a lawyer for eight years, Slade had been singing since high school and appeared onstage at several clubs and sung in local churches. The amateur nature of his work changed when Fred Whitney (of the Whitney Opera House) offered him a contract that led him to New York and a road tour. He continued to work as a professional actor, but he wanted to be able to remain in Detroit permanently, where he became a voice teacher.[185]

SMITH, FRED LOUIS. 1911: Smith was an architect and partner in Smith, Hinchman, and Grylls.[186]

SMITH, HAL HORACE. 1919: Smith was president of Hayes Manufacturing (wheels) and an attorney for the Michigan Manufacturers Association.[187] Smith was also an organizer of the Friends of the Detroit Public Library.[188]

STANDISH, WILLIAM COLBURN (OLIE), SR. 1913: Standish was an advertising executive with an outdoor advertising firm.[189]

STARK, GEORGE W. 1915: Stark was one of the major reporters in Detroit. He was the central force behind the building of the Detroit Historical Museum and was also a Detroit historian.[190]

STEARNS, FREDERICK KIMBALL. 1913: Stearns was the founder of Frederick Stearns and Company, a pharmaceutical firm.

STEARNS, FREDERICK SWEET. 1910: Stearns was a founder of The Players. Son of Frederick Kimball Stearns, he became president and general manager of the family company, Frederick Stearns and Company.[191]

STRINGHAM, JOSEPH S. 1911: Stringham was a Detroit city engineer.[192]

STROH, BERNARD, JR. 1913: Stroh was president and treasurer of the Stroh Casting Company.[193]

STROH, EDWIN R. 1913: Stroh was a vice-president and secretary of the Stroh Casting Company.[194]

STROH, GARI. 1918: Stroh was the president of Stroh Brewing Company. He was also a friend of Edsel Ford.[195]

THOMPSON, HAYWARD S. 1927: Thompson was an insurance executive with General Underwriters, Inc.[196]

TODD, JOHN. 1944: Todd played "Tonto" on *The Lone Ranger* radio program.

TOMS, ROBERT (BOB) M. 1918: Toms performed bit parts for Jesse Bonstelle's theatrical stock company even as he began working as a lawyer.[197] Toms eventually worked his way up to Wayne County prosecuting attorney. In this capacity, he worked on the historic Ossian Sweet Case. Ossian Sweet was an African American physician who moved into an all-white neighborhood in 1925. A mob gathered outside of his home, threw rocks, and threatened his family. Someone in the house fired into the crowd, killing one man and wounding another, and Sweet and everyone else in the house were arrested. The National Association for the Advancement of Colored People (NAACP) brought in Clarence Darrow, for what was to be his last case, to defend Sweet, which he did successfully. Toms remembered that Darrow "complained throughout the trial that my decent treatment of him was purely strategic and that it was working a great hardship on him."[198] Two recent books on the subject can provide additional information: Kevin Boyle, *Arc of Justice: A Saga of Race, Civil Rights, and Murder in the Jazz Age* (New York: Holt, 2004), and Phyllis Vine, *One Man's Castle: Clarence Darrow in Defense of the American Dream* (New York: Amistad, 2004).

Toms was also prosecuting attorney throughout Prohibition, during which he defended the use of the tip-over raid by police. This illegal (and definitely unconstitutional—even according to Toms) practice would allow police who had no evidence to raid an establishment they believed to possess alcohol. According to one Prohibition historian, Toms basically believed that "it would be necessary to break the law to enforce it."[199] In 1927, Toms was the first person to register under a law he had proposed that required anyone who owned a handgun to register the weapon and the owner's fingerprints with the police.[200] He was appointed judge in 1929 and was later elected to the 3rd Judicial Circuit, Wayne County. He was never defeated for his position, and he retired in 1959.[201] He served as a judge during the Nuremberg trials and taught constitutional law at Wayne State University from 1932 to 1946.[202]

TRENDLE, GEORGE WASHINGTON. 1927: Trendle was a co-owner of WXYZ and the originator of *The Lone Ranger* radio program.[203]

TUCKER, VERNON W. 1915: Tucker was the president of Apel-Tucker Studio, an advertising design agency.[204]

VAIL, CLAIR FREMONT. 1943: Vail was a surgeon at Harper and Receiving hospitals.[205]

VANDERKLOOT, ROBERT (BOB) C. 1938: Son-in-law of Player William Knudsen, VanderKloot was an amateur musician who played the handbells at an Afterglow.[206] He served in the Army Air Corps during World War II. He was president of Detroit Colortype and Adland Publishing. He was a founding board member of the Michigan Opera Theatre (founder David DiChiera was his son-in-law) and also was active in the creation of the Center for Hearing Disorders at the Kresge Hearing Research Institute.[207]

VERNOR, JAMES, JR. 1942: Vernor's father invented a popular ginger ale of the same name (currently distributed by Pepsi). Junior was one of the chief organizers of the American Bottlers of Carbonated Beverages and took over the James Vernor Company when his father passed away. During World War II, he served in the Aleutian Islands.[208]

VINCENT, JESSE GURNEY. 1939: Vincent was a mechanical engineer who was the "co-designer of the Liberty Aircraft Engine."[209]

WALKER, ROGER V. 1933: Walker was a surgeon at Providence Hospital.[210]

WATERMAN, CAMERON B. 1913: In 1905, Waterman invented the outboard motor.[211]

WATKINS, JAMES K. 1925: Watkins was a Detroit police commissioner in the early 1930s.[212]

WATKINS, JOHN R. 1928: As an adolescent, Watkins worked with the Wallace Brothers circus as everything from a manual laborer to a sideshow barker.[213] He left the circus for a career in law and was federal district attorney during the Prohibition years in Detroit.[214]

WEBBER, OSCAR. 1923: Webber was a nephew of department store magnate J. L. Hudson and spent his early career as a department manager. After Hudson died in 1912, Webber became vice-president and general manager of the J. L. Hudson Company department store.[215]

WEEKS, ALBERT (AL) LOREN. 1915: Weeks was a reporter for the *Detroit Free Press* and then the *Detroit News*. He was the drama critic for the *News* from 1915 to 1925, moved on to editing *Bridle and Golfer* and *The Playgoer*, and eventually became a writer and narrator for the Metropolitan Motion Picture Company.[216]

WHITCOMB, JAMES S. 1937: Whitcomb was a vice-president of Detroit Brass and Malleable Works.[217]

WHITE, H. KIRK, JR. 1915: White was a vice-president of the D. M. Ferry seed company.[218]

WHITTAKER, ALFRED HEACOCK. 1933: Whittaker was a surgeon at Harper, Childrens, Receiving, and Deaconness hospitals.[219]

ZEDER, FRED M. 1936: Zeder was originally part of the engineering firm of Zeder, Skelton, and Breer. He is largely credited for creating the first car bearing Chrysler's name.[220] Zeder eventually became the vice-president in charge of engineering for Chrysler Corporation.[221]

# Notes

## Introduction

1. E. A. Batchelor, "Only an Elephant Could Remember a Better Players Show," *The Player*, 2 Mar. 1946, 2.

## Chapter 1

1. Peter Clark, *British Clubs and Societies, 1580–1800* (New York: Oxford University Press, 2000), 194.
2. Frank Ernest Hill, *Man-Made Culture: The Education Activities of Men's Clubs* (New York: American Association for Adult Education, 1938), 4.
3. Ibid., 13; John Timbs, *Clubs and Club Life in London* (Detroit: Gale Research, 1967), 1.
4. Clark, *British Clubs*, 13, 20.
5. Ibid., 10; Hill, *Man-Made Culture*, 9.
6. Clark, *British Clubs*, 40.
7. Hill, *Man-Made Culture*, 9.
8. Ibid., 128–29, 155, 158.
9. Donald Finlay Davis, *Conspicuous Production: Automobiles and Elites in Detroit, 1899–1933* (Philadelphia: Temple University Press, 1988), 106–7.
10. Clark, *British Clubs*, 230.
11. Timbs, *Clubs*, 11.
12. James M. Mayo, *The American Country Club* (New Brunswick, NJ: Rutgers University Press, 1998), 8.
13. Kenneth Macgowan, *Footlights across America: Towards a National Theatre* (New York: Harcourt, Brace, 1929), 83, 42.
14. Ibid., 45, 84.
15. Peter Martin Phillips, "A Relative Advantage: Sociology of the San Francisco Bohemian Club" (Ph.D. diss., University of California—Davis, 1994), 17.
16. Ibid., 37.
17. Ibid., 98; W. Hampton Sides, *Stomping Grounds: A Pilgrim's Progress through Eight American Subcultures* (New York: William Morrow, 1992), 33.
18. Phillips, "Relative Advantage," 46.
19. Sides, *Stomping Grounds*, 40–41, 52.
20. Ibid., 31, 56.
21. Ibid., 31.
22. Ibid., 39.

23. "History," *Hasty Pudding Theatricals*, 8 July 2002, www.hastypudding.org.
24. Timbs, *Clubs*, 4.
25. Charles Graves, *Leather Armchairs: The Book of London Clubs* (New York: Coward-McCann, 1963), 52.
26. Timbs, *Clubs*, 219–22.
27. Lewis Hardee, "Here Come the Ladies! The Role of Women in the History of The Lambs," *The Script* (Summer 2002): 3; The Lambs, "What Is the Lambs?" 22 July 2004, www.the-lambs.org.
28. Eugene James Hooks, "The Players: Edwin Booth's Legacy to American Theatre" (Ph.D. diss., University of Missouri-Columbia, 1973), 49.
29. Joey Adams, *Here's to the Friars: The Heart of Show Business* (New York: Crown, 1976), 16–18.
30. Clark, *British Clubs*, 163; Timbs, *Clubs*, 39, 49.
31. Mayo, *American Country Club*, 26.
32. No records of this earlier club are extant.
33. Fine Arts Society of Detroit, membership application, n.d.
34. The Theatre Arts Club, brochure.
35. W. Hawkins Ferry, *The Buildings of Detroit: A History*, rev. ed. (Detroit: Wayne State University Press, 1980), 261.
36. Joy Hakanson Colby, *Art and a City: A History of the Detroit Society of Arts and Crafts* (Detroit: Wayne State University Press, 1956), 4.
37. Ibid., 9.
38. Joy Hakanson Colby, "50th Birthday of an Artful Dream," *Detroit News*, 21 Nov. 1976, 55–56.
39. Reynolds Farley and Judy Mullin, "Scarab Club," *Detroit*, classroom materials, University of Michigan, 23 July 2004, http://detroit1701.psc.isr.umich.edu/ScarabClub.htm.
40. "History of the Scarab Club," The Scarab Club, 13 Jan. 2005, www.scarabclub.org/history.html.
41. Colby, *History*, 36.
42. "The Masque of Arcadia," program, Detroit Arts and Crafts Society Box, Burton Historical Collection, Detroit Public Library.
43. Colby, *History*, 39.
44. Ibid., 40–41.
45. Sheldon Cheney, *The Art Theatre* (New York: Knopf, 1917).
46. James Strasburg, "The Meeting Was a Mite Macabre," *The Player*, 13 Apr. 1935, 2.
47. Sheldon Cheney, *The Art Theatre* (New York: Knopf, 1925), 124.
48. Cheney, *Art Theatre*, 1925 ed., 168.
49. Colby, *History*, 45–46.
50. Robert E. Gard and Gertrude S. Burley, *Community Theatre: Idea and Achievement* (New York: Duell, Sloan and Pearce, 1959), 6.
51. Ibid., 9.

## Chapter 2

1. Fine Arts Society, membership application, n.d.
2. "The Palmy Days," *The Player*, 17 Nov. 1928, 2–3.
3. Albert Nelson Marquis, ed., *The Book of Detroiters* (Chicago: A. N. Marquis, 1914), 91.
4. "A Short History of 'The Players,'" Players Minutes, 14 Nov. 1911.
5. Alexander K. Gage, "Foundations—Traditions," *The Player*, 30 Nov. 1940, 3.
6. "Final Curtain," *The Player*, 27 Mar. 1954, 4.
7. The Players, "Articles of Association," The Players Archives, Detroit, Article II.
8. Players Minutes, 19 Dec. 1911; 27 Feb. 1914.
9. Players Minutes, 12 Jan. 1913.
10. Players Minutes, 3 Mar. 1911.
11. Alice Tarbell Crathern, *In Detroit … Courage Was the Fashion: The Contribution of Women to the Development of Detroit from 1701–1951* (Detroit: Wayne State University Press, 1953), 167.
12. Players Minutes, 14 Nov. 1911.
13. Players Minutes, 2 Jan. 1912; 27 Feb., 4 Dec. 1914; 4 Jan. 1915, 8 Nov. 1916; 22 Jan. 1924; 23 Feb. 1926.
14. Players Minutes, 9 July 1953.
15. Players Minutes, 24 Nov. 1911.
16. Players Minutes, 12 Dec. 1911.
17. Ibid.
18. Players Minutes, 11 Mar. 1915.
19. "The Twenty-fourth of May," *The Player*, 22 May 1917, 2.
20. Crathern, *In Detroit*, 167.
21. Players Minutes, 8 Jan. 1913.
22. W. E. Kapp, "Did You Know That …" *The Player*, 29 Mar. 1952, 4.
23. "Players Give Amateur Performance before Detroit Society Folks," *Detroit News*, 12 Apr. 1913, n.p.
24. Ibid.
25. Program, *Hairlooms*, The Players Archives, Detroit, 11 Apr. 1913.
26. Players Minutes, 19 Apr. 1913.
27. Players Minutes, 23 Apr. 1913.
28. Players Minutes, 19 Apr. 1913.
29. Kenneth Macgowan, *Footlights across America: Towards a National Theatre* (New York: Harcourt, Brace, 1929), 86.
30. Ibid.
31. The Players, *The Players Book of One Act Plays* (New York: Walter V. McKee, 1928), viii.
32. Kapp, "Did You Know," 4. The original Al Weeks quote is from the foreword (vii–viii) to *The Players Book of One Act Plays*.
33. David Lee Poremba, *Detroit in Its World Setting* (Detroit: Wayne State University Press, 2001), 219.

34. Donald Finlay Davis, *Conspicuous Production: Automobiles and Elites in Detroit, 1899–1933* (Philadelphia: Temple University Press, 1988), 105–6; Charles K. Hyde, *The Dodge Brothers: The Men, the Motor Cars, and the Legacy* (Detroit: Wayne State University Press, 2005), 115.
35. Davis, *Conspicuous Production*, 105–6.
36. Ibid., 61–64.
37. Ibid., 57–59.
38. Ibid., 89.
39. Ibid., 88–90.
40. Ibid., 90.
41. John McManis, "Lawrence P. Fisher, Auto Pioneer, Dies," *Detroit News*, 4 Sept. 1961, n.p.
42. Frank B. Woodford and Arthur M. Woodford, *All Our Yesterdays: A Brief History of Detroit* (Detroit: Wayne State University Press, 1969), 259.
43. Frank Donovan, *Wheels for a Nation* (n.p: Thomas Y. Crowell, 1975), 74.
44. Woodford and Woodford, *All Our Yesterdays*, 259.
45. Donovan, *Wheels*, 77.
46. Davis, *Conspicuous Production*, 71.
47. Ibid., 72.
48. Ibid., 73; Marquis, *Book of Detroiters*, 81; *Who's Who in Detroit, 1935–36: A Biographical Dictionary of Representative Men and Women of Metropolitan Detroit* (Detroit: Walter Ronig, 1935), 54.
49. Davis, *Conspicuous Production*, 98.
50. Ibid., 93.
51. Eric Dregni and Karl Hagstrom Miller, *Ads That Put America on Wheels* (Osceola, WI: Motorbooks International, 1996), 9.
52. *Who's Who, 1935–36*, 10.
53. *The Player*, 19 Jan. 1929, 3.
54. "Lee Anderson," Obituary, *Detroit News*, 7 Oct. 1955, n.p.
55. *Who's Who, 1935–36*, 219.
56. Ibid., 311.
57. Ibid., 106–7.
58. Adcraft Club of Detroit Home Page, 12 Aug. 2004, www.adcraft.org/i4a/pages/index.cfm?pageid=1.
59. Players, *One Act Plays*, 335.
60. Marquis, *Book of Detroiters*, 92.
61. Ibid., 472.
62. Davis, *Conspicuous Production*, 105–6, 238.
63. Marquis, *Book of Detroiters*, 407.
64. Players Minutes, 13 May 1915.
65. Oscar J. Brockett and Franklin J. Hildy, *History of the Theatre*, 9th ed. (Boston: Allyn and Bacon, 2003), 549.
66. Poremba, *Detroit*, 171.
67. Clarence M. Burton, ed., *The City of Detroit, Michigan, 1701–1922*, vol. 1 (Detroit: S. J. Clarke, 1922), 853–54. Additional information on the Detroit Institute of Arts can be found in Jeffery Abt, *A Museum on the Verge: A Socioeconomic History of the Detroit Institute of Arts, 1882–2000*

(Detroit: Wayne State University Press, 2001), and William H. Peck, *The Detroit Institute of Arts: A Brief History* (Detroit: Wayne State University Press, 1991).
68. Joy Hakanson Colby, *Art and a City: A History of the Detroit Society of Arts and Crafts* (Detroit: Wayne State University Press, 1956), 37.
69. Ibid., 9; Vivian M. Baulch, "How Arts and Crafts Flourished in Industrial Detroit," *Detroit News*, n.d., accessed 16 Jan. 2006, http://info.detnews.com/history/story/index.cfm?id=75&category=life.
70. Colby, *History*, 4.
71. Ibid., 42.
72. Ibid., 42–43.
73. Ibid., 19.
74. *The Player*, 1 Jan. 1919, 2.
75. Players Minutes, 14 Jan. 1916.
76. Players Minutes, 14 Mar. 1917.
77. "Our Own Playhouse?" *The Player*, 27 Mar. 1917, 2.
78. Players Minutes, 19 Oct. 1915.
79. Players Minutes, 18 Apr. 1917.
80. Players Minutes, 28 Nov. 1917.
81. Harvey Campbell, "Back on the Job," *The Player*, 13 Dec. 1917, 2.
82. "Nunquam Renig," *The Player*, 25 Apr. 1918, 4.
83. Players Minutes, 26 Feb. 1918.
84. *Who's Who, 1935–36*, 107.
85. Players Minutes, 8 May 1918.
86. Players Minutes, 19 Nov. 1918.
87. "Whispers!" *The Player*, 15 Apr. 1925, 4.
88. Players Minutes, 24 Feb. 1925.
89. Players Minutes, 22 Jan. 1915.
90. "The Players of Detroit Stage Their 150th Monthly Frolic," *Life*, 31 Jan. 1938, 50–51.
91. "Greenroom Chat," *The Player*, 25 Dec. 1924, 2.
92. *Detroit News*, 26 Aug. 1963, 24A.
93. *Who's Who, 1935–36*, 338.
94. Russ Legge, cartoon, *The Player*, 11 Mar. 1920, 2–3.
95. Larry Engelmann, *Intemperance: The Lost War against Liquor* (New York: Free Press, 1979), 71.
96. Ibid., 77.
97. Ibid., 186.
98. Ibid., 79.
99. James Strasburg, "Those Big White Pitchers," *The Player*, 30 Nov. 1940, 4.
100. John M. Butterfield, letter to the author, 16 Nov. 1999.
101. "The First Frolic—Curtain at 9:15 p.m.," *The Player*, 5 Dec. 1927, 1.
102. "Players in the City Hall," *The Player*, 16 Jan 1919, 2.
103. Harvey J. Campbell, "Off to a Good Start," *The Player* 14 Dec. 1926, 2.
104. Lee Anderson, *In the Thousands of Years to Come*, ms., The Players Archives, Detroit, 1920, 1.
105. Ibid., 6.

106. Ibid., 3.
107. Ibid., 10.
108. Lynn Dumenil, *The Modern Temper: American Culture and Society in the 1920s* (New York: Hill and Wang, 1995), 231.
109. Ibid., 30.
110. "Dress the Act!" *The Player*, 14 Mar. 1922, 2.
111. Players Minutes, 19 Dec. 1922.
112. "Tucker Procession," *The Player*, 14 Dec. 1926, 2.
113. "'Autumn Fires' Leads in March: Other Shows and Afterglow Please," *The Player*, 19 Apr. 1921, 3.
114. Allen Woll, *Black Musical Theatre: From Coontown to Dreamgirls* (Baton Rouge: Louisiana State University Press, 1989), 7, 34, 49; *Broadway: The American Musical Online*, "Bert Williams," Educational Broadcasting Corporation, 2004, PBS, 23 Jan. 2006, www.pbs.org/wnet/broadway/stars/williams_b.html.
115. Players Minutes, 16 Nov. 1927.
116. Players Minutes, 13 Mar. 1952.
117. Players Minutes, 13 Feb. 1923.
118. Players Minutes, 2 Apr. 1923.
119. Players Minutes, 11 May 1923.
120. James Strasburg, "Bill Kapp Gets Nod at Annual Imbroglio," *The Player*, 2 Nov. 1940, 1.
121. Colby, *History*, 45–46.
122. "A Nice Fairy Story by the Weeks' Family," *The Player*, 15 Jan. 1924, 1.
123. "The Ballad of the Player's Daughter," *The Player*, 21 Feb. 1924, 2.
124. "December Frolic Well Attended and Well Worth It," *The Player*, 21 Feb. 1924, 4.
125. "Jake Hirschfield," Obituary, *Detroit News*, 5 Mar. 1963, n.p.
126. "The 1924 May Frolic," *The Player*, 28 Oct. 1924, 1.
127. Players Minutes, 11 May 1920.
128. Players Minutes, 20 Oct. 1925.
129. Players Minutes, 6 May 1924.
130. Players Minutes, 13 Nov. 1923.
131. Players Minutes, 13 May 1924.
132. Strasburg, "Bill Kapp," 1.
133. Players Minutes, 19 Apr. 1966.
134. George W. Stark, "The Players ... A Dream and the Reality," *Bulletin: Detroit Historical Society*, Nov. 1960, 5.
135. Players Minutes, 11 Nov. 1924.
136. Players Minutes, 19 May 1925.
137. This appears to be an introduction from a copy of the music for *Doing Stratford* published and sold at the 1926 May Show that is reproduced in the program for The Players 90th Anniversary Frolic program, The Players Archives, Detroit, 9 Dec. 2000.
138. Players Minutes, 6 Oct. 1925.
139. Players 90th Anniversary program.
140. Players Minutes, 3 Nov. 1925.

141. Players Minutes, 20 Oct. 1925.
142. J. L. Thornhill, "When the Day Is Done," *The Player*, 26 Jan. 1952, 1.
143. "W. F. Holliday Dead," *Detroit News*, 30 June 1926, n.p.
144. Stark, "Dream and the Reality," 4.
145. Walker R. A. Graham, "Behind Scenes," Golden Anniversary program, 10 Dec. 1960, 1.
146. Ibid.
147. Marleen Tulas, e-mail to the author, 27 Apr. 2006; Thomas Diffendal, e-mail to author, 3 June 2006.
148. Graham, "Behind Scenes," 1.
149. "Decoration Committee," *The Player*, 19 Jan. 1926, 2.
150. *Detroit Times*, 3 Oct. 1960, n.p.
151. Golden Anniversary program; *Detroit Free Press*, 23 Sept. 1956, n.p.
152. Scarab Club Home Page, 3 June 2002, www.scarabclub.org.
153. Willard Rohloff, personal interview, 4 July 2002.
154. "Player Kapp's Symbols," *The Player*, 19 Jan. 1926, 2–3.
155. Rohloff interview, 2002.
156. Players Minutes, 1 June 1926.
157. Players Minutes, 14 Dec. 1926.
158. Players Minutes, 19 Oct. 1927.
159. Players Minutes, 26 Oct. 1927.
160. Players Minutes, 1 May 1928, 3 Mar. 1929.
161. Players Minutes, 31 Jan. 1929.

## Chapter 3

1. David Lee Poremba, *Detroit in Its World Setting* (Detroit: Wayne State University Press, 2001), 257, 259.
2. David M. Kennedy, *Freedom from Fear: The American People in Depression and War, 1929–1945* (New York: Oxford University Press, 1999), 87, 131.
3. Robert S. McElvaine, *The Great Depression* (New York: Times Books, 1984), 73.
4. William E. Leuchtenberg, *The Perils of Prosperity, 1914–1932* (Chicago: University of Chicago Press, 1958), 247.
5. Players Minutes, 1 Nov. 1930, 27 Sept. 1932.
6. Players Minutes, 1 Nov. 1930, 28 Oct. 1930.
7. Players Minutes, 31 Mar. 1931.
8. Players Minutes, 9 Dec. 1930, 22 Dec. 1931.
9. Players Minutes, 26 Apr. 1932.
10. Players Minutes, 15 Nov. 1932.
11. "John C. Lodge," Michigan History and Biography Index, Burton Historical Collection, Detroit Public Library.
12. Kenneth H. Voyles and John A. Bluth, *The Detroit Athletic Club, 1887–2001* (Chicago: Arcadia, 2001), 44.
13. John A. Bluth, *A History of the Detroit Athletic Club, 1887–2000* (Detroit: Detroit Athletic Club, 2000), 42, 47; Charles K. Hyde, e-mail to author,

20 June 2006.
14. Arthur M. Woodford, e-mail to author, 4 Sept. 2006.
15. Players Minutes, 22 Nov. 1932.
16. Ibid.
17. "With The Players: Saturday, February 20th," *The Player* 13 Feb. 1932, 4.
18. Players Minutes, 14 Mar. 1933.
19. "The Playhouse for The Players," *The Player*, 16 Apr. 1932, 2.
20. Players Minutes, 30 Mar. 1926, 22 Nov. 1928.
21. Players Minutes, 18 Dec. 1935.
22. Players Minutes, 16 May 1933.
23. Tom Long, "The Good Ol' Boys Come Here to Play," *Detroit News*, 9 Feb. 2000, n.p.
24. Players Minutes, 1 Apr., 18 May 1954.
25. David Horowitz and Peter Collier, *The Fords: An American Epic* (New York: Summit, 1987), 136.
26. "Clubs and Associations Resigned from March 2, 1933," Accession 6, Box 278, 1933 Clubs and Associations folder, Benson Ford Research Center, The Henry Ford.
27. Larry Engelmann, *Intemperance: The Lost War against Liquor* (New York: Free Press, 1979), 194, 205; Philip P. Mason, *Rumrunning and the Roaring Twenties: Prohibition on the Michigan-Ontario Waterway* (Detroit: Wayne State University Press, 1995), 107.
28. Norman H. Clark, *Deliver Us from Evil: An Interpretation of American Prohibition* (New York: Norton, 1976), 207; Engelmann, *Intemperance*, 220.
29. Albert Loren Weeks, *The Cabinet Meeting*, ms., Players Archives, Detroit, 1933, 8–9.
30. Players Minutes, 11 Sept. 1933.
31. Poremba, *Detroit*, 263.
32. Sheldon R. Noble, *Portrait of a Man*, ms., Players Archives, Detroit, 1934, 2.
33. Ibid., 5–6.
34. "Company History," D'Oyly Carte Opera Company, 19 June 2005, www.doylycarte.org.uk/Inside_doyly_carte/company_history.htm.
35. Lee Anderson, "D'Oyly Carte Blanche," *The Player*, 23 Mar. 1935, 2.
36. "Another Offenbach Show," *The Player*, 8 Feb. 1936, 2.
37. Lee Anderson, "'The Rose of Auvergne,' and an Orchid for Offenbach," *The Player*, 7 Mar. 1936, 2.
38. *Detroit News* article reprinted in *The Player*, 7 Nov. 1936, 2.
39. Players Minutes, 11 Mar. 1936.
40. Players Minutes, 3 July 1936, 21 Sept. 1937.
41. Verne Tucker, "Revival Meeting," *The Player*, 6 Feb. 1937, 1.
42. Harry L. Hosmer, "A Man Writes a Play or Weeks Gets His Buck," *The Player*, 6 May 1960, 3.
43. Ibid.
44. *The Player*, 13 Mar. 1937, 6.
45. Michael Todd, "History Is Made at Night," *The Player*, 17 Apr. 1937, 3.

46. "Noble, Sheldon R." and "Jacobs, Raymond A.," *Detroit City Directory* (Detroit: R. L. Polk, 1932–34), 1109, 781.
47. Sheldon R. Noble and Raymond A. Jacobs, *Men Working*, ms., Players Archives, Detroit, 1937, 25.
48. Players Minutes, 18 May, 6 Oct. 1937.
49. Players Minutes, 25 May 1937.
50. Players Minutes, 27 Nov. 1937.
51. Players Minutes, 2 Feb. 1938.
52. *Detroit News*, 14 Apr. 1929, n.p.
53. Players Minutes, 3 Apr. 1940.
54. Larry Smith, personal interview, 20 Dec. 2005.
55. Francis E. Brossy, "On to the Next 75 Years," *The Player*, 29 Oct. 1976, 1; Another version of this story has the Slade portrait being discovered in the Dumouchelle gallery in downtown Detroit: Glenn Scoles, interview with the author, n.d.
56. Harry W. Kerr, "Two Dead Women and a Wilderness," *The Player*, 3 Feb. 1940, 1.
57. E. A. Batchelor, "Another 'Smash Hit' for Ray," *The Player*, 30 Mar. 1940, 2.
58. Ibid.
59. Players Minutes, 17 Dec. 1940.
60. Players Minutes, 28 Jan. 1941.
61. Alexander K. Gage, "Foundations—Traditions," *The Player*, 30 Nov. 1940, 3.
62. "Those Big White Pitchers," *The Player*, 30 Nov. 1940, 4.
63. "Bill Kapp Gets Nod at Annual Imbroglio," *The Player*, 2 Nov. 1940, 1.
64. Players Minutes, 25 Mar. 1941.
65. Frank V. Martin, "February, Lincoln and Sam," *The Player*, 1 Mar. 1941, 2.
66. Ibid., 1.
67. Players Minutes, 15 Apr. 1941.
68. George W. Stark, "Russ Legge," *The Player*, 1 Nov. 1941, 3.
69. Players Minutes, 17 June 1941.
70. Harry Mitchell, "The Night before December 7, 1941," *The Player*, 3 Jan. 1941, 1.
71. Franklin M. Reck, "The Players and the War," *The Player*, 4 Apr. 1942, 4.
72. Players Minutes, 21 Jan. 1942.
73. Ibid.
74. "'The Players' of Detroit Stage Their 150th Monthly Frolic," *Life*, 31 Jan. 1938, 50–51.
75. "Standish, W. Colburn," *Detroit City Directory* (Detroit: R. L. Polk, 1935), 1686.
76. Players Minutes, 13 May 1941.
77. Players Minutes, 1 July 1942; "Initiation Fee Lowered," *The Player*, 31 Oct. 1942, 4.
78. Players Minutes, 8 July, 9 Sept. 1942.
79. Players Minutes, 7 Oct. 1942.

80. "To Dress or Not to Dress," *The Player*, 30 Jan. 1943, 3.
81. Minutes, 18 Oct. 1942; Mary Ellen Menard, "Players Shatter Time-Worn Tradition," *Detroit Free Press*, 18 Nov. 1942, n.p.
82. Menard, "Time-Worn Tradition," n.p.
83. Ibid.
84. "Sam Slade," Obituary, *Detroit News*, 23 Nov. 1942, n.p.
85. Players Minutes, 8 Nov. 1944.
86. Players Minutes, 30 June 1944.
87. E. A. Batchelor, "Yes, the Players Still Can Do the Grim Things," *The Player*, 3 Mar. 1945, 2.
88. Ibid.
89. Players Minutes, 24 Jan. 1945.
90. "Fireworks at the 1945 Annual Meeting," *The Player*, 20 Oct. 1945, 4.

## Chapter 4

1. Joe Kerr, "Trouble in Motor City," *Autotopia* (London: Reaktion Books, 2002), 131; see also David Lee Poremba, *Detroit in Its World Setting* (Detroit: Wayne State University Press, 2001), 277.
2. Thomas J. Sugrue, *The Origins of the Urban Crisis: Race and Inequality in Postwar Detroit* (Princeton, NJ: Princeton University Press, 1996), 30.
3. David M. Kennedy, *Freedom from Fear: The American People in Depression and War, 1929–1945* (New York: Oxford University Press, 1999), 857.
4. Albert D. Conkey, *On High*, ms., The Players Archives, Detroit, 1946, 2.
5. Ibid., 3.
6. Ibid.
7. Ibid.
8. Ibid., 4.
9. Ibid.
10. Ibid., 6–7.
11. Gordon H. Miller, *The Flame*, ms., The Players Archives, Detroit, 1946, 13.
12. Ibid., 15.
13. Ibid.
14. Ibid., 16.
15. E. A. Batchelor, "Only an Elephant Could Remember a Better Players Show," *The Player*, 2 Mar. 1946, 2.
16. Players Minutes, 6 June 1946.
17. "Good News from Minge," *The Player*, 26 Oct. 1946, 4.
18. E. A. Batchelor, "First Frolic Tops for Amateur Productions," *The Player*, 30 Nov. 1946, 1.
19. Players Minutes, 31 Oct. 1946.
20. Batchelor, "First Frolic," 1–2.
21. Ibid.
22. Louis Tendler, "Judge Toms Finds Readjustment Hard," *Detroit News*, 23 Nov. 1947, n.p.

23. Players Minutes, 13 May 1948.
24. Players Minutes, 6 Nov. 1948; "Beattie, Daniel C.," *Detroit City Directory* (Detroit: R. L. Polk, 1944), 82.
25. Glen Warren, "Last but Not Least," *The Player*, 31 Oct. 1949, 1–2; *The Player*, 28 Nov. 1949, 4.
26. Players Minutes, 13 Jan. 1949.
27. Players Minutes, 3 Feb. 1949.
28. Players Minutes, 10 Mar. 1949.
29. Albert D. Conkey, *"Command Decision* Wins Standing Ovation," *The Player*, 28 Nov. 1949, 1.
30. W. Howard T. Snyder, "Love's Labor Won," *Inside Detroit*, ms., The Players Archives, Detroit, 1950, 3.
31. Ibid., 3–4.
32. Ibid., 5.
33. "Ernest R. Breech," *The Automotive Hall of Fame Home Page*, Automotive Hall of Fame, 16 Jan. 2006, www.automotivehalloffame.org/honors/index.php?cmd=view&id=11&type=inductees; Marie Cahill, *A History of Ford Motor Company* (New York: Smithmark, 1992), 86, 116; Walter Hayes, *Henry: A Life of Henry Ford II* (New York: Grove Weidenfeld, 1990), 14, 75. Breech also served as a mentor to Henry Ford II and as the first chairman of the board in 1955 when the company was going public.
34. W. Howard T. Snyder, "Love's Labor Won," *Inside Detroit*, 5.
35. Ibid.
36. Ibid., 6.
37. W. Howard T. Snyder, "On the Birmingham 8:05," *Inside Detroit*, ms., Players Archive, 1950, 2.
38. Ibid., 4.
39. W. Howard T. Snyder, "Lunch at the Detroit Club," *Inside Detroit*, ms., Players Archive, 1950, 2.
40. Verne W. Tucker, "Life Begins at Forty," *The Player*, 28 Oct. 1950, 1.
41. Ken Howard, "Here's Your Cue …," *The Player*, 25 Feb. 1972, 4.
42. Players Minutes, 22 May 1951.
43. "20 Year Club," *The Player*, 3 Nov. 1951, 4.
44. Players Minutes, 6 June 1955.
45. J. L. Thornhill, "When the Day Is Done," *The Player*, 26 Jan. 1952, 1.
46. Players Minutes, 31 Jan. 1952.
47. Players Minutes, 9 Oct. 1952.
48. Players Minutes, 3 Apr. 1952.
49. Players Minutes, 19 May 1953.
50. Al Shelden, letter to the author, 7 June 2005.
51. James Dresbach, "Blue-Ribbon … Blue Plate," *The Player*, 30 Jan. 1954, 2–3.
52. Players Minutes, 18 Feb. 1954.
53. "Final Curtain," *The Player*, 27 Mar. 1954, 4.
54. William B. Gregory, "The Forsyth Saga," *The Player*, 27 Mar. 1954, 2.
55. George L. Cassidy, "One for the Book," *The Player*, 30 Oct. 1954, 1.

56. Carl Mulls, "Nixon Sees Peace Aid in Bomb Power," *Detroit News*, 4 Apr. 1954, 1; see also Hub M. George "Nixon Calls H-Bomb Greatest Peace Force," *Detroit Free Press*, 4 Apr. 1954, A3.
57. Willard Rohloff, personal interview, 30 Mar. 2005.
58. Cassity, "One for the Book," 1.
59. Gregory, "Forsyth Saga," 1.
60. Players Minutes, 1 Apr., 18 May 1954.
61. Players Minutes, 30 Mar. 1955.
62. Players Minutes, 12 Aug. 1955.
63. "Eddie Guest Night," *The Player*, 1 Jan. 1955, 2.
64. *The Player*, 29 Oct. 1955, 2.
65. "Lee Anderson," Obituary, *Detroit News*, 7 Oct. 1955, n.p.; *Detroit Free Press*, 9 Oct. 1955, n.p.
66. Players Minutes, 18 Nov. 1955, 1 Mar. 1956.
67. Players Minutes, 15 May 1956.
68. Players Minutes, 11 July 1956.
69. Players Minutes, 11 Oct. 1956.
70. Players Minutes, 1 Nov. 1956.
71. "President's Letter," *The Player*, 27 Oct. 1965, n.p.
72. Minutes, 21 May 1957.
73. Charles K. Hyde, e-mail to author, 20 June 2006; Arthur M. Woodford, e-mail to author, 4 Sept. 2006.
74. Players Minutes, 15 May 1957.
75. Players Minutes, 18 July, 14 Aug. 1957.
76. Mark Beltaire, "Gentlemen—The Ladies!" *The Player*, 26 Oct. 1957, 1.
77. W. H. T. Snyder, "Here's Your Cue ...," *The Player*, 26 Oct. 1957, 3.
78. Players Minutes, 21 Nov. 1957.
79. "Bulletin!" *The Player*, 9 May 1958, 4.
80. Players Minutes, 5 Feb. 1958.
81. Players Minutes, 27 Feb. 1958.
82. Players Minutes, 21 Apr. 1958.
83. *The Player*, 25 Jan. 1958, 4.
84. James Dresbach, "Protein and Calories," *The Player*, 5 Apr. 1958, 1.
85. Players Minutes, 14 Aug. 1958.
86. Sugrue, *Origins*, 126.
87. Ibid., 127.
88. Ibid., 128, 151, 138, 131, 130, 135, 142.
89. Ibid., 149, 155, 176–77.
90. Ibid., 149.
91. Ibid.
92. Ibid., 156.
93. Gordon H. Miller, *The Day We Captured the Devil*, ms., The Players Archives, Detroit, 1958, 5–8.
94. Ibid., 9.
95. Ibid., 11.
96. Ibid.
97. Ibid., 12–13.

98. Players Minutes, 1 Nov. 1958.
99. Albert D. Conkey, "Concerning Lustre and a 24 Carat Cadillac Evening," *The Player*, 29 Nov. 1958, 1.
100. Robert L. Greene, "Blood and Thunder, a Pussycat and Pot," *The Player*, 9 May 1975, 1.
101. "Player William H. Elliott," *The Player*, 29 Nov. 1958, 4.
102. Players Minutes, 19 May 1959.
103. Walker Graham, "President's Letter," *The Player*, 31 Oct. 1959, 1.
104. Players Minutes, 11 Jan. 1960.
105. Players Minutes, 25 July 1960.
106. Players Minutes, 22 Aug. 1960.
107. Players Minutes, 22 Feb. 1960.
108. Players Minutes, 20 June 1960.
109. W. H. T. Snyder, "Here's Your Cue …," *The Player*, 6 May 1960, 3.
110. Robert E. Lamb, "Making Hay for May," *The Player*, 30 Jan. 1960, 1.
111. W. H. T. Snyder, "Here's Your Cue …," *The Player*, 28 Nov. 1959, 3.
112. W. H. T. Snyder, "Here's Your Cue …," *The Player*, 2 Jan. 1960, 5.
113. James Strasburg, "Todd-Forsyth-and Alexander Ruelle III," *The Player,* 29 Mar. 1941, 4; Players Minutes, 16 May 1961.
114. Larry Smith, personal interview, 20 Dec. 2005.
115. Players Minutes, 21 Aug. 1961.
116. Players Minutes, 25 Sept. 1961.
117. Players Minutes, 30 June 1964.
118. Players Minutes, 11 Aug. 1961.
119. Players Minutes, 25 Aug. 1961.
120. Players Minutes, 9 July 1962.
121. Players Minutes, 6 Dec. 1966.
122. Players Minutes, 6 Mar. 1961.
123. Players Minutes, 20 Mar. 1961.
124. Players Minutes, 23 Oct. 1961.
125. Players Minutes, 10 Oct. 1973.
126. Players Minutes, 20 Mar. 1961.
127. Players Minutes, 5 June 1961.
128. Willard Rohloff, personal interview, 8 Oct. 2003.
129. Players Minutes, 13 July 1964.
130. Players Minutes, 5 Aug. 1964.
131. Players Minutes, 24 Aug. 1964.
132. Players Minutes, 15 Aug. 1928.
133. Players Minutes, 16 Nov. 1964.
134. Ibid.
135. Ibid.
136. Players Minutes, 12 July 1965.
137. Players Minutes, 8 Nov. 1965.
138. Players Minutes, 10 Jan. 1966.
139. Players Minutes, 16 Oct. 1967.
140. Players Minutes, 18 May 1965.
141. Players Minutes, 20 Oct. 1965.

142. Players Minutes, 8 Nov. 1965.
143. Players Minutes, 11 July 1966.
144. Players Minutes, 31 Jan. 1966.

## Chapter 5

1. Frank B. and Arthur M. Woodford, *All Our Yesterdays* (Detroit: Wayne State University Press, 1969), 350.
2. Thomas J. Sugrue, *The Origins of the Urban Crisis: Race and Inequality in Postwar Detroit* (Princeton, NJ: Princeton University Press, 1996), 259.
3. Joe Kerr, "Trouble in Motor City," *Autotopia* (London: Reaktion Books, 2002), 134.
4. David Lee Poremba, *Detroit in Its World Setting* (Detroit: Wayne State University Press, 2001), 314–15.
5. Woodford and Woodford, *All Our Yesterdays*, 355.
6. Sugrue, *Origins*, 260–61.
7. Ibid., 264.
8. Camilo José Vergara, *American Ruins* (New York: Monacelli Press, 1999), 24.
9. 1950 census data: Sugrue, *Origins*, 23; 2000 and 2005 census data: Oralander Brand-Williams, "Detroit's Population Lowest since 1917," *Detroit News*, 8 Feb., 16 June 2005, www.detnews.com.
10. "Detroit Falls off Top 10 City List," *Detroit News*, 30 June 2005, www.detnews.com.
11. Detroit Factsheet, *U.S. Census Bureau*, 17 June 2005, http://factfinder.census.gov.
12. Sugrue, *Origins*, 269.
13. Jervis B. McMechan, letter to the author, Nov. 1999.
14. "Players in Its Diamond Jubilee," *The Player*, 29 Oct. 1971, 3.
15. Greg R. Thorn, e-mail to the author, 23 May 2000.
16. James Dresbach, "Player Richard A. Forsyth," *The Player*, 7 May 1971, 4.
17. Players Minutes, 15 June 1971.
18. Players Minutes, 14 Aug. 1971.
19. Players Minutes, 15 Nov. 1972.
20. Ibid.
21. Players Minutes, 31 July 1974.
22. Ken Howard, "Here's Your Cue …," *The Player*, 26 Nov. 1971, 3; Players Minutes, 16 Aug. 1972.
23. Players Minutes, 8 Aug. 1973.
24. Allan G. Dick, "It Must Have Been the Meatloaf," *The Player*, 26 Mar. 1982, 2.
25. Richard S. Shannon, "Another Year to Remember," *The Player*, 29 Oct. 1971, 1.
26. Willard Rohloff, personal interview, 30 May 2005; Thomas F. Burns, "Ménage a Trois," *The Player*, 27 Nov. 1971, 2.
27. Players Minutes, 17 Jan. 1973.
28. Ibid.

29. Ibid.
30. Players Minutes, 16 Nov. 1964.
31. Ken Howard, "'This is Players'...*IS* Players," *The Player*, 25 Feb. 1972, 4.
32. F. E. Brassy, "Here's Your Cue ...," *The Player*, 29 Dec. 1972, 3.
33. Players Minutes, 11 Oct. 1972.
34. Players Minutes, 16 Mar. 1970.
35. Jervis B. McMechan, *Running the Gamut, or More Than You Ever Wanted to Know about Human Sensitivity Labs*, ms., The Players Archives, Detroit, 1971, 1.
36. Ibid., 2–3.
37. Jervis B. McMechan, *The Way Cousin Kerby Fought the Steamboat Gambler*, ms., The Players Archives, Detroit, 1971, 9.
38. Players Minutes, 8 Aug. 1973.
39. "Here's Your Cue ...," *The Player*, 28 Dec. 1973, 3.
40. Players Minutes, 24 Sept. 1975.
41. Players Minutes, 14 Nov. 1973.
42. Players Minutes, 17 Apr. 1973.
43. Players Minutes, 9 Jan. 1974.
44. Players Minutes, 14 Nov. 1973.
45. Ibid.
46. Players Minutes, 6 Feb. 1974, 10 Dec. 1975.
47. Loren T. Robinson, "The Players Is Fun," *The Player*, 25 Oct. 1974, 1.
48. Players Minutes, 11 Sept. 1974, 4 June 1975.
49. Players Minutes, 10 Oct. 1974.
50. Players Minutes, 6 Nov. 1974.
51. Players Minutes, 18 May 1976.
52. Players Minutes, 11 July 1973.
53. Thorn e-mail; Ed Priebe, e-mail to the author, 26 May 2000.
54. James Turnbull,"... and Players Now Abed Shall Think Themselves Accurs'd They Were Not Here," *The Player*, Oct. 2005, 2; Larry Smith, interview with author, 21 Dec. 2005.
55. Players Minutes, 18 May 1976.
56. Thom e-mail.
57. Players Minutes, 25 June 1975.
58. Players Minutes, 27 Aug. 1975.
59. Willard A. Rohloff, "Look Up," *The Player*, 24 Oct. 1975, 1.
60. Ibid.
61. Rohloff interview, 2005; W. Howard T. Synder, "It's a Hit! Send Out Your Laundry!" *The Player*, 2 Jan. 1976, 1.
62. Robert L. Greene, "Here's Your Cue ...," *The Player, 2* Jan. 1976, 4.
63. Players Minutes, 23 July 1975; Willard Rohloff, Al Shelden Jr., Ned Schneider, interview with Bill Fitzpatrick for The Players Archives, Detroit, 8 Oct. 2003.
64. Players Minutes, 27 Aug. 1975.
65. Players Minutes, 10 Dec. 1975; Greene, "Here's Your Cue ..."
66. Snyder, "It's a Hit."
67. Players Minutes, 8 Dec. 1976.

68. Players Minutes, 5 Nov. 1975.
69. Players Minutes, 18 Aug. 1976.
70. Players Minutes, 22 Sept. 1976.
71. Players Minutes, 18 Jan. 1978.
72. Players Minutes, 10 Jan. 1979.
73. Jervis B. McMechan, "Moment #4," *Memorable Moments at Players*, ms., The Players Archives, Detroit, 1976, 3.
74. Players Minutes, 17 May 1977.
75. Robert L. Greene, "Christmas Comes but Once a Year," *The Player*, 31 Dec. 1976, 1.
76. Players Minutes, 8 June 1977.
77. Ibid.
78. Thomas F. Burns, "To the Best of All Worlds or 'A Tale of Once Upon a Time,'" *The Player*, 25 Nov. 1977, 1.
79. Players Minutes, 8 June 1977.
80. Martin Schroat, "Renaissance at Players," *The Player*, 27 Oct. 1978, 1.
81. Robert L. Greene, "Here's Your Cue ...," *The Player*, 29 Dec. 1978, 3.
82. Schroat, "Renaissance."
83. Players Minutes, 2 Apr. 1980.
84. Players Minutes, 11 June 1986.
85. *The Player*, 24 Oct. 1980, 2.
86. W. Howard T. Snyder, "Smash!" *The Player*, 26 Nov. 1980, 1.
87. Robert L. Greene, "Here's Your Cue ..." *The Player*, 21 Mar. 1980, 3.
88. Greg R. Thorn, "The Day Allan Believed in Miracles," *The Player*, 26 Jan. 1979, 2.
89. Francis E. Brossy III, "Rohloff, Rohloff, Pearse & McCann," *The Player*, 8 May 1981, 1–2.
90. Douglas F. Rohloff, "Work (Nunquam Renig)," *The Player*, 24 Oct. 1980, 1.
91. Arthur W. Gohle, "All Hail *The Valiant*," *The Player*, 29 Dec. 1980, 2.
92. W. Howard T. Snyder, "Author! Author! Author!" *The Player*, 24 Feb. 1984, 3.
93. Allan G. Dick, "FINAL SCORE: Players 3, Love 0," *The Player*, 8 May 1987, 2.
94. Larry Smith, personal interview, 21 Dec. 2005.
95. Robert L. Greene, "Shower, Anyone?" *The Player*, 27 Nov. 1981, 2.
96. Willard Rohloff, personal interview, 4 July 2002.
97. Robert Musial, "The Players Is Their Thing," *Detroit* [the Sunday magazine], *Detroit Free Press*, 25 Apr. 1982, 24.
98. W. Howard T. Snyder, "PPP Rates the 417th Frolic a Smash," *The Player*, 7 May 1982, 2.
99. Michael Jefferies, "It's an Honor to Be a Player," *The Player*, 27 Oct. 1983, 2.
100. Robert L. Greene, "Here's Your Cue ..." *The Player*, 23 Oct. 1981, 3.
101. Rohloff interview, 2005; Charles Weikel, "Escargot, Champagne and One Big Diamond," *The Player*, 27 Dec. 1985, 2; Robert L. Greene, "Gourmet Group," *The Player*, 27 Dec. 1985, 3.

102. J. J. Jorgensen, e-mail to author, 20 June 2005.
103. Robert L. Greene, "Here's Your Cue ...," *The Player*, 30 Dec. 1982, 3.
104. Glenn Scoles, cartoon, *The Player*, 30 Dec. 1982, 4.
105. Chris Monley, cartoon, *The Player*, 25 Nov. 1983, 4.
106. Players Minutes, 9 July 1986.
107. Players Minutes, 10 Dec. 1986.
108. Charles Weikel, "The Black Formosan Corruption May Be Getting Us All," *The Player*, 1 May 1984, 1.
109. Robert H. Janover, "Players' First Trolley Frolic Right on Track," *The Player*, 23 Nov. 1984, 1.
110. Weikel, "Escargot."
111. John L. Daly, e-mail to author, 26 May 2005.
112. Arthur W. Gohle, "Tragedy and Triumph," *The Player*, 28 Mar. 1986, 1.
113. Cameron Cross, *The Last Flight of the Columbia*, ms., The Players Archives, Detroit, 1986, 3–4.
114. Robert L. Greene, "Here's Your Cue ...," *The Player*, 21 Feb. 1986, 3.
115. Gohle, "Tragedy," 2.
116. Snyder, "It's a Hit!"
117. Kenneth Howard, "Eine Grosse Nachtmusik," *The Player*, 28 Nov. 1986, 1.
118. Ibid., 2.
119. Henry Nelson, e-mail to author, 30 May 2005.
120. Arthur C. Walker, "Make a Lasting Contribution," *The Player*, 25 Oct. 1984, 1.
121. Francis E. Brossy III, "Surprise, Surprise!" *The Player*, 22 Feb. 1985, 2.
122. Players Minutes, 11 June 1986.
123. Players Minutes, 10 Sept. 1986.
124. Players Minutes, 10 Dec. 1986.
125. Players Minutes, 8 Oct. 1986.
126. Bill Rohloff, personal interview, 8 June 2000.
127. Robert L. Greene, "Here's Your Cue ...," *The Player*, 24 Feb. 1989, 3.
128. Players Minutes, 15 Sept. 1986.
129. John A. Bluth, *A History of the Detroit Athletic Club, 1887–2000* (Detroit: Detroit Athletic Club, 2000), 68; Charles K. Hyde, e-mail to author, 20 June 2006.
130. Arthur M. Woodford, e-mail to author, 4 Sept. 2006.
131. Phil Gillis, "Nunquam Renig," *The Player*, 29 Sept. 1989, 1.
132. William L. Robinson Jr., "A Return to Tradition," *The Player*, 3 Sept. 1992, 1–2.
133. Chuck Steltenkamp, personal interview, 10 June 2000.
134. "How the Renaissance Center Changed the Landscape of Detroit," *Detroit News*, n.d. (c. 2001), 19 June 2005, http://info.detnews.com/history/story/index.cfm?id=122&category=locations.
135. Arthur M. Woodford, *This Is Detroit: 1701–2001* (Detroit: Wayne State University Press, 2001), 237.
136. Poremba, Detroit, 331–32.
137. Mark Puls, "Gem Theatre Move Begins," *Detroit News*, 12 Sept. 1997,

1D.
138. Players Minutes, 9 Oct. 1991.
139. Players Minutes, 9 Mar. 1999.
140. Players Minutes, 6 July 1999.
141. Michael T. Maurer, letter to The Players Board of Governors, c. 1991–92, The Players Archives, Detroit.
142. J. J. Jorgensen, e-mail to author, 14 Jan. 2006.
143. Peter Dawson, e-mail to author, 15 Jan. 2006.
144. The Players Strategic Plan: 1994, The Players Archives, Detroit.
145. Michael Goodell, "You Really, Really Like Players!" *The Player*, 1 Nov. 1995, 2.
146. Players Minutes, 10 Nov., 8 Sept. 1998.
147. Players Minutes, 9 Mar. 1999.
148. Players Minutes, 6 Apr. 1999.
149. Charles E. Roberts, "Clucks Revisit the 492nd Frolic," *The Player*, 1 Mar. 1995, 1.
150. For more information on the *Miss Saigon* debate, the two sides are presented rather clearly in Woodie King Jr.'s "Casting 'Miss Saigon' in a Bad Light" in the *The Impact of Race: Theatre and Culture* (New York: Applause Theatre and Cinema Books), 209–10 and Robert Brustein's "Lighten Up, America" in *Reimagining American Theatre* (New York: Hill and Wang, 1991), 227–29. Additionally, the playwright David Henry Hwang was very involved in the debate, and several interviews with him address the issue.
151. Steltenkamp interview.
152. Christopher G. Monley, "This Frolic Gets a 'D,'" *The Player*, 1 May 1996, 1.
153. Ibid.
154. Moore Whaite, "Motown's Pearse Arrow Scores Hit on Big Apple," *The Player*, 23 Nov. 1996, 1.
155. Ibid.
156. Bob Greene letter, *The Player*, 15 Oct. 1996, 1.
157. Mickie Miners, "It's Showtime!" *The Player*, 27 Sept. 1997, 1; John Yavruian, "Curtain Up!" *The Player*, 27 Sept. 1998, 1.
158. J. Robert O'Leary III, "Notes from the President," *The Player*, Oct. 2003, 5.
159. Peter Dawson, e-mail to author, 17 June 2005.
160. Sam Slade, "Wasn't That a Party!" *The Player*, Jan. 2001, 4.
161. Jim Turnbull, The Players 550th Frolic, The Players Archives, Detroit, videocassette, 4 Dec. 2004.

## Chapter 6

1. Glenn Michael Corey, letter to the author, Nov. 1999.
2. Glenn Scoles, personal interview, 12 May 2000.
3. Marianne Shrader, personal interview, 22 June 2005.
4. John Denler, personal interview, 22 June 2005; John Denler, e-mail to the

author, 23 June 2005.
5. D. C. Moon, personal interview, n.d.
6. Moon, interview.
7. Jervis B. McMechan, letter to the author, 8 Dec. 1999.
8. Scoles, interview.
9. J. J. Jorgensen, e-mail to the author, 2 July 2005.
10. Chris Nesi and Bob Zych, *Martha & Me*, ms., The Players Archives, Detroit, 2004, 2.
11. Ibid., 9.
12. Name withheld by request, personal interview, 2000.
13. Denne Osgood, "A Departing Note from Outgoing President, Player Denne Osgood," *The Player*, Sept. 2003, 6.
14. J. J. Jorgensen, e-mail to author, 20 June 2005.
15. Jorgensen e-mail, June 2005.
16. John L. Daly, e-mail to author, 26 May 2005.
17. Geno Pirrami, personal interview, 6 July 2005.
18. Jorgensen e-mail, June 2005.
19. "This Is Players," The Players Archives, Detroit, 1987.
20. Willard Rohloff, personal interview, 12 May 2000.
21. Maureen McDonald, "Club Casts All-Male Plays with Black Ties, Beer," *Detroit News*, 24 Oct. 2001, 12 May 2005, www.detnews.com.
22. Jorgensen e-mail, June 2005.
23. Ruth Scoles, personal interview, 12 May 2000.
24. John M. Butterfield, letter to the author, Nov. 1999.
25. Rohloff, interview.
26. Chuck Steltenkamp, personal interview, 10 June 2000.
27. Willard Rohloff, Al Shelden Jr., Ned Schneider, interview with Bill Fitzpatrick for The Players Archives, Detroit, 8 Oct. 2003.
28. Ibid.
29. Ibid.
30. William Colburn Standish Jr., letter to the author, Nov. 1999.
31. Michael Goodell, "The Players: Frolic #DXII," *The Player*, 25 Oct. 1998, 1.
32. Jorgensen e-mail, June 2005.
33. Greg R. Thorn, e-mail to the author, Nov. 1999.
34. Allan G. Dick, "Behind the Scenes," *The Player*, Mar. 2004, 4.
35. Rohloff, interview.
36. Steltenkamp interview.
37. Larry Smith, e-mail to the author, 16 July 2005.
38. James Turnbull, "… and Players Now Abed Shall Think Themselves Accurs'd They Were Not Here," *The Player*, Oct. 2005, 2.
39. Ibid.
40. Ibid.
41. Greg R. Thorn, "The Day Allan Believed in Miracles," *The Player*, 26 Jan. 1979, 1.
42. Daly e-mail.
43. Kensinger Jones, letter to the author, Nov. 1999.

44. William S. Turner Jr., letter to the author, Nov. 1999.
45. J. Robert O'Leary III, "Let's Continue the Momentum," *The Player*, Sept. 2003, 1.
46. "Wassailfest Seats & Tables Now on Sale!!" *The Player*, Nov. 2003, 3.
47. "Wassailfest '04 ... A Cast of Thousands!" *The Player*, Jan. 2005, 2.
48. Jim Jorgensen, "How to Live with a Necessary Evil," *The Player*, Oct. 2004, 6.

## Conclusion

1. Robert D. Putnam, *Bowling Alone: The Collapse and Revival of American Community* (New York: Simon and Schuster, 2000), 16, 55, 59–61.
2. Ibid., 100, 105, 109, 111, 114.
3. Ibid., 283.
4. Mary Ann Clawson, *Constructing Brotherhood: Class, Gender, and Fraternalism* (Princeton, NJ: Princeton University Press, 1989), 260.
5. Putnam, *Bowling Alone*, 62–63.
6. James A. Vela-McConnell, *Who Is My Neighbor? Social Affinity in a Modern World* (Albany: SUNY Press, 1999), 5–6.
7. Ibid., 221, 139.
8. Ibid., 3.
9. Anthony P. Cohen, *The Symbolic Construction of Community* (New York: Tavistock, 1985), 9.
10. Gregory J. Shepherd and Eric W. Rothenbuhler, eds. *Communication and Community* (Mahwah, NJ: Lawrence Erlbaum, 2001), 16.
11. John G. Bruhn, *The Sociology of Community Connections* (New York: Kluwer Academic/Plenum, 2005), 13, 15.
12. Jonathan Barry and Christopher Brooks, eds., *The Middling Sort of People: Culture, Society and Politics in England, 1550–1800* (New York: St. Martin's, 1994), 106, 104.
13. Shepherd and Rothenbuhler, *Communication*, 27.
14. Putnam, *Bowling Alone*, 96.
15. Cohen, *Symbolic Construction*, 50.
16. Clawson, *Constructing Brotherhood*, 13, 18.
17. Patricia Anne Masters, "The Philadelphia Mummers Parade: A Sociological Study of Play and Community" (Ph.D. diss., American University [DC], 1998), 330.
18. Shepherd and Rothenbuhler, *Communication*, 9.
19. Cohen, *Symbolic Construction*, 91, 94.
20. Ibid., 102.
21. Ibid., 98.
22. Michael Jeffries, "It's an Honor to Be a Player," *The Player*, 27 Oct. 1983, 1.
23. Shepherd and Rothenbuhler, *Communication*, 187.
24. Vela-McConnell, *Who Is My Neighbor*, 34.
25. Bruhn, *Sociology*, 12.
26. Vela-McConnell, *Who Is My Neighbor*, 30.

27. Diane Blake, personal interview, date unknown.
28. Edward T. Hall, *Beyond Culture* (Garden City, NY: Anchor, 1976), 6.
29. Putnam, *Bowling Alone*, 288–89.
30. Bruhn, *Sociology*, 188.
31. Masters, "Philadelphia Mummers Parade," 391–93.
32. Ibid., 394.
33. Ibid.
34. Ibid., 335–36.
35. Ibid., 325, 306.

## Appendix C

1. Theodore F. MacManus and Norman Beasley, *Men, Money, and Motors: The Drama of the Automobile* (New York: Harper and Brothers, 1929), 48.
2. Donald Finlay Davis, *Conspicuous Production: Automobiles and Elites in Detroit, 1899–1933* (Philadelphia: Temple University Press, 1988), 238.
3. MacManus and Beasley, *Men, Money, and Motors*, 11–15, 27.
4. The Players, *The Players Book of One Act Plays* (New York: Walter V. McKee, 1928), 335.
5. Charles Fey, "Joseph Boyer," ms., Joseph Boyer file, Michigan and Detroit Biography Index, Burton Historical Library, Detroit, 1949; Davis, *Conspicuous Production*, 147.
6. *Who's Who in Detroit, 1935–36: A Biographical Dictionary of Representative Men and Women of Metropolitan Detroit* (Detroit: Walter Ronig, 1935), 23.
7. Willard Rohloff, Al Shelden Jr., Ned Schneider, interview with Bill Fitzpatrick for The Players Archives, Detroit, 8 Oct. 2003.
8. David H. Shayt, "Hi-Yo, Silver! Away!" *Smithsonian*, Oct. 2001, 28–30.
9. Robert L. Greene, "Here's Your Cue …," *The Player*, 21 Mar. 1980, 3.
10. *Who's Who, 1935–36*, 31.
11. Ibid., 35.
12. Ibid., 39.
13. Ibid.; Davis, *Conspicuous Production*, 257.
14. Obituary, *Detroit Free Press*, 2 May 1946, Michigan and Detroit Biography Index, Burton Historical Library, Detroit.
15. Davis, *Conspicuous Production*, 62–63.
16. Ibid., 58.
17. "New Service Manager of Local Ad Agency," *Detroit Times*, 3 Jan. 1922; "Boynton Dies in Washington," *Detroit Free Press*, 24 Sept. 1934; and "France Gives Writer Medal," *Detroit Free Press*, 23 Nov. 1928, Walter C. Boynton file, Michigan and Detroit Biography Index, Burton Historical Library, Detroit.
18. Larry Engelmann, *Intemperance: The Lost War against Liquor* (New York: Free Press, 1979), 133.
19. *Who's Who, 1935–36* 49; MacManus and Beasley, *Men, Money, and Motors*, 49.

20. Davis, *Conspicuous Production*, 257.
21. Kenneth H. Voyles and John A. Bluth, *The Detroit Athletic Club, 1887-2001* (Chicago: Arcadia, 2001), 68.
22. *Who's Who, 1935-36*, 49.
23. Laurena Pringle, "A Man in the Middle Is 'Spike' Briggs," *Detroit Free Press*, 16 May 1953, n.p.; and "Spike Briggs Dies at 58," *Detroit News*, 3 July 1970, A1, Walter O. Briggs Jr. file, Michigan and Detroit Biography Index, Burton Historical Library, Detroit.
24. George Weeks, *Stewards of the State: The Governors of Michigan* (Ann Arbor: *Detroit News* and the Historical Society of Michigan, 1991), 90.
25. Ibid., 91.
26. *Who's Who, 1935-36*, 52.
27. Louis L. Richards, "Arthur H. Buhl," ms., Michigan and Detroit Biography Index, Burton Historical Library, Detroit, 20 July 1929, 2-3; Clarence M. Burton, *The City of Detroit, Michigan, 1701-1922*, vol. 4 (Detroit: S. J. Clarke, 1922), 261; *Who's Who, 1935-36*, 53.
28. *Detroit City Directory* (Detroit: R. L. Polk, 1931-32), 412; Davis, *Conspicuous Production*, 73.
29. Unidentified article, *Detroit Free Press*, 17 Sept. 1946, Michigan and Detroit Biography Index, Burton Historical Library, Detroit.
30. Ibid.; Burton, *City of Detroit*, vol. 4, 683.
31. Burton, *City of Detroit*, vol. 5, 676.
32. Ibid., vol. 4, 595-96.
33. Bob Carlson, e-mail to author, 26 May 2005.
34. Carlson e-mail.
35. MacManus and Beasley, *Men, Money, and Motors*, 44; Davis, *Conspicuous Production*, 89.
36. Davis, *Conspicuous Production*, 89.
37. According to Alan Schwarz in his book on statistics (note 38), most people found Cobb "loathsome" while Lajoie was "immensely popular."
38. Alan Schwarz, *The Numbers Game: Baseball's Lifelong Fascination with Statistics* (New York: St. Martin's, 2004), 29.
39. Voyles and Bluth, *Detroit Athletic Club*, 36.
40. MacManus and Beasley, *Men, Money, and Motors*, 39-45; *Who's Who, 1935-36*, 66; Davis, *Conspicuous Production*, 88, 91.
41. Davis, *Conspicuous Production*, 257.
42. Norman Beasley, *Knudsen: A Biography* (New York: McGraw-Hill, 1947), 59.
43. *Who's Who, 1935-36*, 68; Engelmann, *Intemperance*, 194.
44 "Apropos," *Michigan Motor News*, n.d., Howard A. Coffin file, Michigan and Detroit Biography Index, Burton Historical Library, Detroit.
45. Peter Gavrilovich and Bill McGraw, eds., *The Detroit Almanac: 300 Years of Life in the Motor City* (Detroit: Detroit Free Press, 2000), 269.
46. Harry Barnard, *Independent Man: The Life of Senator James Couzens* (1958; repr., Detroit: Wayne State University Press, 2002), 49-50.
47. Ernest A. Baumgarth, "James Couzens' Life Story, From Car Checker to Fame," *Detroit News*, 23 Oct. 1936, 56.

48. Richard Barry, "Newberry's Successor: A Study of Senator Couzens," *The Outlook*, 20 Dec. 1922, 696.
49. MacManus and Beasley, *Men, Money, and Motors*, 154–61; Charles W. Wood, "He Had Millions, But Wanted a Job," *Colliers*, 5 Aug. 1922, 10; Barnard, *Independent Man*, 88–89, 94.
50. *Who's Who, 1935–36*, 88.
51. Burton, *City of Detroit*, vol. 4, 595–96.
52. Davis, *Conspicuous Production*, 93; MacManus and Beasley, *Men, Money, and Motors*, 84.
53. Michael S. Frank, *Elmwood Endures: History of a Detroit Cemetery* (Detroit: Wayne State University Press, 1996), 190.
54. Davis, *Conspicuous Production*, 257.
55. David DiChiera, *Michigan Opera Theatre Home Page*. Michigan Opera Theatre, Detroit, 8 July 2002, www.michiganopera.org; Arthur M. Woodford, *This Is Detroit: 1701–2001* (Detroit: Wayne State University Press, 2001), 239.
56. Unidentified article, *Detroit Free Press*, 9 Sept. 1943, Joseph Morell Dodge file, Michigan and Detroit Biography Index, Burton Historical Library, Detroit.
57. "Detroit Banker Reaches Japan," *Detroit Free Press*, 29 Oct. 1943, Joseph Morell Dodge file, Michigan and Detroit Biography Index, Burton Historical Library, Detroit.
58. Obituary, unidentified newspaper, 12 June 1914, Michigan and Detroit Biography Index, Burton Historical Library, Detroit.
59. *Who's Who, 1935–36*, 102–3.
60. "Ewald Will Be Host at Dinner," *Detroit Free Press*, 9 Feb. 1941, n.p., Henry T. Ewald file, Michigan and Detroit Biography Index, Burton Historical Library, Detroit.
61. Memorial card, Henry T. Ewald file, Michigan and Detroit Biography Index, Burton Historical Library, Detroit.
62. Henry Dominguez, *Edsel: The Story of Henry Ford's Forgotten Son* (Warrendale, PA: Society of Automotive Engineers, 2002), 119.
63. Davis, *Conspicuous Production*, 257.
64. "L. P. Fisher, Auto Pioneer, Dies at 73," *Detroit News*, 4 Sept. 1961, n.p., Lawrence P. Fisher file, Michigan and Detroit Biography Index, Burton Historical Library, Detroit.
65. Kay Houston and Linda Culpepper, "The Most Beautiful Building in the World," *Detroit News*, n.d., 19 June 2005, http://info.detnews.com/history/story/index.cfm?id=32&category=locations.
66. Vivian M. Baulch, "Lavish Grayhaven Community Was Crippled by Great Depression," *Detroit News*, c. 2001. 19 June 2005, http://info.detnews.com/history/story/index.cfm?id=128&category=locations.
67. Barnard, *Independent Man*, 106; "Eddie Fitzgerald, After 7 Years of Public Life, Quits to Enter Business," *Detroit Journal*, 2 Aug. 1919, Edward T. Fitzgerald file, Michigan and Detroit Biography Index, Burton Historical Library, Detroit.
68. *Who's Who, 1935–36*, 116.

69. Ibid., 161.
70. "Richard E. Byrd's North Pole Flight," Byrd Polar Research Archival Center, the Ohio State University, 15 May 1996, accessed 18 Dec. 2006, http://polarnet.mps.ohio-state.edu/Archival/Diary.html; "The Papers of Admiral Richard E. Byrd," Byrd Polar Research Center Archival Center, the Ohio State University, 3 Mar. 2004, accessed 18 Dec. 2006, http://library.osu.edu/sites/archives/polar/byrd.php.
71. Dominguez, *Edsel*, 179–81; William Greenleaf, *From These Beginnings: The Early Philanthropies of Henry and Edsel Ford, 1911–1936* (Detroit: Wayne State University Press, 1964), 160–61.
72. Greenleaf, *From These Beginnings*, 163.
73. Patrick Marnham, *Dreaming with His Eyes Open: A Life of Diego Rivera* (New York: Knopf, 1999), 240; Diego Rivera, *My Art, My Life: An Autobiography* (New York: Citadel, 1960), 191.
74. Greenleaf, *From These Beginnings*, 166–67.
75. Davis, *Conspicuous Production*, 257.
76. *Who's Who, 1935–36*, 116.
77. Davis, *Conspicuous Production*, 233, 98.
78. "Detroiter Assigned to Stockholm Post," *Detroit Free Press*, 26 Oct. 1944, Michigan and Detroit Biography Index, Burton Historical Library, Detroit.
79. *Who's Who, 1935–36*, 118.
80. Ibid., 123.
81. Ibid., 124.
82. Ibid., 129.
83. Ibid., 134.
84. Ibid., 137.
85. W. Hawkins Ferry, *The Buildings of Detroit: A History Revised* (Detroit: Wayne State University Press, 1980), 262.
86. "Legacy," The SmithGroup Home Page, the SmithGroup, 16 Jan. 2006, www.smithgroup.com/AboutUs/Legacy.asp.
87. Royce Howes, *Edgar A. Guest: A Biography* (New York: Reilly and Lee, 1953), 1, 27–28, 30, 6.
88. Ibid., 4.
89. Ibid., 177.
90. *Who's Who, 1935–36*, 147.
91. Barnard, *Independent Man*, 7; Louis L. Richards, "Norval A. Hawkins," ms., Norval A. Hawkins file, Michigan and Detroit Biography Index, Burton Historical Library, Detroit, 11 Dec. 1929, 1.
92. Davis, *Conspicuous Production*, 71.
93. Dominguez, *Edsel*, 119.
94. Davis, *Conspicuous Production*, 257.
95. "Earl Holley Funeral Monday," *Detroit Free Press*, 7 Dec. 1958, Earl Holley file, Michigan and Detroit Biography Index, Burton Historical Library, Detroit.
96. "W. F. Holliday Dead," *Detroit News*, 30 June 1926, n.p., William F. Holliday file, Michigan and Detroit Biography Index, Burton Historical Library,

Detroit.
97. *Who's Who, 1935–36*, 164.
98. Malcolm W. Bingay, "C. A. Hughes of DAC, Dies at 71," *Detroit Free Press*, 30 Jan. 1953, n.p., Charles Hughes file, Michigan and Detroit Biography Index, Burton Historical Library, Detroit.
99. Voyles and Bluth, *Detroit Athletic Club*, 26, 24.
100. MacManus and Beasley, *Men, Money, and Motors*, 113.
101. Ibid., 258; *Who's Who, 1935–36*, 171.
102. John F. Nehman, "Funeral Monday for Judge O. Z. Ide," *Detroit News*, 6 Sept. 1957, n.p.; unidentified article, *Detroit Free Press*, 28 June 1933; and "Birthday of O. Z. Ide," *Detroit News*, 26 May 1933, n.p., O. Z. Ide file, Michigan and Detroit Biography Index, Burton Historical Library, Detroit.
103. *Detroit Free Press* Biography Index and unidentified newspaper article, *Detroit Free Press*, 7 Nov. 1927, Michigan and Detroit Biography Index, Burton Historical Library, Detroit.
104. *Who's Who, 1935–36*, 172.
105. Francis E. Brossy III, "Two Simons and a Coble! Quel Bon Soir!" *The Player*, 1 May 1993, 1; Greg R. Thom, "The More Things Change …" *The Player*, 27 Nov. 1993, 1; John L. Daly, "Old Favorites, Well Performed," *The Player*, 1 Dec. 1995, 1; Greg R. Thorn, "In Like a Lion …" *The Player*, 28 Mar. 1984, 1.
106. "Joy, Henry Bourne," *National Cyclopedia of American Biography* (New York: James T. White, n.d.), n.p., Henry B. Joy file, Michigan and Detroit Biography Index, Burton Historical Library, Detroit.
107. MacManus and Beasley, *Men, Money, and Motors*, 48–50.
108. Davis, *Conspicuous Production*, 58.
109. Frank, *Elmwood*, 185.
110. Engelmann, *Intemperance*, 102–3, 194–210.
111. "Henry B. Joy Dead; Motor Car Leader," *New York Times*, 6 Nov. 1936, Henry B. Joy file, Michigan and Detroit Biography Index, Burton Historical Library, Detroit.
112. Davis, *Conspicuous Production*, 238; "Joy Memorial," n.p., 1 July 1939, Henry B. Joy file, Michigan and Detroit Biography Index, Burton Historical Library, Detroit.
113. Davis, *Conspicuous Production*, 58.
114. Ibid., 102.
115. Peter Dawson, e-mail to author, 17 June 2005.
116. Barnard, *Independent Man*, 215.
117. Davis, *Conspicuous Production*, 126; Dominguez, *Edsel*, 111.
118. Dominguez, *Edsel*, 119.
119. Davis, *Conspicuous Production*, 257.
120. Ibid.
121. Tim Kiska, *Detroit's Powers and Personalities* (Rochester Hills, MI: Momentum, 1989), 115–16.
122. Gerald Scott, "WW II Exhibit Honor's GM's Knudsen," *New Center News*, 24 Oct. 1994, 1, 4.

123. Harold C. Livesay, *American Made: Men Who Shaped the American Economy* (New York: HarperCollins, 1979), 174; Robert VanderKloot, "To Denmark a Good Son: The William S. Knudsen Story," ms., William S. Knudsen file, Michigan and Detroit Biography Index, Burton Historical Library, Detroit, 9. One particularly interesting aspect of the moving assembly line was the addition of a moving overhead trolley system that was borrowed from the meat packing industry.
124. H. C. Garrison, "New GM Head Began Career as a Mechanic," *Detroit News*, 4 May 1937, n.p.; MacManus and Beasley, *Men, Money, and Motors*, 245.
125. Barnard, *Independent Man*, 188; *Who's Who, 1935–36*, 192.
126. *Who's Who, 1935–36*, 195.
127. Davis, *Conspicuous Production*, 238.
128. *Who's Who, 1935–36*, 198.
129. Ibid., 200.
130. *Detroit City Directory* (Detroit: R. L. Polk, 1925), 1289.
131. *Detroit City Directory* (Detroit: R. L. Polk, 1911), 1596.
132. MacManus and Beasley, *Men, Money, and Motors*, 89.
133. Barnard, *Independent Man*, 222.
134. MacManus and Beasley, Men, *Money, and Motors*, 150–51, 202–3; Frank, *Elmwood*, 190.
135. Davis, *Conspicuous Production*, 257.
136. "City to Hail Gen. Knudsen," unidentified newspaper, William S. Knudsen files, Michigan and Detroit Biography Index, Burton Historical Library, Detroit.
137. *Who's Who, 1935–36*, 218–19.
138. MacManus and Beasley, *Men, Money, and Motors*, 194.
139. *Who's Who, 1935–36*, 221.
140. Burton, *City of Detroit*, vol. 4, 523.
141. Dominguez, *Edsel*, 76; Richard Bak, *Henry and Edsel: The Creation of the Ford Empire* (Hoboken, NJ: John Wiley and Sons, 2003), 173.
142. *Who's Who, 1935–36*, 210.
143. "Is Found Dead in His Garage," *Detroit News*, 29 Feb. 1928, and E. A. Batchelor, "Personal and Confidential: Joseph Meadon," *Detroit Saturday Night*, 19 July 1924, Joseph Meadon file, Michigan and Detroit Biography Index, Burton Historical Library, Detroit.
144. *Who's Who, 1935–36*, 231.
145. Davis, *Conspicuous Production*, 72.
146. "Michael Case Miners, 1941–1999," plaque over the bar in the lobby of the Playhouse.
147. Davis, *Conspicuous Production*, 257.
148. MacManus and Beasley, *Men, Money, and Motors*, 243.
149. *Who's Who, 1935–36*, 237.
150. "Michael Murphy Is Praised as B. of C.'s First President," *Detroit Free Press*, 20 Feb. 1938; and "M. J. Murphy" *Detroit News*, 6 Sept. 1932, Michael Joseph Murphy file, Michigan and Detroit Biography Index, Burton Historical Library, Detroit.

151. Davis, *Conspicuous Production*, 62.
152. *Who's Who, 1935–36*, 242.
153. Phelps Newberry file, Michigan and Detroit Biography Index, Burton Historical Library, Detroit.
154. MacManus and Beasley, *Men, Money, and Motors*, 48.
155. Davis, *Conspicuous Production*, 58.
156. *Who's Who, 1935–36*, 245; Engelmann, *Intemperance*, 169.
157. Burton, *City of Detroit*, vol. 3, 670.
158. "Fred A. Nolan," obituary, *Detroit News*, 14 Dec. 1946, Michigan and Detroit Biography Index, Burton Historical Library, Detroit.
159. *Detroit City Directory* (Detroit: R. L. Polk, 1938), 1291.
160. "Owen, John L." Obituary, *Detroit News*, 23 Nov. 2003, accessed 21 June 2005, www.detroitnewspapers.com/deathnotices/print.cfm?id=44049.
161. Davis, *Conspicuous Production*, 68.
162. *Who's Who, 1935–36*, 253.
163. MacManus and Beasley, *Men, Money, and Motors*, 58; Davis, *Conspicuous Production*, 107.
164. *Who's Who, 1935–36*, 256.
165. Frank, *Elmwood*, 200.
166. Obituary, *Detroit Free Press*, 11 Nov. 1938, Michigan and Detroit Biography Index, Burton Historical Library, Detroit.
167. *Who's Who, 1935–36*, 259.
168. Ibid., 264; "Michigan Author Reck Dies at His Typewriter," *Detroit News*, 15 Oct. 1965, Franklin M. Reck file, Michigan and Detroit Biography Index, Burton Historical Library, Detroit.
169. Voyles and Bluth, *Detroit Athletic Club*, 70.
170. "Ad Man Robinson Dies at 72," *Detroit Free Press*, 26 Oct. 1963, Loren T. Robinson file, Michigan and Detroit Biography Index, Burton Historical Library, Detroit.
171. "William L. Robinson, title firm executive," *Detroit News*, 15 Sept. 1974, W. L. Robinson file, Michigan and Detroit Biography Index, Burton Historical Library, Detroit.
172. Davis, *Conspicuous Production*, 48.
173. *Who's Who, 1935–36*, 276.
174. "Walter S. Russel, Engineer and a City-Builder, Is Dead," *Detroit Free Press*, 18 Aug. 1935, Walter S. Russel file, Michigan and Detroit Biography Index, Burton Historical Library, Detroit.
175. Burton, *City of Detroit*, vol. 5, 17.
176. *Who's Who, 1935–36*, 278.
177. "Schantz, Retired Head of D & C Line, Dead at 73," unidentified newspaper, n.d., n.p., A. A. Schantz file, Michigan and Detroit Biography Index, Burton Historical Library, Detroit.
178. Jay M. Grossman, "Vet brings Personal Perspective to Ceremony," *Birmingham Eccentric*, 29 May 2005, A1.
179. *Who's Who, 1935–36*, 280.
180. "Life of William E. Scripps a Monument to His Widespread Interests," *Detroit News*, 12 June 1952, W. E. Scripps file, Michigan and Detroit Bi-

ography Index, Burton Historical Library, Detroit; Kay Houston, "How the Detroit Zoo's First Day Was Almost Its Last," *Detroit News*, n.d., accessed 23 July 2004, http://info.detnews.com/history/story/index.cfm?id=204&category=locations.

181. "William J. Scripps Gets Air Force Post," *Detroit News*, 26 May 1942; and "William J. Scripps' Funeral on Tuesday," *Detroit News*, 12 Dec. 1965, William John Scripps file, Michigan and Detroit Biography Index, Burton Historical Library, Detroit.
182. Richard Bak, *Detroit: Across Three Centuries* (Chelsea, MI: Sleeping Bear, 2001), 173.
183. Willard Rohloff, personal interview, 30 Mar. 2005.
184. *Who's Who, 1935–36*, 289; Frank, *Elmwood*, 190.
185. George W. Stark, *In Old Detroit* (Detroit: Arnold-Powers, 1939), 119–22.
186. "Fred L. Smith Dies in Crash," *Detroit Free Press*, 26 Feb. 1941, Fred L. Smith file, Michigan and Detroit Biography Index, Burton Historical Library, Detroit.
187. Davis, *Conspicuous Production*, 253; Barnard, *Independent Man*, 169.
188. Unidentified article, *Among Friends*, Spring 1957, Michigan and Detroit Biography Index, Burton Historical Library, Detroit.
189. *Who's Who, 1935–36*, 301.
190. Frank, *Elmwood*, 183; MacManus and Beasley, *Men, Money, and Motors*, 58.
191. *Who's Who, 1935–36*, 303.
192. Ibid., 308.
193. Burton, *City of Detroit*, vol. 3, 728.
194. Ibid., 720.
195. Obituary, *Detroit Free Press*, 27 June 1950, Michigan and Detroit Biography Index, Burton Historical Library, Detroit; Dominguez, *Edsel*, 33.
196. *Who's Who, 1935–36*, 315.
197. "Toms to Retire," *Detroit Times*, 27 Dec. 1959, Robert M. Toms file, Michigan and Detroit Biography Index, Burton Historical Library, Detroit.
198. Irving Stone, *Clarence Darrow for the Defense* (Garden City, NY: Garden City Publishing, 1941), 479, 483–84.
199. Engelmann, *Intemperance*, 130.
200. "Coin Toss Won by Toms," *Detroit Free Press*, 24 Sept. 1927, Robert M. Toms file, Michigan and Detroit Biography Index, Burton Historical Library, Detroit.
201. *Who's Who, 1935–36*, 317.
202. Robert D. Kirk, "Ex-Judge Toms, 73, Dies of Heart Attack," *Detroit News*, 7 Apr. 1959, Robert M. Toms file, Michigan and Detroit Biography Index, Burton Historical Library, Detroit.
203. David H. Shayt, "Hi-Yo, Silver! Away!" *Smithsonian*, Oct. 2001, 28–30.
204. Burton, *City of Detroit*, vol. 3, 938.
205. *Who's Who, 1935–36*, 324.
206. Richard S. Shannon, "Something for Everyone," *The Player*, 30 Mar.

1973, 2.
207. Douglass Dowty, "Robert VanderKloot," obituary, *Detroit News*, 16 June 2005, www.detnews.com.
208. "James Vernor, Jr.," ms., and "James Vernor Dead at 39," *Detroit Times*, 9 Apr. 1957, James Vernor Jr. file, Michigan and Detroit Biography Index, Burton Historical Library, Detroit.
209. *Who's Who, 1935–36*, 329.
210. Ibid., 332.
211. Frank, *Elmwood*, 199.
212. Barnard, *Independent Man*, 252.
213. Unidentified newspaper article, *Detroit Free Press*, 7 Sept. 1932, John R. Watkins file, Michigan and Detroit Biography Index, Burton Historical Library, Detroit.
214. *Who's Who, 1935–36*, 335; Engelmann, *Intemperance*, 117.
215. *Who's Who, 1935–36*, 336.
216. Ibid., 338.
217. *Detroit City Directory*, 1938, 1810.
218. Louis L. Richards, "H. Kirke White, Jr.," ms., 4 Jan. 1930, H. Kirke White Jr. file, Michigan and Detroit Biography Index, Burton Historical Library, Detroit.
219. *Who's Who, 1935–36*, 342.
220. MacManus and Beasley, *Men, Money, and Motors*, 251–58.
221. *Who's Who, 1935–36*, 354.

# Index

*References to illustrations are in bold*

Abbey Players of Dublin, 30
Alexander, Kirkland B., 18, 21, 29
Alger, Frederick, 25–26, 63
*Alice in Playerland*, 136
*All Aboard*, 74–75
American Motors, 26
Anderson, Lee: building the Playhouse, 42; career, 28; death of, 99; *In the Thousands of Years to Come*, 1, 39–40; *Is Peculiar*, 109
*Annie*, 136
Art Theatre movement. *See* Little Theatre movement
*Art Theatre, The*, 14–15, 30–31
Arts and Crafts, Detroit Society of: donating materials to Playhouse, 48; founding of, 5, 12; Hume, Sam, 13–14, 29; Hume models of stage craft, 13; masques, 13, 14; and Player ties, 30, 42–43; problems with Players, 33; *Theatre Arts Magazine*, 14–15, 30; theatre at, 12, 14–15, 30, 32, 37, 42–43, 52
Arts and Crafts movement, 12
Austin, Ronald H., 145

"Ballad of the Player's Daughter," 43–44
*Bardell vs. Pickwick*, 61
Batchelor, Edward (Ned) A., 28, 86
Beattie, Daniel C., 88, 110
Bel Geddes, Norman, 189
Bellanca, Peter J., 140, 142–43
Blenkle, Oren W., Jr., 143, 165
Bohemian Club, 8–9, 17
*Book of Etiquette, The*, 70
Booth, Ralph W. H., 30
Bowen, Edgar W., 23, 46, 69
Bowen, Lem W., 25
*Bowery Burlicue Moves Uptown*, 141
Boyer, Joseph, 25–26

Boynton, Walter C., 18, 61
Brandel, Tom, 157
Brossy, Francis E., III, 144
Bruce, Marshall, 136
Brucker, Wilber, 95, **97**
Brunk, Thomas W., 152
Buchinger, William G., 121
Buhl, Arthur H., 27
Buhl, Theodore D., 27
Burns, Thomas F. 135
Burroughs, Cldye H., 30
Butterfield, John M., 38, 170
Byrd, Richard E., 122, 240

*Cabinet Meeting, The*, 63, 67
Cadillac Automobile Company, 25, 26
Cady, Guy Brewster, 17–18, 29, 75, 95
Campbell, Harvey J., 33, 80, 170–71
Canty, Alan, 95
Carley, Leonard R., 18
Carroll, Leona (Lee), 79–80, 138, 146, 147, 172
Chalmers, Hugh, 26
Chalmers-Detroit Motor Company, 26, 27
Chapin, Dallas, 90, 95
Chapin, Roy D., 26
Cheney, Sheldon, 14–15, 30
Chrysler Corporation, 244, 256
Clark, Emory, 63
Clark, Frank Scott, 53
Coffin, Dean, 114
Coffin, Howard E., 26
Comedy Club, the, 11, 17, 22
*Command Decision*, 89
Community Theatre movement, 16
Conkey, Albert D.: *All Aboard*, 74–75; *On High*, 83–85; and Players Foundation, 102; review, 105; *There Once Lived a King*, 94
Coppin, John S., 56, 73, 114
Coppin nude, 56, 114

Corey, Glenn (Fuzz) M., 161, 175
Corrigan, Al M., 28
Couger, Warren, 142
*Coup/Clucks*, 154
Couzens, James, 27, 33, 38–39
Cross, Cameron, 141–42
Crow, Allen, 95
Cullen, Countee, 41

Daly, John L., 141, 167
Davies, Lewis, 143
Dawson, Peter W., 151, 157
*Day We Captured the Devil, The*, 104–5
Denby, Edwin, 249
Deneen, William F., 101
Detroit Athletic Club (DAC): exclusivity, 24; first president of original club, 238; founding of, 7; and Hughes, Charles, 243; membership numbers, 60, 100, 145; nude above bar, 73; and wartime, 34; women (opening doors to), 3
Detroit Automobile Company, 25
Detroit Club: exclusivity, 24; *Inside Detroit*, 91; membership numbers, 60, 100, 145–46; relation to DAC, 7
Detroit Historical Museum, 24, 47
Detroit Institute of Art, 12, 24, 29–30, 239, 240, 248
Detroit Museum of Art. *See* Detroit Institute of Art
Detroit Orchestral Association, 24,
Detroit Public Library, 24, 253
Detroit Society of Arts and Crafts. *See* Arts and Crafts, Detroit Society of
Detroit Zoo, 24, 233
Denby, Edwin, 28
Dick, Allan, 141, 176–77
Diedrich, Arthur V., 113
Di Lorenzo, Thomas, 52
Dodge, Horace, 25
*Doing Stratford*, 2, 48–49, 110, 132, 133
*Down to Rio*, 88, 110
D'Oyly Carte Opera Company, 67–68, 70
Dresbach, James, 109, 120–21

Eddy, Frank W., 25
Edgett, Richard J., 143
Eldredge, Gordon C., 109
Elliot, William (Bill) H., 79, 106, 171
E-M-F Company, 27

E. R. Thomas-Detroit Company, 26
Ewald, Henry T., 29, 33, 53

*Fair Enough*, 39
Fellows, Waldo E., 109
Ferguson, Homer, 96–97
Fine Arts Society: combining with Players (possibility of), 32, 130–31; discount at Playhouse, 57; founding of, 5, 11, 17; and gender, 20; and Gourmet Group, 139; today, 162; and Tri-Effort, 99–101, 108, 110, 131–32, 133, 162; and war relief, 33
Fisher Body Company, 26
Fisher, Lawrence P., 26–27
Fitzgerald, Edward T., 38–39
*Flame, The*, 85
Ford, Edsel B., 28, 44, 46, 63, 122
Ford, Harry W., 27, 34
Ford, Henry, 27, 44, 246, 249–50
Ford, Henry, II, 90, 149
Ford Motor Company, 27, 44, 59, 89, 236–37, 240, 244, 245, 246
Forsyth, Richard A.: death of, 120–21; dressing room door, 110, 171–72; ghost of, 170; *On Borrowed Time* (director), 79; Players Foundation, 102; *There Once Lived a King* (actor), 94; *What the Heil* (actor), 73
Forsyth, Sandy, 79
Frear, Robert G., 165
Friars Club (NY), 10–11

Gage, Alexander K., 17–18, 75, 80
Garrick, the (club), 10
Garrison, Robert (Bob) L., 96, 165, 171
General Motors, 25, 26, 44, 59, 246
Gillis, Philip A., 146, 148
*Glad Tidings*, 100–101
Graham, Murry, 123
Graham, Walker, 101, 107, 109
Granse, William H., 73
Greene, Robert L., 105, 128, 131, 134, 139, 156–57
Greenfield Village, 24
Gregory, William B., 18
Groesbeck, Alex, 27
Grylls, H. J. Maxwell: Arts and Crafts connection to, 30; building Playhouse, 46–47, 75; death of, 78; as a

# INDEX

founder, 18; resignation attempt, 61
Guest, Edgar, 95, 98–99
Guest, Harry, 95, 100, 101

Habel, Mark, 148
Haberkorn, C. H., Jr., 46
Haidt, Ruth. *See* Hughes, Ruth Haidt
*Hairlooms*, 21–22, 110
Harfst, Richard, 80
Hartigan, Joseph J., 114
*Hasty Heart, The*, 86–88, 87
Hasty Pudding Club, 10, 17
Hawkins, Norval A., 44, 236
Hawksley, Christopher R., 167
Heaslet, James G., 27
Henry Ford Company, 25
Henry Ford Museum, 24
*Her Family Tree*, 35
Hiers, Walter, 40–41
Hill, Willard S., 21
Hirschfield, Francis, 113, 138, 172
Hirschfield, Jake, 44, 72, 95, **112**, 113, 172
*Hitchhiker, The*, 108–9
Hodges, Walter, 196
Holliday, William F., 2, 41, 44, 48–19, 92–93, 110, 132–33
Honoré, Paul, 53, **54**
Hopkins Club. *See* Scarab Club
Houston, Henry A., III, 114
Howard, Ken, 124, 143
Hudson, J. L., 13, 26
Hudson, J. L., Co., 52, 57
Hudson Motor Car Company, 26
Hughes, James, 101
Hughes, Robert T., 135
Hughes, Ruth Haidt, 92, 98
Hume, Sam, 29, 43
Hupp Motor Car Company, 28

*I Killed the Count*, 101
*If a Little Ford Should Lead 'Em*, 44
*In the Thousands of Years to Come*, 1, 39–40
*Inside Detroit*, 89–92
*Is Peculiar*, 109

Jacobs, Raymond (Ray) A.: *All Aboard*, 74–75; background, 70–71; *Men Working*, 71–72, **72**, 110; *Rose of Auvernge, The*, 68; *What the Heil* (music), 73
Jeffries, Micheal L., 123, 130, 137, 172, 183–84
Jendrzejewski, Roy A., 177
Jones, Kensinger, 177
Jorgensen, J. J., 139, 151, 164, 167, 168, 173
Joy, Henry B., 7, 25–26, 63
Joy, Richard P., 25–26
Judge, Frank T., Jr., 157, 170–71

*Kaleidoscope 76*, 133
Kane, Frank G., 28
Kapp, William E.: banners, 53; building Playhouse, 46–47, 75; history of Players, 98; *Nunquam Renig*, 23; and steins, 113; *Trial of Anne Boleyn* (design), 95, **96**
Kerr, Harry W., 73
Knudsen, William S., 238
Knudson, Eric J., 143
Koch, Henry, 37–38
Kummerow, Arnold, 143
Kurtz, Jeffrey, 130
Kurtz, Kenneth, 130

Lahr, Bert, 122
Lambs, the (club), 10, 17
Larned, Charles P., 11, 18, 20
Larned, Lillie Whitney, 11, 20
*Last Flight of the Columbia, The*, 141–42
*Last Meeting of the Butler's Club*, 122
Legge, Russell H., 36, **64**, **69**, **71**, **74**, 76, 86
Lerchen, William G., 46, 48, 72, 109
*Lights of the Apocalypse, The*, 86
Little Theatre movement, 13–14
Lodge, John C., 38–39, 60, 109
Love, Harold O., 133

Macklin, Charles, 45
MacManus, Theodore F., 28–29
Malcolmson, Alexander T., 27
*Martha & Me*, 164
Martin, Frank V., 75
Matheson, Charles W., 53
Maurer, Michael T., 150
Maxwell Briscoe, 27
Maxwell Motor Company, 26
May Show. *See under* Traditions
McKee, Walter V., 57

McMechan, Jerry: *Last Meeting of the Butler's Club*, 122; rejected script, 125; retirement, 136; *Running the Gamut*, 126; *Way Cousin Kerby Fought the Steamboat Gambler, The*, 126
Meadon, Joseph, 42
*Memorable Moments at Players*, 133–34
*Men Working*, 71–72, **72**, 110
Merrill, William W., **87**, 87–88
Miller, Gordon H., 85, 104–5
Mills, Joseph B., 57
Minge, LaVerne (Verne), 86–87, **87**, 106–7, 114, 127
*Minus Zero*, 93–94
Monley, Christopher G., 139–40, **140**
Montgomery, Jeffrey M., 137
Moock, Harry, 96
Murphy, C. Hayward: building the Playhouse, 42; joining club, 35–36; Players Holding Company, 46, 52
Murphy, William H., 25, 29, 46, 72

Nash Motors, 26
Nastfogel nude, 73
Nawrocki, Henry, 133
Nawrocki, Lorraine, 133
Nelson, Henry, 143, 175
Nesi, Christopher, 164
Newberry, Phelps, 34, 46, 47, 51, 56
Newberry, Truman H., 25–26, 27, 45, 237, 238
Ninetieth anniversary, 3
Nixon visit. *See under* Players, The
Noble, Sheldon R.: *All Aboard*, 74–75; background, 70–71; *Men Working*, 71–72, 72, 110; *Portrait of a Man*, 66–67; *What the Heil*, 73–74, **74**

Ohio Automobile, 25
Oldsmobile, 26, 235
*On High*, 83–85
Osgood, Denne, 166–67
*Outside Looking In*, 61
Owen, John L., 51, 152

Packard Motor Company, 26, 232
Paige-Detroit, 27
Parducci, Corrado, 50, 51
Peabody, Eddie, 122–23
Peabody, Horace B., 21

Pearse, Bud: *Alice in Playerland*, 136; *Bowery Burlicue Moves Uptown*, 141; death of, 157; donating heels, 197; *Memorable Moments at Players*, 133–34; *Players Diamond Review*, 141; *Players Take Manhattan*, 154, 156
Pearse, Isabelle, 101
Pearson, Alan H., 74
Phelps, George Harrison, 37, 46
Piper, Walter C., 53
Pirrami, Geno, 168
Pitkin, Maxwell Irving, 29
*Players Book of One Act Plays*. *See under* Players, The
Players, The: amateur status, 22–23; Articles of Association, 18; Associates get vote, 76–77; building Playhouse, 32, 42–53, 50, 51, 52, 55, 56; burning mortgage, 51; combining with Fine Arts and Theatre Arts, 32, 130–31; crest, 23; fiftieth anniversary, 101, 107–8, 109–10; Glowworm, 32; Gourmet Group, 139; and history, 98, 110–11, 169–70; honorary life, 98; humor at, 44–45, 70, 109, 133–34, 137; *Life* magazine article, 72; life membership, 62–63; Michigan historic site, 141, 153; Millionaire's Party, 115; mortgage burning, 80; Nixon visit, 95–97, 97; nonprofit status, 152; *Nunquam Renig (see under* Traditions); one-act play competition, 108, 115; orchestra, 71, 136, 166; and philanthropy, 33, 57, 60, 75; 78, 79, 88–89, 94–95, 100, 121, 133; *Players Book of One Act Plays*, 24, 57; Players Foundation, 101–2; Players Holding Company, 46, 62; Players' Song, 48–49, 92–93; and Prohibition, 1–2, 36–38, 37, 40, 63; scholarship, 178; seventy-fifth anniversary, 141; Singing Players, 135–36, 166; sixty-fifth anniversary, 2, 132; sound at Playhouse, 93–94; "This Is Players," 124; Traffic Hour, 130, 167; Tri-Effort, 99–101, 108, 110, 131–32, 133, 162; Twenty Year Club, 92, 102; Willie Awards, 130, 137; and women, 17, 20, 39–40, 93, 128–29, 164

Players Club (NY), 10–11
*Players Diamond Review*, 141
Players' Song. *See under* Players, The
*Players Take Manhattan*, 154, 156
*Portrait of a Man*, 66–67
Potter, Ray, 114
Pringle, Andrew C., 125
*Producers, The*, 142–43
Pulcher, Martin L., 46
Putnam, Karen, 101
Putnam, Leslie C., 102

Rader, Todd, 175
Reck, Franklin M., 74–75, 77
*Reclining Figure*, 101
*Re-Doing Stratford*, 158
*Re-Doing Stratford—1986*, 142
*Red Peppers*, 96–98
Reliance Motor Car Company, 27
Remick, Jerome H., 29
Rivera, Diego, 241
Robinson, Loren T., Jr., 129
Robinson, Loren T., Sr., 113
Robinson, William L., 111
Robinson, William L., Jr., 148
Rohloff, Douglas F., 122, 123, 130, 136–37
Rohloff, Willard A.: and afterglows, 173; ashes of, 51; and community of Players, 169; dressing room door, 137, 172; and Forsyth, Dick, 171–72; and ghosts, 170; glowworm, 123; and Gourmet Group, 139, 176; "Great Lady," 53; *Hitchhiker, The* (director), 108–9; Honoré murals, 53; *Last Meeting of the Butler's Club* (director), 122; Nixon visit, 96; and *Nunquam Renig*, 174; president, 131–32; and Project R, 174–75; and rookie show, 155; and steins, 113; Willie Awards, 130
*Rose of Auvernge, The*, 68
*Running the Gamut*, 126

Sanger, Harry, 53
Saxon Motor Car Company, 27
Scarab Club: Burroughs, Clyde and, 234; founding of, 5, 12–13; and Paul Honoré, 53; *Life* magazine article, 72
Schafer, Robert, 106, 106–7

Schneider, Edward (Ned) N., 171
Scoles, Glenn, 139, 163
"Seven Stages of Man," 52
Shannon, Richard, 125
Shelden, Al, Jr., 93–94, 172
*Shock of Recognition, The*, 140–41
Sinclair, Sid, 115
Sinischo, William R., 137, 177
Slade, Sam I.: career, 35; dressing room, 79, 171; ghost of, 170; ghostwriting, 157; joining club, 35; life membership, 62–63; Lincoln performance, 72, 75–76; popularity, 72–73, 76; and *Roller Skates Must Be Mended*, 69–70
Smith, Hinchman, and Grylls (architectural firm), 46
Smith, Lawrence L., 137, 174
Snyder, W. Howard T., 89–92, 93
Society of Arts and Crafts. *See* Arts and Crafts, Detroit Society of
*Solid Gold Cadillac*, 105
Spring Invitational. *See* Traditions: May Show
Standish, Marion Eddy, 34
Standish, W. Colburn, Jr., 113, 172–73
Standish, W. Colburn (Olie), Sr. 34, 37, 61, 78, 98, 113
Stark, George W., 109
Stearns, Frederick K., 30
Stearns, Frederick S., 18, 30, 72
Steele, Charles M., 34
Steltenkamp, Charles J., 148, 155, 170–71, 174
Stevens, Henry G., 42, 46
Strasburg, James, 29, 37–38, 46, 75
Stratton, William B., 30
Stringer, Charles, 33
*Summer Comes to Diamond O*, 175

Talman, William W., 18, 108
Thalian Association, 8
Theatre Arts Club: combining with Players (possibility of), 32, 130–31; discount at Playhouse, 57; electric chimes donation of, 56; founding of, 5, 11; and gender, 20; today, 162; and Tri-Effort, 99–101, 108, 110, 131–32, 133; and war charities, 75
Theatre Arts Magazine. *See under* Arts and Crafts, Detroit Society of

*There Once Lived a King*, 94
Thorn, Greg, 123, 130, 137, 143, 172, 173
Thompson, Hayward S., 73
Thornhill, John L., 92–93
*Tinder Box, The*, 43
Todd, Michael, 61
Toms, Robert M., 38, 88, 94, 98
*Tonight's the Night*, 74
Traditions: Afterglow, 32; beer at the frolics, 11, 37–39; business suits at frolics, 155; caricatures, 86; Frank Judge *Nunquam Renig* Award, 157, 173; male only, 128–29; May Show, 19–20, 22, 166; November Invitational, 124; *Nunquam Renig*, 23–24, 61, 78, 114, 127, 140, 172–77; plaque for deceased Players, 93; renaming dressing rooms, 79, 106, 110, 137, 138, 171–72; revivals, 69; steins, 11, 47, 113–14; Turnbull's "A Selkirk Christmas," 157–59, 159; tuxedos, 2, 40, 79, 83, 119, 166–67
*Trial by Jury*, 98
*Trial of Anne Boleyn*, 95–96, 96, 98
*Tridget of Greva, The*, 125
Trombly, Barry A., 170
Tucker, Verne W., 91–92
Turnbull, James (Jim), 148, 157–58, **159**, 175
Turner, William S., Jr., 177
Tuxedos. *See under* Traditions

VanderKloot, Robert (Bob) C., 238
Van Deusen, Francois (Fran), 183

Walter, William, 113
*Way Cousin Kerby Fought the Steamboat Gambler, The*, 126
Webb, Jefferson B., 45, 48
Webber, Oscar, 52
Weeks, Albert Loren: *Cabinet Meeting, The*, 63, 67; career, 28, 35; death of, 113; *Doing Stratford*, 2, 48–49, 110, 132, 133; *Her Family Tree*, 35; joining club, 35; *Nunquam Renig*, 23–24; *Players Book of One Act Plays*, 99; Players' Song, 48–49, 92–93; *Roller Skates Must Be Mended*, 69–70; and Sam Slade, 62–63; *Tinder Box, The*, 43; and Williams, Bert, 41
Weeks, Vera, 43
*What the Heil*, 73–74, **74**
"When the Day Is Done." *See* Players' Song
White, Craig, 156
Williams, Bert, 41–42
Winningham, C. C., 51
Witbeck, Ernest S., 18
*Whispers*, 34

Yondotega, the, 24

Zych, Robert, 164

www.ingramcontent.com/pod-product-compliance
Lightning Source LLC
Chambersburg PA
CBHW070753230426
43665CB00017B/2344